## 1979-80 EDITION OF

# Arthur Frommer's Guide to

# ATHENS

### by
### IAN KEOWN

Published by
**THE FROMMER/PASMANTIER PUBLISHING CORPORATION**
380 Madison Avenue
New York, New York 10017


Distributed by
**SIMON & SCHUSTER**
**A GULF+WESTERN COMPANY**
1230 Avenue of the Americas
New York, New York 10020
0-671-24905-3


Distributed outside the U.S.A. and Canada by
**FLEETBOOKS**
c/o Feffer and Simons, Inc.
100 Park Avenue
New York, New York 10017


Distributed in Canada by
**P J PAPERBACKS LTD.**
330 Steelcase Road East
Markham, Ontario L3R2M1


Motif drawings by Paul Berkow

**NOTE:** Although every effort was made to insure the accuracy of price information appearing in this book, it should be kept in mind that prices can and do fluctuate in the course of time.

Manufactured in the United States of America

# CONTENTS

# MAPS

## Inflation Alert

It is hardly a secret that a wave of inflation has battered the countries of Europe, and Greece has not escaped. The author of this book has made every effort to insure the accuracy of prices appearing in this guide. As we go to press, we believe we have obtained the most reliable data possible. However, we cannot offer guarantees for the tariffs quoted, and so in the lifetime of this edition the wise traveler will add 10 to 15% to the prices quoted.

## The Dollar and the Drachma

Where currency conversions from drachmas to dollars appear in parentheses on these pages, they were prepared on the basis of 36 drachmas = $1. That rate may not be accurate by the time you travel, as it varies from day to day, depending on the relative values of both currencies on world markets. Use our currency conversions, therefore, only as a gauge for what you'll be spending and check with a banker before you leave for Greece to determine what the actual rate of exchange is at that time.

# Chapter I

# THE GREEK IN ALL OF US

GREECE IS THE CRADLE of civilization, the origin of the West, the birthplace of democracy . . . etcetera, etcetera. That gets the clichés out of the way. Nevertheless, it's hard to imagine what civilized life would be like today without the influence of Ancient Greece. The Greeks invented drama, and amphitheaters to perform it in. They invented the Olympic Games. Euclid and Pythagoras formulated the theories geometry students slave over to this day. And there isn't a computer programmer who hasn't studied the logic of Aristotle. Ancient Greece created a style of architecture which was the model for the White House, the Lincoln Memorial, and state capitols all across the land. Doctors still take the Hippocratic Oath, named for the father of medicine, a Greek, of course. Children learn about the ant and the grasshopper and other characters from the fables of Aesop. And Greek myths have become so interwoven with our civilized consciousness that we sometimes forget where they came from. Oedipus, after all, was a Greek, not a character living in Freud's Vienna.

And then there's the Greek language. It doesn't exactly sound like poetry when spoken in the streets of Athens, but what a debt we owe to it! Sophisticated, metropolitan, aristocratic, philanthrophy, gymnastics, pornographic—are all from the Greek. Even ecology, our newest "in" word, comes from the Greek words *oikos,* meaning house, and *logos,* meaning word or thought.

The mighty Romans, conquerors of almost the entire ancient world, were so awed by the accomplishments of Ancient Greece that they copied its art, its architecture, and in general acted as if they had been conquered by the Greeks rather than the other way around. Perhaps in a way they were. Perhaps in a way we *all* were.

In fact, the Greek influence has been so strong throughout our heritage, so ubiquitous in our everyday lives, that a visit to Greece is like a prodigal's return. So as the Greeks tell their visitors, "Welcome home. You've been away too long!"

# Chapter II

# A REFRESHER COURSE IN GREEK HISTORY

ANCIENT GREECE, rather than modern Greece, is what brings most visitors to Athens (the Greek Islands are something else again), and since you're going to be looking at quite a lot of ruins you might as well take a quick refresher course in Minoans, Myceneans, and Macedonians. After all, the more you remember, the more you'll enjoy.

**THE BULL DANCERS:** Around 3000 B.C., the most ancient civilization of Greece began to flourish. The **Minoan** civilization of Crete is one of the oldest civilizations in Greek history, and this civilization, with Crete at its center, lasted almost two thousand years.

The Minoans were generally peace-loving people. They lived in cities without protective walls, and they were never invaded. They were an artistic people, but didn't develop a script until some time around 1700 B.C. Their art, which you can still see in some of the ruins at Knossos in Crete, was colorful and sunny—red columns and sky-blue temple walls.

One of their favorite pastimes was bull jumping (the bull dancers would grab the bull's horns and flip themselves over its back, etc.), a sport that makes today's bullfighting look like a sheepdog trial. Bulls, in fact, were a key part of the culture, and were worshipped by the Minoans. The most famous bull of all, the Minotaur, was a creature with a bull's head and a human body, the mythological offspring of a bull sent from the sea as a sign to prove King Minos' right to the throne of Crete. Unfortunately, when the king refused to sacrifice the bull to the god Poseidon, his queen was cursed with a passion for it. Her child, the Minotaur, was then imprisoned by King Minos in the center of the Labyrinth, a maze so convoluted no one could reach the center to kill it and thus free the people from the influence of the monster. Except the great Theseus, of course, but even he couldn't kill the Minotaur without the help of Minos' daughter, Ariadne. We'll come back to Theseus in a minute.

**THE FAMILY THAT SLAYS TOGETHER . . .** On mainland Greece the first civilization you have to contend with is the Mycenean, which started to make its presence felt about 1400 B.C. It was focused on the city of Mycenae, about 25 miles from Corinth in the region known as the Peloponnese. Mycenae was the home of that happy family headed by Agamemnon, who was put to death by his wife Clytemnestra and her lover, who in turn were wiped out by her son Orestes at the instigation of her daughter Electra. The Trojan War was launched from here.

Then about 1100 B.C. a people called the Dorians invaded Mycenae and other cities of Greece, and crushed them. Almost overnight, the great "palace bureaucracies" disappeared, and the Greeks were reduced to small, illiterate communities. This was the Dark Age of Greece.

**THE YARN SPINNERS:** Throughout history the Greeks have been nothing if not hardy, and at this time they began to develop the *polis* that was to become the central political unit in the upcoming classical period. The polis was a cluster of houses around a "palace" that stood on a safe hill, called an Akropolis, and its inhabitants usually had a common family relationship. Apart from that, they had nothing—no culture, no literature, only memories of past glories. So they got together on their akropolis and consoled themselves by singing songs and reciting poetry extolling the heroism of their ancestors. Two of these songs were the *Iliad* and the *Odyssey.* No one knows for sure in what form Homer learned the legends he wrote about in the *Iliad,* but no matter how he received them he handed the legends along in a great new art form that excites scholars to this day.

Around this time, 800 B.C., the Greeks came into contact with the Phoenicians, who did have an alphabet and knew how to put things in writing; so the Greeks adapted it, just in time for Homer to polish up his spoken poetry and get it down on stone.

**THE SPARTANS:** Slowly, aristocracy began replacing monarchy (except in Sparta and Macedonia); trade was flourishing, slavery increasing, and coined money was introduced to simplify trading throughout the entire Mediterranean. Revolutionaries came along, roused the slaves, and overthrew governments. Except in Sparta, where two kings ruled, and reared their people to live frugally (hence the word "spartan") and cultivate physical discipline. From the age of seven, Spartan youths were given military training. All men of military age lived in barracks and were not allowed to live with their wives until they were 30. Thus, when any revolutionary tried to start anything in Sparta he was quickly put down by the militaristic establishment.

**THESEUS RIDES AGAIN:** The scene now shifts to Attica, which is the part of mainland Greece where Athens, and several other small independent cities, were located. These city-states were being united by King Theseus (this is the same Theseus who penetrated the Labyrinth and killed the Minotaur—the Minoan civilization was still there all this time). No sooner had Theseus finished with the Minotaur than he was off battling the Centaurs. Somewhere along the way he became king of Athens, married an Amazon, conquered Thebes, and united Attica.

Sometime around 621 B.C. a legislator named Draco appeared on the Athenian scene and codified laws that substituted public justice for personal revenge, and thus outlawed the feuds that were a popular Greek pastime. His laws were so severe that the legislator has been immortalized by the word "draconian." The laws were said to be written in blood rather than ink, because he rewarded many types of crime (such as stealing a cabbage!) with the death penalty. These laws held for only a quarter of a century until Solon, who came to be called the founder of Athenian democracy, abolished the death penalty for everything but murder. Shades of 1972! Solon also instituted constitutional reforms that set up free elections and brought all classes (except slaves) into the process of government. And so democracy began.

**MARATHON AND SALAMIS:** A hundred years later democracy and everything else Greece had built up were threatened by Persia. The first of Persia's expeditions took place in 490 B.C., when its army arrived at Marathon. This was the event where a Greek soldier ran the 27 miles back to Athens, managed to gasp "We have won," then collapsed and died. In their second expedition the Persians were matched by the genius of Themistocles, an Athenian leader who made his people nervous by going out and building a huge fleet rather than an army. However, he turned out to be right: the Persians were blasted off the sea at the battle of Salamis. When the Greeks, and their Spartan allies, turned to the attack on land at the pass of Thermopylae, they trapped the Persians for four days. But the Persians eventually gained the upper hand, and rather than retreat, the Spartans remained and died to the last man. A Greek poet composed one of history's most famous epitaphs for them: "Stranger, go tell the Spartans that here we lie in obedience to their wishes."

**THE GOLDEN AGE:** Athens, now a naval power, was headed for its golden age. Its ruler at this time (the middle of the fifth century B.C.) was **Pericles,** the most dazzling orator in a city of dazzling orators. He practiced democracy at home, imperialism abroad. One of his wisest decisions was to pay jurors, so that even the poorest citizens could sit on juries. One of his not-so-smart decisions was to restrict Athenian citizenship to people whose mother and father were both Athenians. This would have been fine if he hadn't at that time fallen under the spell of Aspasia. Aspasia had been born in Mileta but had migrated to Athens because that was where the action was in those days; she quickly established herself as a beautiful and intelligent courtesan, who taught rhetoric on the side. One of her students was Socrates, and another was Pericles. Pericles took her as his mistress, promptly divorced his wife, but he couldn't marry Aspasia because of the new law he himself had brought into being. So they lived together. Aspasia became the uncrowned queen of Athens, and their son was later honored with citizenship by a special act of the Athenians. Aspasia was later condemned to death for impiety, a trumped-up charge, and Pericles had to muster all his dazzling oratory to save her. It was Pericles who built the Parthenon, the Propylaea, the long walls to Piraeus, and many of the temples you'll see on your strolls around town. This was quite a time in Athens. Aspasia was right—Athens was *the* place. While Pericles was building his Parthenon, Aeschylus, Sophocles, and Euripides were writing their plays, and Socrates and Plato were teaching. But Sparta was smouldering with jealousy, and became increasingly worried about Athens' imperialistic policies.

Now we get involved with another series of wars. Or rather one long, lingering, 27-year war—the **Peloponnesian War.** Pericles led Athens, avoiding battles on land, attacking the Peloponnese from the sea, because Athens ruled the waves. Pericles, unfortunately, saw only two years of the war—he died of a plague which struck Athens in 429 B.C. A host of demagogues and lesser leaders followed, who eventually brought Athens to defeat in 404 B.C. But victorious Sparta's influence lasted only 30 years after that, at which time it was superseded by Macedonia, a kingdom in the north of Greece.

**THE PRINCE AND THE HORSE:** Philip of Macedon's ambition was to unify all of Greece, restore Greek culture to Macedon, and eliminate Persia as a lingering threat. But before he could do that he too divorced his wife, who thereupon hatched a plot and had him assassinated because she was jealous of his new consort. His nephew was next in line to the throne, but the crown went instead to his first wife's son, **Alexander.** One of the first legends about Alexander began when he fulfilled an oracle's prediction by succeeding in mounting a high-spirited horse named Bucephalus. Philip had intended to destroy this horse because he was unmountable, but the clever Alexander noticed that the problem with Bucephalus was that he was literally afraid of his own shadow; so Alexander turned the horse's eyes into the sun and mounted. At the age of 20, Alexander became king, and Bucephalus would soon carry him across an empire.

**ALEXANDER THE GREAT:** Alexander, as you know, conquered Greece, united it against Persia, then marched his armies across continents, conquering Asia, Syria, Egypt, Babylon, Susa, Persepolis. He was on his way to conquer India when his troops finally became so exhausted they compelled him to return to Macedon. He was a humane man (he had studied under Aristotle), who maintained the civil liberties of all the peoples he conquered, honored their gods and their customs. He even went so far as to adopt one Oriental custom for himself, and married several Eastern princesses. In 323 B.C. Alexander the Great caught a fever and died. He had lived an extraordinary life, and died when only in his early thirties.

Alexander's death marked the end of the great classical period of Greece—in literature, philosophy, and art. The city-states withered, the upper classes took over, and there was constant bickering and battling until 146 B.C. when Greece was conquered by the powerful and indomitable armies of Rome.

**CENTURIONS AND CHRISTIANS:** Although the Romans, as we noted earlier, admired the art and culture of Greece, they had no respect at all for its countryside. Rather than fight all their battles on Roman soil they tended to move them to neutral territory. Mark Antony and Octavius fought it out with Brutus and Cassius in Greece, at Philippi; Octavian then routed Antony and turned back Cleopatra's ships in Greek waters.

For five hundred years, right through the early era of Christianity, Greece was subject to the power of Rome. It also became a stronghold of Christianity. Saint Paul preached in Greek, and his famous epistles were written to the Greek communities of Corinth, Thessalonika, and Ephesus.

For most practical purposes the history of classical Greece ends at this point. Tourists come to Greece mainly to see the remains of the classical ruins, and relive the days of glory of Pericles and the Athenians. That's what Greece is all about. Obviously, though, its history continues, and there are many people who want to see the country's examples of Byzantine art and culture (which you'll read about next)—but that's not the essential Greece. From the time of Saint Paul and the Apostles, the history of Greece is a chronicle of sieges, battles, and struggles to regain independence. The struggle was heroic enough but it lacked the grandeur of Ancient Greece. Or maybe they just didn't have a Homer to glorify it.

**BYZANTIUM:** In 330 A.D. the Roman emperor Constantine chose a fishing village on the Bosphorus, the channel leading to the Black Sea, to be his eastern capital. He named it Constantinople. Eventually it became the capital of its own empire, the Byzantine, and managed to resist invasions and maintain its hold on the Balkan Peninsula, Asia Minor, Cyprus, the Middle East, and Egypt. Rome at the time was slowly succumbing to invasions of barbarians. Greece was a mere province.

For many hundreds of years, Byzantium was the only civilized part of Europe. Art, especially religious art, flourished, and churches, monasteries, and palaces were going up everywhere. Then the Eastern and Western churches separated; Venetians, Franks, and soldiers from other countries in Western Europe formed their crusades and pillaged Constantinople. The city eventually fell to the Ottoman Turks, Greece was reduced to an even more insignificant province, and Athens became a small town. The Parthenon was turned into a Turkish mosque.

# A Ready Reference for Ancient Greek History

| Period | Approx. dates | Key events and people |
|---|---|---|
| Minoan | 3000 to 1400 B.C. | Knossos (Crete) King Minos The Minotaur Theseus |
| Mycenean | 1400 to 1150 B.C. | Agamemnon Jason and the Argonauts Achilles Troy |
| Dark Age | 1200 to 1100 B.C. | |
| Aristocratic Age | 800 to 600 B.C. | Athens unites with towns of Attica Draco proclaims severe laws Solon reforms constitution Homer composes the *Iliad* and the *Odyssey* |
| Persian Wars | 520 to 480 B.C. | Themistocles fortified Piraeus Greeks win at Marathon and Salamis Aeschylus wins Athens drama festival |
| Classical Age | 480 to 430 B.C. | Parthenon built Pericles in power Aeschylus, Sophocles, and Euripides at work |
| Peloponnesian War | 430 to 400 B.C. | Naval battle of Syracuse Erechtheum on Acropolis completed Aristophanes writes comedies Pericles dies Socrates drinks hemlock Sparta triumphs |
| Macedonian Age | 360 B.C. to 300 B.C. | Alexander the Great conquers Aristotle founds school |
| Roman | 200 B.C. to 300 A.D. | Rome sacks Corinth |
| Byzantine | 300 to 1200 A.D. | Constantine builds Constantinople Crusaders build forts, sack Constantinople |

For the next 400 years, Greece remained under Turkish rule. In the early 1600s, Venice tried to move in, without success (although you can still see the Venetian influence in places like Corfu). In the early 1800s, the Greeks started to muster groups of revolutionaries, and in March, 1821, they formally began their struggle for independence when an archbishop raised a new blue-and-white flag at a monastery near Patras. (The date, March 25, is now Greek Independence Day.)

This was the period when Lord Byron and other volunteers rallied to the Greek cause. Byron died at Missolonghi in 1824, but in the end, with the help of Britain, Russia, and France, Greece finally defeated the Turks in a spectacular sea battle off the Bay of Navarino—spectacular and extraordinary because the Turks lost 53 ships with 6,000 men on board but the allied fleet didn't lose a single vessel.

GETTING TO ATHENS

**INDEPENDENCE, DEFEAT, INDEPENDENCE:** In 1829, the "protecting powers" declared Greece an independent nation. Unfortunately, they couldn't agree among themselves on territorial and legal conditions (some of these problems remain undecided to this day). A year later, Greece became a kingdom; a 17-year-old Bavarian prince was named to the throne, Prince Otto (or

Othon). He lasted until 1862, when he was replaced by the Danish ruling house. Thessaly, Macedonia, and Thrace meantime remained under Ottoman rule, but after the Balkan War of 1912-13 they became part of Greece, leaving Turkey with only the eastern half of Thrace, including Constantinople (which was then renamed Istanbul). We can leave Greek history there, at least until October 28, 1940, when an emissary from Mussolini demanded that the Greek-Albanian border be opened to Italian troops. The Greek patriot, General Metaxas, replied "Ohi," or no, and thereby brought Greece into World War II. (October 28 is now celebrated as Ohi Day.) Greece was invaded by the Nazis, freed by its own Resistance and the Allies, and settled down once more to the intramural squabbles characterizing the period.

Regimes may come and regimes may flounder, but the glory that was Greece remains. Or as Pericles once said, "Future ages will wonder at us, as the present age wonders at us now."

# Chapter III

# MOUNTAINS, ISLANDS, AND RUINS

## An Outline of Modern Greece

ON A MAP, Greece looks almost like an inkblot that landed in one large glob and burst into a score of splotches. The glob is the mainland, the splotches the islands. The total land area of Greece is 51,182 square miles—roughly the size of Louisiana. One quarter of this area is islands, the remainder is mountains. The island quarter we leave to later chapters in this guide; right now we'll examine the three-quarters that make up the land mass.

It's a complicated land, so let's begin by dividing it, like Gaul, into three parts: the Olympian north, central Greece, and the Peloponnese.

**THE OLYMPIAN NORTH:** This region includes Epirus, Thessaly, Macedonia, and Thrace. Mount Olympus, the dwelling place of the gods, is up there; so is Mount Athos, with its famous monastery. Thessaly is considered the breadbasket of Greece, supplying most of its wheat, corn, barley, and cotton.

**CENTRAL GREECE:** This region can be subdivided into six areas —Aetolia, Acarnania, Phthiotis, Phocis, Boeotia, and Attica. The first four names you can forget for the moment, but Attica is the land around Athens (you'll probably be seeing quite a bit of it), and Boeotia is where you'll find Delphi of oracle fame.

GREECE

Filippi
THESSALONIKI
Kastoria
Karial
AGIONOROS
Ioanning
Meteora
KERKIRA
Kalampaka
Arta
Nea Anchialos
Nikopolis
Delfi
Ossios Loukas
KIOS
KEFALLINIA
Egosthena
Dafni
ZAKINTHOS
Korinthos
ATHENS
Vravrona
Olympia
Epidauros
SALAMIS
Ermioni
Mistra
Kranidi
PATMOS
Sparta
PAROS
MILOS
Monemvasia
Rodos
Lindos
Apolakia
CRETE
Iraklion
Potamies
Gortis
Kritsa
LASSITHION

**THE PELOPONNESE:** To the southwest is a peninsula known as the Peloponnese, which can almost be considered an island since the completion of the Corinth canal which separates it from central Greece. The canal, incidentally, was begun by Nero, way back then, but not completed in its present form until 1893. It's a spectacular tourist sight in its own right.

The Peloponnese is where you find such haunts of the ancient Greeks as Corinth, Mycenae, Epidaurus, Olympia, and Sparta, 4,000 years of history, and mountains rising to almost 8,000 feet.

**THE COUNTRYSIDE:** Greece is a land of bleached limestone ridges, brown hills, olive groves, and an incredible collection of bays and coves lapped by green and turquoise sea. In the north, Greece is cut off from Albania, Yugoslavia, and Bulgaria by mountains; in the west, she's isolated by the Ionian Sea; in the south, by the Mediterranean; and in the east, by the Aegean. Because of the mountains and valleys, communities have historically been cut off from each other and have tended to retain their own individual characteristics, and Greeks still tend to identify themselves as Cretans, Athenians, Rhodians, and so forth. This individuality has helped make the country's folk art and folklore so varied and fascinating.

All the groups still retain their rivalries, as you'll find out if you go to a taverna and the singer announces a song from beautiful Thessalonika (cheers!), then a song from beautiful Rhodes (hurrahs!), and a song from Macedonia (whistles!). The most reliable, charming, tolerant, intelligent of these groups is the one you happen to be talking to at a particular time.

**GREEK HOSPITALITY:** Over all, however, the Greeks are a lively, friendly, fun-loving, sometimes exuberant, people. And Greek is the only language in the world in which the word for stranger is also the word for guest—*xenos.* They take a great delight in the fact that so many tourists appreciate their country, and a great pride in their country, its heritage, and its ruined symbols of glory.

Hospitality has always been an admirable Greek trait. From the fishing families who open their homes to tourists on the islands (it's more than just that they can use the money) to the hotel clerk who acts like he's always known you, the Greek actually seems to like visitors.

Perhaps it's because Herodotus, one of the first world travelers, was so tolerant of other races, and because for centuries Greeks have roamed the world and come back home to settle with a less insular view of things than many other nations. (In almost every small village, there's a local Greek-American—an older man who spent his youth in the U.S., made his "fortune," and came back to settle and be the ultimate arbiter of all arguments about that country and its doings. Sometimes he's living on weekly Social Security checks.)

But perhaps it's nothing more than the innate native sense of drama—the opportunity to take the stage at somebody else's prompting. To any Greek all the world's a stage, just as it always has been—especially the marketplace, the main square, or the cafes along the harbor.

Stop and ask for directions in the street and everybody gathers around and puts in their two-bits' worth. At last, weary of making yourself understood or getting any uniformity out of the replies, you walk away and leave the discussion. When you look back, they're still arguing.

Friendliness, in short, is a characteristic, and you'll often be encountered with the all-purpose greeting *Yiasu!* (good health) by people you don't know. *Kalimera* (good morning) and *kalispera* (good evening) are useful greetings to sprinkle around, too.

The Greek government is also trying to be friendly, and has launched an all-out drive to attract tourists. It's done a lot to make them welcome. Overseas, it has opened new offices to tell people about Greece, and has stocked the offices with lavishly enticing brochures. In Greece, it has streamlined arrival and customs facilities, put up hotels where they were needed, built new highways to get you to the new hotels. The tourists have responded. In 1978, for the first time in history, *five* million tourists visited Greece—more than double the number who came in 1974. That's good news for the hotels and the tour operators, but it causes increasing soul-searching among people who care about Greece's ruins and once unspoiled charm.

# Chapter IV

# THE ACROPOLIS—AND THE CITY AT ITS FEET

## Getting To Know Athens

EVERYONE'S IMAGE of Athens is a white, rocky hill with a ruined, but glorious, temple on top. Or maybe a soldier in a skirt with pompoms on his shoes. But your first impression of Athens will be nothing like that.

Your introduction to Athens is a marble parthenon of the 20th century—a gleaming, elegant airport terminal that puts you in the atmosphere of a big, modern, successful city.

On your ride in from the airport you pass through disheveled suburbs of two-story white houses, by women dressed in black, and despite the alien but unmistakable injunction to drink Coca-Cola you're left with no doubt that you're now in a Mediterranean country.

When you get to your hotel in the heart of the city, you're in a sophisticated European city of avenues, jewelry shops, spacious squares, and terrace cafes.

Step a few streets from this chic city and you're treading in the marbled steps of Aristotle, Pericles, and Sophocles.

In other words, there's no point in trying to put Athens into any kind of category. It's unique. It's a city where you brush shoulders with Ancient Greece, Rome, Sparta, Macedonia, Byzantium, the East, the West, Venice, Germany, France, Italy, America. They've all left their imprint, and what you're treated to is a fascinating, intriguing, unbelievably historic but not particularly beautiful city.

Let's pinpoint it. Athens is roughly on the same latitude as Louisville, Kentucky; San Francisco; and Tokyo. Its climate is considered mild, and probably is except when you're trudging around town looking for a hotel at high noon in August. Rainfall is a skimpy 15 inches a year, most of it in short showers in winter (if it rains in summer before the last week of August, it's news). June, July, August, and September are hot, but bearable because the air is so dry. On the other hand, don't try to fit in half a dozen temples between noon and 2 p.m.; try to confine your sightseeing to the early morning or late afternoon. That's the way the Athenians organize things (but we'll come back to that later). In winter, specifically January and February, things can get a little chilly. The cafes and tavernas move indoors, and occasionally you may have to hold on tight for fear of being blown off the Acropolis.

## ATHENS: AVERAGE MONTHLY TEMPERATURES

|  | Low | High |  | Low | High |
|---|---|---|---|---|---|
| January | 45.0 | 56.3 | July | 73.6 | 90.1 |
| February | 44.6 | 57.7 | August | 73.8 | 90.1 |
| March | 47.7 | 61.9 | September | 68.0 | 83.8 |
| April | 53.4 | 68.7 | October | 60.6 | 75.4 |
| May | 60.8 | 75.9 | November | 52.0 | 66.6 |
| June | 68.5 | 84.2 | December | 48.2 | 59.5 |

But all the statistics in the weather bureau will never do justice to the Athenian evenings. The air is soft, scented, seductive, scintillating—even alliteration doesn't do it justice. The best part of a summer day in Athens is the evening: plan your schedule accordingly.

**WHAT TO WEAR:** Since what you wear in Athens relates to the climate more than anything else, we'll deal with it right now. In summer, wear your lightest clothes. Wear comfortable, *sturdy* shoes for scrambling over all those marble ruins. Men rarely need a jacket, except in the evening for the smarter restaurants or nightclubs. Ladies should bring along a sweater or stole (you can buy one there inexpensively) for evenings, cruises, or the mountains. But, generally, how you dress is up to you. The Greeks dress casually. Short skirts, slacks, and long hair are now acceptable, although sometimes startling to the peasants in the countryside. You're expected to dress in a respectable manner when you enter a cathedral or church, but there are no hard and fast rules.

**WHEN TO COME:** As soon as you can get away—now, if you can. From the point of view of things to see and do, any time of the year is fine. For dogged sightseeing, in fact, winter might even be best. On the whole, the best times are April, May, June, September, October, November. Those are the months when the weather is gentlest and the ruins are not swamped (not only by Americans, remember, but also by Germans, British, Dutch, Scandinavians, French, Japanese, and the Greeks themselves). You'll have a better choice of hotels then, also. (Remember, that we're talking here only about Athens; some of the islands, particularly Crete and Rhodes, are almost as busy in winter as in summer.) If you're on a tight budget, you'll find at least one advantage in coming in winter: many hotels lower their rates then.

**THE LAYOUT OF ATHENS:** Let's begin where Athens began— with the **Acropolis.** From the summit of the hill you get the second best view of the city. Around the base of the Acropolis is the **Plaka,** built on the ancient city (you'll be reading more about it later), with some of the most notable archaeological finds—the Agora and the Temple of Theseus. To the northeast is the **Hill of Lycabettus;** and beyond that the spreading suburbs and the ring of mountains separating Athens from the rest of Attica. Between Lycabettus and the Acropolis is the heart of the city, distinguished from this height (about 450 feet) mainly by the green patch of the National Gardens and the hint of broad avenues radiating from **Syntagma,** or Constitution Square. To the other side, the west and south, the avenues and suburbs lead off to the coast and the Saronic Gulf, with Piraeus hidden behind a couple of hills.

At street level, the focal point of Athens is Syntagma (which, as you've just read, is also called Constitution Square, but if you want to ask directions of an Athenian, call it Syntagma). Syntagma is a large square, sloping in the direction of the Acropolis. At the upper end is the neoclassical shuttered facade of the Parliament Building, which used to be the the Royal Palace. The other three sides are surrounded by hotels and office buildings (including several airline offices and travel agencies). The great attraction of Syntagma, however, is its cafes. There are cafes on three sides and in the middle. In fact, it has been estimated that there are almost 3,000 chairs here (and most of them really are chairs, upholstered and with arm rests).

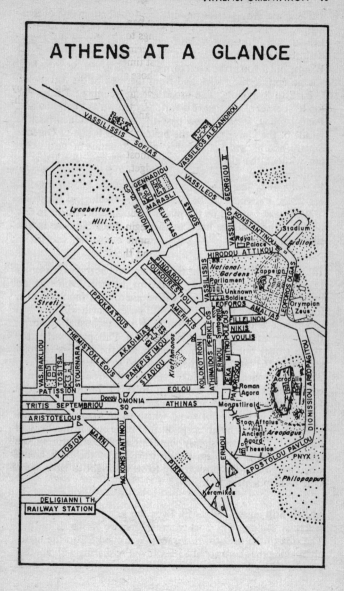

# ATHENS AT A GLANCE

There are three streets running from the bottom end of Syntagma, all laden with shops and hotels: **Karageorgi tis Servias, Ermou,** and **Mitropoleos.** Mitropoleos leads you to the cathedral, the Agora, the Temple of Theseus, and the Temple of the Winds; and if you make a left turn when you get to the cathedral, you go up into the Plaka, and from there up to the Acropolis.

Back to Syntagma. The broad avenue running off from the top-left corner of the square is variously known as **Venizelou** and **Panepistimou;** it takes you past the magnificent neoclassical facade of the University to the helter-skelter bustle of **Omonia Square,** another swirl of greenery, with a fountain in the middle, but without the elegance of Syntagma. Omonia Square is to Syntagma what Times Square is to, say, Rockefeller Center. From Omonia Square you can follow the avenue known as October 28 or Patission to the National Archaeological Museum.

We've just touched on the major landmarks of Athens in this chapter, and will get back to them in detail later on in the sightseeing chapter.

**TROLLEYS AND BUSES:** The trolley bus and bus routes crisscross the city, and you can get to all the main tourist haunts for no more than 6 drachmas. Some of the main routes from Syntagma, for example, are the #3/7 and #12 buses, which will take you to Omonia Square and the National Archaeological Museum; the #16 goes to the Acropolis, the Pnyx, Philopappos Hill; the #1/5 trolley bus to Omonia Square and the Larissis railroad station; #163 bus to Faleron; and #165 to Piraeus. *Procedural Note:* You board at the back, get off at the front, and pay the conductor as you get on, except on trolleys #7 and #12, which you board at the front and on which you need the exact fare.

If you're in any doubt about which route to take and where to get off, ask your hotel receptionist to write out the number and the stop in Greek and simply show this to the conductor, or one of the passengers (unless you're traveling at the peak hours, when everyone's too busy trying to stay upright to have much time to help a stranger).

**TAXIS:** Still incredibly cheap. Even the ride from the airport is less than you'd pay in most cities for the fare on the airline bus. The ride to the next town, Piraeus, is around $4, to the night-clubs along the shore about $3.50. If you're sharing with another couple, taking a taxi in Athens is like taking a bus back home.

You don't have to tip the drivers, although they've got into the habit of expecting to keep the small change at least; and a few of them seem to have trouble counting out your change in the hope that you may just tell them to forget it. The drivers are, on the whole, honest—but erratic. Shut your eyes and don't look. They also have a tendency to have conversations with other cab drivers as they ride along, since most of them can't converse with their foreign passengers. If you're setting off for a night on the town, it's wise to have the doorman or receptionist at your hotel write down the address in Greek for the benefit of your driver. And, of course, like cab drivers everywhere they disappear at rush hours (in the case of Athens, there are *four* busy periods). The taxis are usually small and relatively new, or large and relatively old, and any day now their exhaust fumes are expected to tumble the Acropolis.

The latest development in taxi-riding is that a new law allows drivers to pick up additional passengers going in the same direction; conversely, you can now try to flag down a taxi that's already taken. This is a very practical idea intended to save gasoline and space; but the problem is defining "same direction" and you may find yourself making a few unscheduled detours that add minutes (though *not* drachmas) to your trip. If you concur in sharing your taxi, try somehow, stumblingly but politely, to insist that you get to your destination first.

Although taxi fares are still inexpensive, they have gone up again. The meter now starts at 10 drachmas, then ticks over at the rate of 7½ drachmas a kilometer; there's an additional charge of 5 drachmas between midnight and 6 a.m., and each piece of luggage is an additional 5 drachmas.

**THE SUBWAY:** It goes in a straight line—from Omonia Square to Piraeus and from Omonia Square to the hill town of Kifissia (10 drachmas in each direction). You probably won't have too many occasions to use it, unless you're staying around Omonia Square and you want to get to Piraeus to catch a ferry boat or cruise ship, in which case it's the fastest and cheapest way to get there.

**RENTING A CAR:** You could, of course, rent a car, but even a small European runaround won't free you from the frustrations of one-way streets, blue zones, and parking places. While you're sightseeing in the city forget about a car; if you're planning to do some trips out into the country or along the coast, then a car makes more sense. That's a subject we'll come to in the chapter "Touring the Hinterlands."

**GREEK MONEY:** Most other currencies in Europe went through convulsions in recent years, but Greece's **drachma** remained true to the dollar.

One drachma is currently worth roughly 2.78 U.S. cents, which means that the dollar is worth 36 drachmas, or thereabouts.

The drachma is made up of 100 **leptas.** There are copper coins for 50 leptas, and for 1, 2, 5, 10, and 20 drachmas. Bills are worth 50 drachmas (blue), 100 drachmas (red), 500 drachmas (green), and 1,000 drachmas (brown).

Some coins may seem to be worth peanuts but you'll need them for tipping, telephones, and trolleys.

*Note:* In the following pages, the dollar equivalents have been rounded off to the nearest half-dollar for the sake of simplicity.

Regardless of the color of the currency, prices have a habit of changing. We've tried to be as accurate about prices as possible. We've checked and double-checked, and, to the best of our knowledge, all these prices were accurate at press time (late 1978). Rumors are that the authorities will try to hold hotel and restaurant prices steady in 1979/80, but we can't guarantee it. SO PLEASE: CHECK ALL PRICES IN ADVANCE.

Also at press time, the U.S. dollar is worth 35.87 drachmas; since most people find it more convenient to convert drachmas

*Academy of Science*

into dollars by dividing by 36 rather than by 35.87, that's what we've done throughout this guide. So for all practical purposes, 36 drachmas equals $1. Check rates and prices in advance. Use the figures in these pages *as a guide only.*

# Chapter V

# WHERE TO STAY IN ATHENS

WHAT'S THE HOTEL situation in Athens? Most people visiting Athens for the first time naturally have this question on their minds. After all, Athens is a very, very old city—does it have very old hotels? Do they have private baths? And since summers are hot in Athens, do the hotels have air conditioning?

Well, here's the surprise—most hotels in Athens seem to have been built in the past decade, and those that weren't have been renovated and modernized in the past ten years. Most of them (except in Class D and E) have private bathrooms; most of them have air conditioning.

Nevertheless, the outstanding attraction of hotels in Athens is their relatively low rates. In Athens you can live in the style you always knew you were intended to live in. The Hotel Grande-Bretagne and the King George Hotel, for instance, have been entertaining kings, queens, and other heads of state for years; they're grand hotels on a par with the finest in Europe, but you can get a double room at one of them, in the peak season, for only $61. A double room in a medium-class downtown hotel will cost you only $15 to $20, and there are hundreds of other modern rooms for under $12 a night. Where else in Europe can you get a room with private bath, smack in the center of a capital city, in peak season, for under $20 a night?

If you're seeing Europe on a tight budget, you can probably get a better room, dollar for dollar, in Athens.

If you're traveling on a shoestring, you can survive longer in Athens.

But you'd better hurry: three years ago the deluxe rooms were going for $37, and you could get simple but comfortable rooms for as little as $6 a night. In addition, the quality of hotel services seems to be declining, and staffs are eager to get their tips despite the fact that a 15% service charge is already included in the bill.

Before going on to individual hotels, here are some general notes on the hotel situation in Athens today.

**CATEGORIES:** All hotels in Greece are classified by the Greek Government. There are six official categories—beginning with L for Deluxe running through Class A and ending with E. In this guide, we will confine our reviews to the first four categories, with a quick look at some hotels, guest houses and hostels in the lowest price ranges. The factors the Government uses in judging hotels are the "existence of restaurants, availability of private baths, degree of comfort, and excellence of service."

In reality, the formula for determining the categories must have been devised by the Oracle at Delphi. For example, in Class B hotels every room must have hot and cold running water, at least half of them must have private bathrooms, most of them must have central heating and a telephone, and the staff must speak at least one foreign language (which need not, of course, be English). In Class C hotels, private bathrooms are not compulsory for any of the rooms, and there must be at least one toilet for every six rooms. But in some cases the designations are a holdover from seasons long gone; consequently, some Class C hotels are better than some Class B hotels, and the Class B Athens Gate Hotel, for example, is better value than, say, the Class A Attica Palace. Again, the relatively new Electra Palace Hotel offers more comfortable rooms than most of the accommodations in the traditional King's Palace Hotel. In the following pages, you'll read about a few hotels which seem to offer outstanding values.

**RATES:** The Government also establishes and enforces the rates for each category. The price and what it includes must be posted in each room—service, taxes, handling of luggage, central heating, air conditioning, meals, and so on. Usually these signs are in English as well as Greek. When you come to pay your bill you should have no problem with overcharging; if you're in a Class B hotel you *know* you'll be paying no more than $23 in a double room, with service charge, in season. However, this does not mean you will not encounter misunderstandings here and there, because hotel keepers are allowed to tack on a few extras: 50 drachmas in a double room for central heating, 75 drachmas for air conditioning; "an increase of 10% may be added to room rates if the stay is two days or less"; "the room rates of hotels located in summer holiday areas, or spas, may be increased by 20% during the period July 1st to September 15th"; "the use of the public bath or shower will be charged at 10 drachmas for cold water, or 20 drachmas for hot water." Throw in a slight language problem and there could be a minor international incident. You can avoid any misunderstandings if you reserve your room in advance (preferably through a travel agent) and have a written confirmation in your hand.

With all these rules and controls you might think that getting accurate up-to-date hotel rates would be a simple matter. It isn't. When this guidebook was being updated in October 1978, the Greek National Organization for Tourism didn't know the hotel rates for 1979. Neither did the Hellenic Chamber of Hotels, nor did most of the hotel keepers in Athens, although the Government had by that time authorized an increase of 15% on 1978 rates.

*Therefore, we must report, with regret, that many of the rates included in the following pages are estimates based on information supplied by the appropriate authorities. The figures take into consideration the authorized 15% increase, so they should be accurate to within two or three percentage points; however, you should check with your travel agent, or with individual hotels, to determine the precise rate in effect at the time you plan to visit Greece.*

**TAX AND SERVICE CHARGE:** As of this writing, the Government tacks on a 6% tax to all hotel rates. In addition, hotels are allowed to add a 15% service charge to the bill. Many hotels, however, quote rates which include both service charge and tax. *All the rates quoted in these pages include the 15% service charge.*

**BREAKFAST:** Some hotels also quote a rate which includes service charge, tax, *and* breakfast. That is—continental breakfast, which consists simply of coffee with rolls or toast and butter or marmalade or jam. If you want orange juice, you'll probably have to pay extra. If breakfast is served in your room, you may have to pay a few extra drachmas. When a hotel quotes "English breakfast" this means eggs and bacon with your coffee and rolls. If you're on a very tight budget, you may prefer a rate that does *not* include breakfast, since you can probably walk around the corner to a neighborhood cafe and have the same thing for half the price.

**HALF-BOARD, FULL-BOARD:** The Government also controls the prices of meals served in hotels, and one way a hotel keeper will try to boost his income is to insist on guests paying a rate that includes meals—half-board, with breakfast and lunch or dinner (the equivalent of modified American Plan, and sometimes also known as demi-pension), or full-board, with breakfast, lunch, and dinner (the equivalent of American Plan). This may be an advantage if you're staying in a hotel like the Astor and can dine in the Roof Garden; in most hotels it will probably be a drawback. On the one hand, the tourist organization advertises tempting waterfront tavernas, on the other the hotel keepers force you to dine where *they* want you to dine. Whenever possible, resist half-board and full-board rates and leave yourselves the option of dining out.

**SEASONS:** There are basically two seasons for hotels in Athens: the off-season usually runs from November 1 through March 31, but in some cases it may begin on October 1 and in others end on May 31, while a few hotels no longer distinguish between the seasons, so steady is the stream of visitors to the city. Get your travel agent to look closely into precise dates, because this may save you several dollars.

**CHOOSING A HOTEL IN ATHENS:** Once you've determined what price you want to pay, the situation is fairly simple. Most of the hotels are in one of two clusters in the center of town— either around Syntagma (Constitution Square) or around Omonia Square. A few, like the Hilton and the Alkistis, are a few blocks farther away, but still convenient to the center of town. Most hotels in Athens are within walking distance of almost everything you want to see, and in any case, taxis are so cheap that getting around the city is not much of a problem.

**COMPARE BEFORE BUYING:** If you come in the off-season, when the choice of rooms is greater, it's a perfectly acceptable practice to inspect rooms before taking one. If you give yourself half an hour or an hour, you can walk from hotel to hotel, looking at locations, checking out facilities and the view from the balconies or roofs. Even in the hotel you finally decide on, check out the room, because the standards in some of the older hotels vary considerably from one room to another.

**THE VIEW FROM THE TOP:** The Acropolis is one of the most stunning sights in the world. Every corner you turn in Athens brings you another glimpse of this sacred hill. You'll probably want to sit on your balcony at sunset and watch the sunset turn the Parthenon to a glowing honey color. You may even want to sit on your balcony in the morning and watch the Parthenon's columns loom through the morning light. There's nothing like it, so try to get a room with a view, even if you have to give up luxury or space or a private bathroom. And one of the surprising facts about hotels in Athens is that you generally pay no more for a room with a view.

**RESERVATIONS:** During the peak season don't go near Athens without a reservation. You may end up like the Parthenon—without a roof over your head. In the end, you'll very likely find a place to stay, but you may spend half your day finding it. Make a reservation. And if you want a room with a view, be sure to specify. In recent years, with more and more visitors flocking to the city, it's wise to make reservations well in advance even during the off-season, if you want to be sure of staying in the hotel of your choice. (This is true not only of Athens but of places like Delphi and Nauplion.)

**LONGER STAYS:** Because hotel rates in Athens are so low, you may be tempted to linger a while in that city. If you do, consider renting an apartment, rather than staying in a hotel room. Apartments are usually cheaper, well equipped, and they give you a chance to live a more truly Athenian life. It's a particularly economical idea if you have a family. The **Delice Hotel Apartments** and **Riva Hotel Apartments** both offer one-bedroom and two-bedroom suites with fully equipped kitchenettes and air conditioning, 24-hour reception, and telephone service; the Riva also has bar and restaurant service. The Delice is at 3 Vassileos Alexandrou Street, the Riva at 114 Michalakopoulou Street, both near the Hilton Hotel. Double rates are in the region of $45 to $60 per night for stays of a month or longer.

**SERVICE CHARGE AND TIPPING:** A service charge of 15% is included in your hotel bill. The theory behind a service charge was to avoid the confusion resulting from having to tip different members of the hotel staff; the service charge would be added to the bill and that would take care of all tipping. Except that it doesn't. The staff still expects tips. Don't encourage this. Tip only for small *extra* services like shining shoes and fetching cabs.

Here are some tips on tipping in hotels: according to the sign in your room, luggage handling is included in the service charge built into the room rate. So you're not obliged to tip any more, but if you feel like it, offer 10 drachmas a bag (the same rate as porters at airports and stations). In a deluxe hotel you may want to double that. You're also expected to tip the waiter who brings you breakfast in bed. Some people will recommend 15 to 20 drachmas, but this seems unnecessarily high since you're already paying a special charge for room service. Tip what you can get away with.

**THE ROOMS:** Greeks are traditionally people who like to get out into the open air. And why not, with a climate as balmy as theirs? They'd rather spend a summer evening sitting beneath an olive tree discussing politics or soccer than being cooped up at home watching the telly. Since they spend so much time outdoors, they don't bother about spending a bundle furnishing their homes. By American standards, Greek homes are bare. Ditto Greek hotels, especially the older ones. The lobbies may be like marble palaces, but upstairs the corridors may be spartan, and the rooms furnished only with the essentials. No frills. So don't come to Athens expecting all the trimmings you'd normally find in an American hotel. The rooms will be spotlessly clean and comfortable, but in many cases they won't have wall-to-wall carpeting, armchairs, radios, and writing desks. You may be discouraged at first, but you'll soon discover that it doesn't matter, because you, too, will soon prefer to spend your evenings beneath an olive tree.

**AIR CONDITIONING:** The majority of Athens hotels now have air conditioning, at least in the *L, A,* and *B* categories. Hotels in other categories probably have air conditioning in *some* of the rooms, and you will have to request one of these rooms—and pay an additional charge of around $2 a day. Temperatures in Athens in midsummer go up into the 90s by day, and linger in the 70s at night. If you're accustomed to air conditioning back home, you'll probably want it in Athens also, at least in July and August.

**BATHS AND SHOWERS:** There are two types of bathtubs in Athens—the regular kind and the sit-in kind. The sit-in type is about three feet by three feet. It's fine for feet that have trudged all the way up the Acropolis and back, but inadequate for weary shoulders that have carried camera bags and shoulder purses. If you want a real bath, tell the reception clerk when you're checking in. Most hotels have both types. Most baths of either dimension also have hand-held showers, which have one advantage—when you're in your bath you can also switch on the shower *underwater* and use it for a whirlpool bath, or to massage your weary thighs. If you do get an overhead shower, you may not get a shower curtain. The technique is to let the water splosh onto the floor which has been angled to drain off the surplus. It makes sense—but just remember not to leave your slippers or bathrobe on the floor.

**TELEVISION:** Don't expect TV in your room. Even at the Hilton. Greece has had television transmission for only nine years, and it's still not the big thing it is in the U.S. (Many new hotels have TV sets in the lobby or the lounge—but that's it. Many hotels don't even have radios in the room.)

**SWIMMING POOLS:** You'll find few hotels with pools in Athens. Of the ones listed in this guide, only the Athens Hilton, Caravel, Royal Olympic, St. George Lycabettus, Chandris, President, Stanley, Electra Palace, Dorian Inn, and Sirene have pools. Many hotels have sundecks on the roof. But, generally speaking, people come to Athens for sightseeing rather than a tan. If you do want to get in some swimming and sun, stay at one of the nearby resorts—like Glyfada and Vouliagmeni. They're both close enough for jaunts into town for sightseeing and dining.

### Deluxe "L" Hotels
### (from $40 to $100 double, peak season)

The **Athens Hilton,** Vassilissis Sophias Avenue (tel. 720-201), is not so much a hotel as a city. On weekends its lobby is filled with wide-eyed Athenians who can't afford a trip to New York but want to see what America is like. There's plenty for them to see—but it's not America. Not with all that marble. There's probably enough marble in the new Athens Hilton to have built a second Parthenon—30,000 square meters of it, of 11 types, from Arta, Timos, Pendeli, Yannina, and Salamis. You arrive at the hotel beneath a great curving portico with brown and white marble (a work of art which later centuries may dig up and prize as highly as we prize fragments from Knossos). You walk through hallways with marble floors and marble pillars, down marble steps to a lounge with dozens of plush armchairs, then down a few more marble steps to another wider furnished lounge that looks over the marble pathways leading to the swimming pool. Just inside the hotel entrance are two courtyards (the traditional Greek atrium), 200-year-old olive trees in the middle, and boutiques and shops around the sides—six fashion shops, an antique store, a bank, post office, telegraph office, beauty salon, barbershop, florist, drugstore, travel agencies, airline office, Avis Rent-a-Car office. Without ever leaving the Hilton you can buy designer clothes, records, jewelry, flowers, books, souvenirs, handicrafts, copperware, rugs, bags, cigars.

One of the favorite spots for the Athenian sightseers is the Byzantine Cafe—an arena of a coffeeshop dominated by a 20-foot-wide copper chandelier. This is where Greeks sample American coffee, American hamburgers, and American apple pie. The Taverna ta Nissia, downstairs, is also full of Athenians, who've come in this case to sample authentic Greek cooking (see the chapter on "Dining Out in Athens"). Next door to the Taverna there's the smart late-night Trattoria, and above both

*Evzones (Greek soldiers)*

the Pan Bar, a softly lit watering place that's cool in the summer, snug in winter.

On the Hilton roof, 12 floors above the city, you'll find a mini-Las Vegas of entertainment—the Supper Club restaurant/nightclub, and Galaxy Bar with dancing to a live band. But these are no ordinary night spots. When you step off the elevator you'll see why. Ahead of you, through floor-to-ceiling windows, lies one of the most spellbinding views in Europe—the black, star-speckled mass of the Mediterranean sky, the twinkling lights of the city, and, smack in center stage, the floodlit Acropolis and Parthenon. In summer, of course, you can sit outside on the terrace itself and soak in the view and the soft Athenian air.

All the guest rooms at the Hilton have views of either the Acropolis or Mount Pentelicon, and a few have views of both the Acropolis and Lycabettus Mountain. The Hilton's rooms are spacious and comfortable, as you've come to expect of Hilton hotels everywhere: five-channel radio, direct-dial telephones, wall-to-wall carpeting, and, of course, sliding glass doors opening onto spacious balconies. The bathrooms (more marble, this time gray) have ice-water taps and American-style shower-baths. The Hilton's maids fix your room twice a day, and turn back the sheets while you're up on the roof dancing. Other Hilton facilities include a swimming pool, sauna, massage parlor, photostat service, typewriter rental, garage, and photographer.

The Hilton is located in one of the smart residential districts, among the embassies, beyond the National Park. It's only a 15-minute walk or a 75¢ cab ride from Constitution Square.

The Athens Hilton is the most expensive hotel in town: singles 2,255-3,072 drachmas ($62 to $85), doubles 2,804-3,657 drachmas ($78 to $102) including service charge and tax; these rates, moreover, are in effect *all year*, and if you think the Hilton people are crazy, just try to get a room there.

The **Hotel Grande Bretagne**, Syntagma (tel. 3230-251), is the Dowager Duchess of Athens' hotels. It was built in 1862 as a 30-room annex to the royal family's summer palace across the street (now the Houses of Parliament), and put in the care of Eustace Lampsa, chef to the royal household who knew all the preferences of the royal visitors who'd be staying there. It's still a family-run hotel, with long-serving staff (its two classic concierges retire this year after 50 years of service apiece), but the original three-story building is now seven stories with a total of 450 rooms. Generations of distinguished guests have created a unique atmosphere at the GB (no one refers to it as the Grande

Bretagne). Its doors have been whisked open by uniformed attendants for princes, czars, tycoons and millionaires, for composer Richard Strauss, the Grand Duchess Helen, and, more recently, Sir Laurence Olivier, Henry Fonda, and Paul Newman. During World War II, the GB was Nazi headquarters; at the end of the war, Sir Winston Churchill stayed here for a few nights and narrowly escaped an assassination attempt which involved using the labrynthine sewers of the hotel. Today the GB is virtually a "reviewing stand" for state occasions at the Parliament Building and the Tomb of the Unknown Soldier across the street.

The lobby of the GB is one of those monumental Athenian halls of marble—marble floors, green marble walls, marble pillars, Oriental carpets and plushly upholstered sofas and fauteuils; beyond it is an equally comfortable and spacious lounge with a decorative glass ceiling, and beyond that the dignified, classical dining room. Two contemporary touches are the intime, dimly lit cocktail lounge in one corner, and the new GB Corner cafe-restaurant in the other. If you simply want to sample the opulence of the GB's public quarters, drop into the lobby for a coffee; it costs a few drachmas more than it would cost in one of the cafes in the square, but it comes to you in a silver pot, on a silver tray, with a silver milk jug and silver sugar bowl—with a wine glass of chilled water, served with great dignity by a waiter in immaculate white uniform.

The GB is one of *the* grand hotels of Europe (it's just been elected to something called the "Golden Chain" of the world's best hotels); but it is a traditional *Greek* hotel, and although it was completely upgraded a few years ago, the style of the guest rooms may not be as "fluffy" as you expect (wooden floors and rugs rather than wall-to-wall carpets); but they're immaculate, and beside each bed are three buttons to summon waiter, maid, or porter. The prize rooms are those facing the square, with terraces where you can have morning coffee or afternoon tea as you watch the light change on the Acropolis; but you should be warned that with the pell-mell clutter of traffic in modern Athens, these rooms can be noisy and you may have to keep your terrace doors closed in the interest of sanity. Summer rates are 1,690 to 2,070 drachmas ($47 to $57) for single rooms, 2,200 to 2,640 drachmas ($61 to $74) for double rooms; suites are $115. Off-season rates are 25% less.

When Greece's former King Constantine was married to his Danish princess several years ago, the **King George Hotel,** Constitution Square (tel. 3230-651), became an official annex of the Royal Palace, complete with sentries at the door. The KG is accustomed to entertaining royalty and the aristocracy of Europe. It's the second of the grand hotels facing onto Constitution Square. It has an entrance of glass flanked by Grecian urns on marble pedestals and French sculptures worth millions of drachmas. The palatial lobby is decorated with five types of marble. Chinese screens, Chinese vases, and dazzling chandeliers. The King George even has its own art gallery. The pictures are not for sale; they're there simply for the pleasure of the guests (the bulk of the collection is made up of Greek masters of the 18th and 19th centuries).

The breakfast room, by the way, with its two enormous tapestries, is the big-windowed, glittery room overlooking the square; if you want to pretend you're a prince waiting for a royal wedding, come over here someday for breakfast, or afternoon tea. Either one will cost you around $3.

The front office staff at the KG is impeccable. The concierge wears wing collar, the clerks wear striped trousers, and everyone talks in whispers. The elevators are plush little vehicles with black leather walls, mirrors, and bronze trim. The ninth floor of the KG is famous for its magnificent Tudor Hall restaurant, which is a bit like having a stately home in your attic. (More about the Tudor Hall in our chapter on dining.)

The rooms at the King George are what you'd expect in a luxury hotel: rich furnishings mostly in the styles of Louis XV and Louis XVI (the chairs and stools are kept covered with plastic covers to protect the expensive fabric until the guests arrive). Rooms are heavily draped and carpeted, and all at the front have balconies overlooking the square with views of the Acropolis and the Royal Palace. The suites are equipped with Directoire writing desks, armchairs so elegant they have to be called *fauteuils,* chandeliers, and the inevitable marble bathrooms. Summer rates are from 1,320 drachmas to 1,680 drachmas single ($37 to $46), 2,032 drachmas to 2,360 drachmas double ($57 to $66).

**St. George Lycabettus Hotel,** 2 Kleomenou Street, (tel. 790-711), is a four-year-old with 150 rooms, as many balconies, located on a residential street in the foothills of Lycabettus. Crowning it all is a rooftop pool and restaurant. Glass doors open to cool, spacious elegance. Gleaming black marble floors are highlighted with upholstered chairs and couches in blends of caramel, pumpkin, and gold, and smoky-glass tables with brass accents. Tony's Bar is down a few stairs to the left, and a full floor down there's a cool dining room with gold tablecloths and olive antiqued chairs (prix-fixe lunch or dinner, 340 drachmas). One floor below that, going down the hill, there's a patisserie/coffeeshop. But most guests will probably opt for the rooftop restaurant—green chairs among potted oleanders in the summer, indoors in winter in the Grill Room (dinners average around 400 drachmas, with dancing to a combo). The 30-foot-long pool is surrounded by "astroturf"-style matting, with comfortable chaises and poolside showers.

The accommodations are plush—gold wall-to-wall carpeting, coral upholstery, wood paneling, furniture with brass trim, luxurious bathrooms with tile walls and marble floors, radio, and direct-dial telephones. The plushest rooms are the corner suites, especially those on the fourth and fifth floors which have balconies on two sides, breathtaking views, two rooms, two bathrooms, and a sense of spaciousness that you might miss in the basic rooms. The St. George Lycabettus (don't get it confused with the plain Lycabettus Class B hotel farther down the hill) is managed by the French chain—Etap-Hotel—which has a fine reputation throughout Europe; it will probably be popular with visitors (especially businessmen) who want modern facilities and comfort in a quieter location than Syntagma (a seven-minute walk downhill and 60¢ cab ride back up). Other facilities include TV, garage, beauty parlor, barbershop, bank. Rates: singles 1,139 to 1,370 drachmas ($32 to $38); doubles 1,672 to 2,025 drachmas ($46 to $56); 20% less during the off-season.

Americans will probably feel at home at the **Amalia Hotel**, 10 Amalias Avenue (tel. 3237-301), even before they step inside because it looks like a modern American resort hotel, and the sign that greets you as you go through the door says "Air Conditioning by Carrier."

The Amalia is just off the National Garden. The lobby is airy, with tall ceilings, lots of wood paneling, and a marble stairway leading up to the mezzanine. Off the lobby there's a neat little bar (shielded from the outside world by lacy drapes), a tearoom, and a restaurant with wooden Grecian-style chairs, chandeliers, and flowers. The lounge in the lobby is as large as you'll find in most hotels, but take the elevator or the marble stairway to the mezzanine floor and you'll find three more lounges—one on a terrace overlooking the palm trees of the National Garden, another with a 23" TV, and the third a quiet room that can be shut off for meetings. They're all furnished with softly upholstered

### The Athens Chandris Hotel

Syngrou, the long straight avenue that links the city with the sea, is currently undergoing a major facelift, and one of the landmarks in this new-style Athens is the glistening new 354-room **Athens Chandris Hotel,** which opened its automatic doors in August 1977. The city's 12th deluxe hotel, it's close to the sea, equidistant from downtown Athens, downtown Piraeus and the airport, and facing the Ippodromo, or race track. The interior is a glistening Art Deco extravaganza of holiday colors, marble, and contrasting textures. The furniture, imported from Italy, is all Milan Modern—the bedside lamps are like giant ice cubes, the chrome trim of the headboards has a built-in radio, and the ultra-modern suites (26 in all) must be among the most luxurious in Athens. On the roof, eight floors up, guests can cool off in a small pool, get a suntan, or enjoy vast views of the city, the mountains, and the Saronic Bay; many guests also have a grandstand view of the races from their balconies. Other Chandris features include a trio of smart restaurants and a 24-hour coffeeshop. Room-only rates for summer 1979 are 1,450 drachmas single ($40), 1,650 drachmas double ($46); off-season, 1,050 drachmas single ($29), 1,250 drachmas double ($35)—surely a bargain.

couches and arm-chairs that are paradise for people who've spent the morning hiking around the Acropolis.

The rooms, like the facade, come closer to American ideas than most Athens hotels. You'll find paneled headboards, modern table lamps, armchairs, throw rugs, and those cute, new, one-piece telephones with the dial on the bottom; and the bathrooms have fixed overhead showers. The Amalia also has a hairdressing salon and round-the-clock room service. Of the 100 rooms, 38 have private balconies, and of these 34 face the National Garden. Only six of the rooms are singles, so if you're lucky you'll get a double at the single rate. High-season rates are 989 drachmas ($27) for a single, and 1,454 drachmas ($40) double.

Most tourists, and even a few Athenians, have never heard of the **Royal Olympic Hotel,** 28 Diakou (tel. 9226-411). It's slightly off the beaten track, which by the pampered standards of Athens means it's all of six blocks from Constitution Square. But what a location! If you have a room facing the front, you can throw back the drapes, open the sliding windows, step out onto your balcony, and there in live wide-screen cinemascope is the entire

Temple of Olympian Zeus spread out in front of you. And right behind it, almost growing out of the temple's cluster of columns, is the mountain of Lycabettus, with the greenery of the National Garden filling the gap between. It's a breathtaking sight. And well worth the six blocks between you and Constitution Square. Into the bargain, this new hotel is beautifully furnished—the 235 bedrooms as well as the public rooms.

The hotel's main doors are opened by bellboys who look like airline pilots. The steps up to the lobby, the floors and pillars, are inevitably of marble. The luxurious bar separates the lobby from the small swimming pool at the back of the hotel, and on the left of the lobby, there's an elegant new dining room decorated with engravings of old Athens. One of the most attractive of the public rooms is the lounge, up a few marble steps, to raise it above the level of the traffic so that you can get an undisturbed view of the temple. (Even if you're not staying at the Royal Olympic, remember this grandstand lounge is a place to drop into for morning coffee or afternoon tea.)

The Royal Olympic's guest rooms are American-style. There are carpets or fluffy scatter rugs on the floor, computerized direct-dial telephones, radio, air conditioning, balconies, sliding doors of double-glaze glass, amply fitted closets, chairs, coffee tables, well-equipped bathrooms, complete down to a second phone, and big towels. The hotel's corner suites can keep an entire family in comfort, with even an icebox attractively disguised as a woodgrained cabinet. There are also a few "businessmen's studios" with sliding screens to separate sleeping area from working area, and equipped with a full-sized desk, studio couch, refrigerator, and coffee table. The most luxurious rooms are on the sixth floor. They're a shade more "designed," and they have larger balconies—and, of course, the higher you are the more stunning the view and the more muffled the sound of the traffic. But take a room on any floor as long as it's at the front.

The hotel's management is youthful and alert, the front desk staff especially cordial, efficient, and bilingual. The dining room is a spruce, chandelier-bright place; there's also a specialty restaurant, the Templar's Grill, which you'll read about in the next chapter. The fixed meals, lunch or dinner, cost 350 drachmas.

The Royal Olympic's rates are 1,548 drachmas ($43) single, 1,878 drachmas ($52) double—all year. A full breakfast costs 200 drachmas ($4), a continental breakfast half that amount.

The **Athenée Palace**, 1 Kolokotroni Square (tel. 3230-791), is the elegant building on the corner across from the National

Historical and Ethnological Museum—just one block behind Constitution Square. It's one of the grand old hotels of Athens, but a few years ago it was completely refurbished, air-conditioned, and brought into line with modern hotels. The lobby is a cathedral-like place, with marble floors and columns, and a grand stairway leading up to a mezzanine balcony lounge. Over in one corner, down a few steps, there's a snug bar and cocktail lounge; in the opposite corner, a souvenir-and-postcard shop. Above the mezzanine (where you'll find a 23" television set), one entire floor is given over to lounges, a beauty parlor, and the dining room. The lounges have big club-like armchairs, Oriental carpets, soft colors on the walls and ceilings to offset the vivid prints on the chairs. The dining room has a red carpet, sparkling table linens, immaculate waiters, and a wall covered with murals of Arcadian scenes.

The Athenée Palace has 150 rooms and 150 full-length, stretch-out-and-wallow-type baths. The rooms are spacious, and the bathrooms are as large as many single rooms in other hotels. (The bathrooms, incidentally, follow a precise hierarchy in marble: in the suites, they have marble floors and marble walls; in the deluxe rooms, marble floors and tiled walls; in the superior rooms, linoleum floors and painted walls.) The rooms are furnished throughout in period style—slightly Victorian, with floral-print covers in an exuberance of reds, yellows, and greens. Some of the rooms have small balconies with a view of Lycabettus popping up over the tops of office buildings, but this is a hotel where the eye-popping attractions are inside.

The Athenée Palace also boasts a quietly efficient front-office staff, and a concierge who seems to be able to handle six problems at once without any trouble whatsoever. Summer rates are 1,150 drachmas single ($32); 1,610 drachmas ($44) double; 2,090 less in the off-season.

The **King's Palace Hotel,** 4 Venizelou Avenue (tel. 623-231), is more or less a contemporary of the Hilton, but they're decades apart in styling. Where the Hilton goes for marble, the King's Palace, right off Syntagma, gleams with dark, highly polished wood. The main lounge, to the right of the lobby and along the Promenade, has high ceilings, artificial sunlight, wooden walls, and a large multicolored glass vitrine running from floor to ceiling at one end. It's for all the world like being on an old ocean liner. Even the furniture has the solid, plump look about it that reassures you it won't pitch around in heavy seas. (Maybe this is why the hotel is often host to shipping magnates who arrive in convoys for a conference.)

The front-desk staff is efficient, and apparently able to speak any language. The lobby usually has an airline crew arriving or waiting for pickup. But there's no hubbub here—it's a gentlemanly hotel. Many Athenians come here in the morning or afternoon to sip coffee in the Cafe Belvedere, facing the avenue, with a view almost all the way to Omonia Square.

The rooms at the King's Palace have, let's say, a Grecian simplicity. The chairs and tables are in Grecian style, the kind with curved legs like a fawn's. The beds are low and curlicued, like the divans you see Grecian maidens lolling around on on old Greek pottery. Some of the rooms have tubs, some have full-scale baths. Not sumptuous, but perfectly good, comfortable rooms.

One special feature guests enjoy is the Roof Garden. It's one level above the top of the GB and the King George, both of which very kindly block out the neon signs between the hotel and the Acropolis. The King's Palace Roof Garden is also one of the best places for watching the Changing of the Guard at the Tomb of the Unknown Soldier—you get a grandstand view without having to crane your neck to see over the heads of the crowd. The menu up there features Greek, French, and American dishes (80 drachmas for lunch, 120 drachmas for dinner) but you can also just have drinks and snacks. If you're staying at the hotel, you can use the roof as a sundeck.

The King's Palace has 230 air-conditioned rooms. Ask for a room on the seventh or eighth floors, facing west. You won't get a view of anything in particular, but you will get fairly large balconies high above the traffic—with room enough to stretch and sunbathe, and watch the sun set as you sip your ouzo. In high season, singles are 1,230 drachmas ($34); doubles, 1,585 drachmas ($44). In off-season rates are 1,095 ($31) and 1,425 ($40) drachmas respectively.

While you're thinking in this price range, keep in mind the luxurious resorts described in the chapter "Athens by the Sea"— the **Astir Palace** in Vouliagmeni and the **Apollon Palace** in Kavouri.

The **Acropole Palace,** 51 Patission (tel. 523-851), probably has the most elegant facade of any hotel in Athens. It was built at the turn of the century, with some of the embellishments you'd find in a French hotel of that period—bay windows, tiny iron balconies, and a curved corner. But it's beginning to show its age:

rooms are still furnished as they were originally, and there are many antique items in the rooms—but several of the rooms are looking dowdy and threadbare. The main lobby has a marble and wrought-iron stairway that sweeps gracefully up to the air-conditioned lounges and the circular, domed dining room. Downstairs there's the oddly named Sky Room Bar and the winter nightclub. In summer the dining room and the nightclub are on the Roof Garden, eight high-ceilinged floors up, where you can dine with style and dance to the hotel's two orchestras—one Greek, one British.

The Acropole Palace has all the facilities you'd expect of a long-established, fine hotel—tearoom, beauty parlor, barbershop, American Bar, air conditioning. It's a quiet hotel in a convenient location—opposite the National Archaeological Museum, about five minutes on foot from Omonia Square and seven minutes by cab from Constitution Square. If you don't want to be surrounded by tourists, souvenir shops, and cafes, the Acropole Palace might be the answer. Summer rates are 1,085 drachmas ($30) single, 1,497 drachmas ($42) double, with breakfast. Fall rates are 15% less, winter rates 20% less.

The **Park Hotel,** 10 Leoforos Alexandras (tel. 883-2711), is smaller, more intimate, welcoming guests with a club-like lobby of wood paneling and leather decorated in muted colors. It's across the street from one of the city's most spacious parks, and many of the upper rooms have pleasant views overlooking the treetops. Pampering seems to be the philosophy here: bar/refrigerators in all the rooms (plus 24-hour room service), marble bathrooms with extension telephone, fingertip bedside controls for the gadgetry—message light, wake-up alarm, door lock, "Do Not Disturb" sign, heating and air conditioning, radio, and music channels.

In addition to a round-the-clock coffeeshop, the Red House, the Park has, of all things, a pizzeria; but the Latina is like no other pizzeria you've seen—unless you know another one with ovens covered by handhammered copper. In summertime, the Blue Peacock bar on the roof garden gives you an even better view of the treetops and a refreshing breeze. The Park's 113 double rooms cost 1,215 drachmas ($34) to 1,780 drachmas ($49) in summer, 25% less during the off-season.

The four-year-old 520-room **Caravel Hotel** 2 Vas. Alexandrou Avenue (tel. 79-07-21), is a near neighbor of the Hilton. The two hotels seem to be competing on the spaciousness and grandeur of their lobbies; both of them have handsome, contemporary-style tavernas and round-the-clock coffeeshops (at the Caravel's bright-and-airy Night-and-Day, you can have dishes like paillard de veau until 7 in the morning); both have lobby-level shopping galleries and beauty parlors. The Caravel's rooftop cocktail lounge, the Horizon, has a spectacular view of the Acropolis and Lycabettus Hill; likewise, the sunning terrace around the full-size heated pool. Up here you'll also find saunas and an indoor gymnasium, with windows to let you admire the view of the Acropolis when you come up for breath. The Caravel's guest rooms are spacious, colorful, and tasteful, with small balconies, individual room controls for heating and air conditioning, marble bathrooms, and small refrigerator/bars (in addition to 24-hour room service). Summer rates are singles from 1,391 drachmas ($39), doubles from 2,035 drachmas ($57) to 2,288 drachmas ($64) and suites to over $100.

Your main interest in Parnes is probably the Casino (discussed further on), but we'll list a hotel here in case you want a change of pace at some point. The **Mount Parnes Hotel-Casino,** Parnes (tel. 249-111), is located on the 3,000-foot mountain 22 miles from midtown Athens. It's comfortable and clean, the rooms have private baths and showers and central heating, and although it's officially classed as a Deluxe hotel there are no frills here. Except that view! All the rooms face Athens, and they all have big terraces (big enough to have a meal on) overlooking the valley and the city, Piraeus and the sea. You get an identical view from the pool terrace. The hotel has a restaurant, snackbar, nightclub, and, of course, the casino. Also a seven-day beauty parlor, TV room, and gardens. What's the point of staying way up there? It's cooler, it's by the casino. Otherwise it's quite dull. The half-board rates in summer are around $35 in a single, $48 in a double.

While you're thinking in this price range, keep in mind the luxurious resorts described in the chapter "Athens by the Sea"— the **Astir Palace** in Vouliagmeni and the **Apollon Palace** in Kavouri.

## Class A and B Hotels
## (from $15 to $30 double, peak season)

There's a large selection of hotels in these two categories, including one of the city's newest, the high-rise **President.** In the following pages, you'll read first about A and B hotels in and around Syntagma (Constitution Square), then those in the general area of Omonia Square.

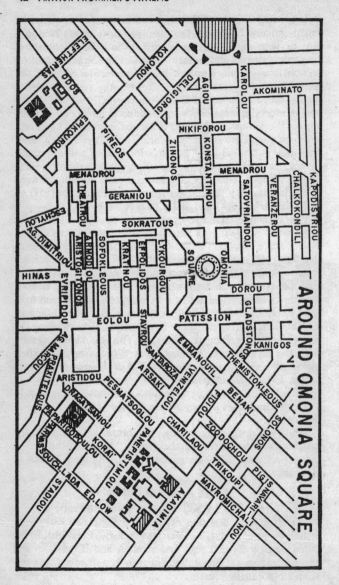

**The newest Class A Establishment**

The high-rise, 530-room **President Hotel** at 43 Kifissias Avenue is Athens' newest Class A establishment, although its stylishly modern lobby (acres of marble in earthy colors, concealed lighting, pop music) might lead you to believe you'd stepped into a Deluxe hotel. Bars, lounges, and dining facilities are equally spacious; the guest rooms, on the other hand, are dainty, although pretty to look at and fitted with direct-dial telephone, air conditioning, radio, and balcony. The 22nd floor is given over to a swimming pool, sun terrace, and disco-theque, but the President's basement may be the best feature if you plan to do a lot of driving—it has space for 500 cars. Room rates for summer 1979 are 760 drachmas single ($21), 1,065 drachmas double (about $30), including service and taxes. The President is located on one of the main avenues leading north from Athens (convenient for touring by car), but a ten-minute to 15-minute taxi ride from Syntagma.

The ten-story **Attica Palace Hotel,** 6 Karageorgi ti Servias (tel. 3223-006), is only a few yards down from Syntagma; there's a big sign outside, but many people seem to miss it, and in case you do too, the entrance is in an arcade, among a row of shops, usually clustered with shoppers, office workers, and dispensers of lottery tickets. The lobby is hardly big enough for you and your luggage, the "lounge" is a niche beneath the stairs, and you may begin to wonder if this really is a Class A hotel. Upstairs is a different matter. No scrimping on space up there. The first floor has not one but *three* spacious lounges, one with a bar, and all of them with contemporary furnishings, big modern paintings and sculpture. The dining room is bright and spacious. The upper floors with the guest rooms have hallways of marble—green, red, beige—and each one would be big enough for Socrates and his pupils to sit around in. Guest rooms have contemporary-style desk and dresser units, couches, armchairs, coffee tables, air conditioning, telephone, and private bath and shower. Some rooms have dividers with abstract paintings giving the impression of a small studio apartment; all rooms facing the street have balconies, and from the seventh floor up you get a view of the Acropolis (the top two floors actually have three rooms with big terraces rather than balconies—great place to sunbathe).

Ninety percent of the Attica Palace's 78 rooms are doubles:

966 drachmas ($27) for two, and the few singles are 690 drachmas ($20) during the summer.

Still another relatively new hotel, still another American-style facade. The **Astor Hotel,** 16 Karageorgi tis Servias (tel. 3224-971), is right in the center of one of the busiest areas of town, with taxis and people constantly passing up and down Karageorgi tis Servias on their way from the Plaka to Constitution Square. Once inside, however, you're not too conscious of noise. The hotel sits back from the street, with its entrance under an arcade that blocks out the traffic noises as well as the harsh sun.

The Astor has 11 air-conditioned floors, with the top floor given over to the Roof Room. This is one of Athens' few year-round roof gardens, in fact. It sprawls over the terrace in summer, but in winter it's enclosed in glass that doesn't confine the view. And what a view! Look up from your table and there's the Acropolis looking as though it's across the street. Over on the right you can see Lycabettus Hall, and over on the left Mount Pentelicon. You can have lunch or dinner up here for around $6, even less if you order budget items like spaghetti ($2) or omelets ($1 to $1.50).

The Astor has 133 rooms and suites, and most of the rooms above the sixth floor have views (except for the singles, which are all at the rear), and most of them also have balconies. The fuurniture is nothing to write home about, but again, you'll be too busy looking at the view from your balcony to care much. Down in the basement, there's a well-stocked souvenir shop and beauty parlor, and just off the lobby, a small bar.

Even in high season, you don't have to pay more than $19 for a single, $28 for a double.

**Esperia Palace,** 22 Stadiou Street (tel. 3238-001), is on one of the big thoroughfares that link Syntagma with Omonia Square, and #22 is closer to Syntagma than Omonia. It's a convenient location, but it can get noisy at rush hours so ask for a room high up or at the rear. (There are balconies of sorts, but only for standing on, so they're not worth making a hassle over.) The Esperia is another of those Athenian palaces with acres of marbled space—a two-story lobby with marble floors and columns, marble hallways on each floor—and the inevitable highly polished floors. The 185 rooms have fresh wallpaper, prints or pictures to brighten them up, colorful bedspreads and curtains, and furniture that's a shade more substantial and comfortable than usual in Greece. The 12-year-old Esperia is owned by the King's Palace people, so service is attentive and efficient. High-season singles are in the $20 region, doubles around $25.

The **Hotel Electra,** 5 Ermou Street (tel. 3223-223), is another of those new hotels that look more like office buildings than hotels—especially at street level where the narrow glass door is surrounded by shops and cafes. Once you step through into the lobby, however, you're unmistakably in a grand hotel. The lobby is two-tiered, with a fishtank set in a marble divider, and a solarium-like bar in a small patio at the rear. To the left, the doors marked Ambrosia lead you into another of those well-tended restaurants you find in Athens hotels.

The balcony around the lobby is really the hotel's lounge, and like most first-class hotels in Athens, it's a lounge generously furnished with couches and armchairs and a big-screen television set. A neat touch: a telephone corner with desk, directories, and chairs.

The corridors on the guest-room floors have olive carpets, dark-green ceilings, and gray floral wallpaper. The floral paper overflows into some of the rooms, which all have polished parquet floors or spotless linoleum with scatter rugs, marble-floored bathrooms with tiled walls, twin beds arranged head-to-head, a desk/dresser unit, armchair, phones, and individual air conditioning controls.

On the eight floor there are four rooms with 8′ x 8′ terraces. The hotel is air-conditioned throughout, and all 110 rooms have massage units attached to the beds (10 drachmas per massage). The Electra's singles are from $20, doubles from $25, in summer.

Turn right into Filellinon Street from the Mitropoleos Street corner of Syntagma, and three blocks later you come to a small square with an old Byzantine church and tower; and three palm trees. The **Olympic Palace Hotel,** 16 Filellinon (tel. 3237-611), is the modern building just acrosss the street, with the neat square verandas on three sides. The lobby is the usual palace of marble, leading into a larger lounge with almost enough armchairs to seat every guest in the hotel. There's also a small bar with comfy upholstered chairs, and, one floor up, a big bright dining room with lots of windows and flowers.

All the Olympic Palace's rooms have private baths, music, telephones, air conditioning, modern (if not exactly brand-new) furniture, and the bathrooms have marble floors and floral wallpaper. There are corner suites that sleep three. Despite its location close to Constitution Square, the Olympic Palace is a quiet hotel. Its summer rates 863 drachmas ($24) for a single, 1,231

Imagine staying in a modern hotel five minutes from Syntagma, on the edge of the Plaka, in the shadow of the Acropolis, *and being able to have a swim in a rooftop pool before your siesta*. Then check into the **Electra Palace Hotel**, 18 Nicodimou Street (tel. 3241-401), and have your dreams come true. It is here that you may also find yourself sitting at sundown in a swinging, canvas loveseat, sipping an ouzo and watching the light fade on the Parthenon. This roof garden, with its loungers, bamboo chairs, elevated pool and bar, is reason enough for staying at the opened-in'74 Electra Palace, but it's by no means the only one. Even without its roof, this would be one of the best values in the city, a Class A hotel with more attractive rooms than many Deluxe hotels. For a start, the 118 rooms are "warmer," less institutional than most of the city's hostelries—with brown-gold-red wall-to-wall carpeting, matching headboards, twin beds plus a sofa and armchair, occasional tables, desk/dresser, and fitted closets all in warm-hued wood. The tile-and-marble bathrooms have some of the most sophisticated fixtures anywhere; chambermaids and room waiters are announced by door chimes rather than a rat-ta-tat, and hallways are carpeted for soundproofing. All the rooms have air conditioning, radios, telephones; most of them also have balconies with sliding glass doors and sliding screens, and the suites on the upper floors have big terraces rather than balconies. Nikodimou Street is only one-car wide, a trifle noisy at times, so ask for a room high up or at the rear. In any case, you have to be above the third floor to get the best view. But even if you can't have one of the upper rooms, stay there anyway—you can always spend your spare hours on the roof. The Electra Palace is owned by the same people who run the highly regarded Electra Hotel a few streets away, so the service is efficient, polite, and friendly. Other facilities include a sunken lounge in a handsome marble-and-mahogany lobby, a cozy bar, a mezzanine dining room and lounge/card room, and adjoining garage. Summer rates are 690 drachmas single ($19), 966 drachmas double ($27); during the busiest months you may be expected to take a half-pension or MAP rate, an additional $8 per person.

drachmas ($34) for a double, breakfast included.

A Class B choice, **Hotel Lycabettus**, 6 Valaoritou Street (tel. 633-514), is a five-minute walk from Syntagma, on one of the quieter shopping streets. The Lycabettus is relatively new and all the rooms on its seven floors have bathrooms, telephones, radio, balconies, and air conditioning. The best of the bunch are on the upper floors (where the balconies are bigger). It's a friendly little place, with a TV bar, coffeeshop, and a breakfast room. Room rates here are 580 drachmas ($16) for a single, 848 drachmas ($24) for a double, including breakfast. It's not a steal, but it is good value considering the location and the coziness.

**Athens Gate Hotel,** 10 Syngrou Avenue (tel. 9238-302), is one of Athens' top values. Location first: a five-minute walk from Syntagma and directly across the avenue from the Temple of Olympian Zeus and its attendant Hadrian's Gate. The entrance to the hotel is surrounded by a terrace cafe sheltered throughout the day by a two-story stoa. There's also a gleaming black-leather, chrome, and marble bar and lounge on the ground floor, but don't linger—head straight for the elevator and press the top button. The roof is eight stories up, a walk-around marble sun-deck with lounges and a view! Probably the most all-embracing view of any hotel in Athens, regardless of category and price. All the sights are there—Olympian Zeus and Hadrian's Gate just across the street, the Zappeion and Parliament to the left, Lyca-bettus in the distance, the Hilton, the Olympic Stadium, and the Royal Palace; then on the other side, the towering Acropolis, and away in the distance the Gulf of Saronica.

Most of the 106 rooms come with balconies, and depending on location, you'll probably have some part of this vista without leaving your room. Get your reservation in early, ask for a room on the seventh floor at the rear, and you'll get a terrace rather than a balcony with room for breakfasting or sunning while you look up at the looming Acropolis. The rooms themselves are much livelier than the usual in Athens—with razzle-dazzle wall-papers and drapes, carpeted floors, functional mahogany furni-ture (desk/dresser, armchair), radio, bedside lamps, modern tiled bathrooms, and a couple of features you don't normally find in Class B hotels—air conditioning and direct-dial telephones. Other facilities include room service until midnight, a 30-car garage, a 100-seat restaurant on the second floor. The manager here is Spiros Zervos, who's been looking after American tourists for years at some of the best hotels in Greece. High-season rates are 860 drachmas for a single ($24), 1,380 drachmas for a double ($38), MAP; off-season, the rates drop to $16 in a single and $24 in a double, EP, including tax, service, and air conditioning. Outstanding value by any yardstick.

The outside of the **Hotel Arethusa,** corner of Mitropoleos and Nikis (tel. 3229-431) is gift-wrapped in what looks like Rey-nolds-Wrap aluminum foil, the interior decor is a lively blend of

Kolonaki is one of the most fashionable neighborhoods in Athens, much sought after by bankers and novelists, and now you can stay there in a quiet residential street, surrounded by high-rent apartments, for only $25 a night double. The **Athenian Inn**, entered by a flower-decked entrance at 22 Haritos (just two blocks from Kolonaki Square) is owned by a Greek-American couple who've decorated it tastefully in "Greek village" style (dark beams, white stucco walls, tile floor). The lounge-breakfast-room-bar features an open fire, rustic furniture, and watercolors by local artists; the 288 guest rooms have wall-to-wall carpeting, quaint rustic-style wooden beds, radios, telephones, and bath or shower; 23 of the rooms have balconies, some with a view of Lycabettus Hill. Summer rates: 603 drachmas single ($17), 878 drachmas double ($25), including service charge, taxes, and breakfast in the pretty rustic lounge.

marble, polished hardwoods, and fabrics in sprightly colors. All 87 rooms in this attractive hostelry are smartly decked out with contemporary furniture, wall-to-wall carpets, air conditioning (with individual controls), radio, telephone, big bathroom. Up top there's an indoor-outdoor roof garden (superb view, drinks, dinner for around $6), and you can have an after-drink in the modern bar (with TV), one hushed floor above busy Mitropoleos. This is an unusually handsome Class B hotel, and until now it has been a bargain; but for 1979, management threatens to raise prices 25% above 1978 levels—to 729 drachmas (around $21) single, 1,069 drachmas double (around $30).

One of the newer hotels in Athens, the **Sirene Hotel** at 15 Lagoumtzi Street (tel. 922-9311), also features a pool and view of the Acropolis from its seventh-floor roof. It's only a medium-sized pool, of course, but then you're not here for the Olympics. You can also stretch out on the sundeck, and there's a bar within hailing distance. The remainder of the hotel is no letdown either: rooms are trimly furnished, with carpets, bath or shower, radio, telephone, big closets, and individual air conditioning controls. The comfy lounge includes a writing room, TV, and bar; lunch or dinner in the cool, modern restaurant is less than $6. The Sirene doesn't have the most convenient location in town (you can't have everything), but it's still only a ten-minute bus ride to Syntagma, or a five-minute ride plus a ten-minute walk to the

Acropolis. The Sirene's summer rates are 544 drachmas single ($15), 790 drachmas ($22) in doubles.

You can't get a much more central location than the **Minerva Hotel**, 3 Stadiou Street (tel. 3230-915)—the upper floors of the business center above the arcade that runs from Syntagma to Stadiou Street. The Minerva was transformed into a Class B hotel in 1960, 50 rooms on three floors (7, 8, 9), all with private tub or shower, room phones, and three of them with air conditioning. No restaurant. A spiral staircase leads from the arcade-level lobby to a small lounge where you can sit down to the continental breakfast that's included in the room rate—578 drachmas ($16) for a single, 795 drachmas ($22) for a double, in-season.

Appollonos is hotel row. It runs for half a dozen blocks from the Plaka to the rear of the TWA office at Constitution Square, and it's full of good budget hotels. The **Omiros Hotel**, 15 Apollonos Street (tel. 3235-486), is one of the newer and smaller ones. It has 37 rooms, all with pink or green tiled bathrooms, telephones, radios, and air conditioning. It's a dapper little hotel. The lobby has handsome wood paneling with Ancient Greek ceramic decorations on the walls, and a coffee corner at the back. There's also a small but uncongested bar-and-restaurant one floor up. The rooms are equally compact, some with head-to-head beds along one wall, a small couch along the other. The rooms facing the street have balconies overlooking the narrow, typically Athenian street, with balustrades, arcades, shutters, and pots of flowers. Most of the rooms have scatter rugs on linoleum floors, and the furnishings are standard. There's taped pop music everywhere at the Omiros—in the lobby, in the elevator, in the rooms, on the roof. The pride and joy of the Omiros is its Roof Garden, which has one of the most unsullied views of the Acropolis in the entire city (it's amazing how a modest little hotel can take on a new dimension of majesty with a superb Roof Garden vista of that omnipresent sacred hill). You can have dinner up there for 197 drachmas ($5.50), or you can just sit on the swing chairs with your date/wife/husband/boyfriend and a Coke and while away the hours gazing at the great white flank of the Acropolis rock.

The Omiros' rates are 526 drachmas ($15) for a single, 741 drachmas ($21) for doubles.

**King Minos Hotel**, 1 Piraeus (tel. 5231-111), is a Class A hotel, close to Omonia Square. It's only a few steps from the square, but its glass-and-grillwork facade is more reminiscent of the Caribbean. The hotel has a spacious lobby, with a marble frieze of King Minos' Palace in Knossos dominating one wall. Up on the mezzanine floor are acres of lounges, two desks with typewriters, an American bar, fountains, birds in gilded cage, and a restaurant. There are seven floors of rooms, and since this ten-year-old was recently refurbished, the furnishings are fresh and modern, with roomy closets, chairs and desks, and marble balconies. Bathrooms have full-size bathtubs, marble floors and walls, and piles of towels; studios have twin beds arranged at right angles, around a brace of chairs and a coffee table. It you feel cramped, you can always sit out on the balcony and watch the action in Omonia Square. Or go up to the roof to sunbathe. The King Minos is air-conditioned throughout. Peak season rates are 848 drachmas single ($24), 1,225 drachmas double ($34), including breakfast.

**Hotel Ambassadeurs,** 67 Socratou Street (tel. 5234-321), is another Class A hotel to go with the King Minos in the Omonia Square area. Socratou Street is only one block from the bustle but you'd never know it from the peaceful, spacious lobby of the Ambassadeurs. It's only 20 years old, but it gives the impression of having been built in a different age, creating a club-like atmosphere with its pleasant  salons" with deeply upholstered French-style furnishings. Fully air-conditioned throughout, and all the rooms have private bath or shower. Rates are 690 drachmas ($19) single, 966 drachmas ($27) double.

**Hotel Stanley,** 1 Odysseos Street (Karaiskaki Square; tel. 541-611), is another hotel with a pool on the roof—this time a Class B. It's a slight distance from the center of town, but its roof is one of the coolest, breeziest places in town at high noon. The 351-room Stanley dominates the big square at the end of Aghiou Konstantinou Avenue, between Omonia Square and the Larissis railroad station. It's a modern air-conditioned hotel, where every room has a bath or shower, balcony, and telephone. The rooftop pool and garden are open from May through October; the attractive first-floor cafeteria with Scandinavian decor and mottled marble floor is open year round—with three-course meals for less than $6. Despite its size, the Stanley is usually full, so if you don't have a reservation call ahead first. The Stanley's rates are 691 drachmas ($19) single, 984 drachmas ($27) double, 20% less in fall, 40% less in winter. The #1 yellow bus will take you from the Stanley to Omonia Square or Syntagma for 8 drachmas.

Two of the best values in and around Omonia Square are relatively new Class B Superior hotels—the Titania and the

Dorian Inn, both opened in 1976.

A stylish tinted glass facade rising eight floors above a street-level shopping arcade identifies the **Hotel Titania** at 52 Panepistimiou Avenue (tel. 360-961). Up on the roof, the terrace and bar have impressive views of Lycabettus Hill and the Acropolis. The Titania's 400 rooms and a score of suites fill six floors with bright colors and trim design; all the rooms have telephones, individual heating/cooling controls, fitted wall cabinets and tiled bathrooms with tubs and hand-showers. Public facilities include a 24-hour coffeeshop (there's also room service from 7 a.m. to 7 p.m.), spacious restaurant (lunch or dinner for $5.50), and lounge-writing room on the second floor. Summer rates are 613 drachmas ($17) single, 848 drachmas ($24) double. Good value in a convenient location (the traffic hurtling along Panepistimiou is not too intrusive with the windows closed, but if you want complete quiet, ask for a room at the rear).

The **Dorian Inn Hotel** is located on the far side of Omonia Square at 15-17 Piraeus Street (tel. 523-9782). Its 117 rooms and 29 junior suites have balconies, direct-dial telephones, individual controls for heating and air-cooling; there's 24-hour room service, a restaurant, a bar-lounge with TV and another bar on the roof, 12 floors above the city. But the Dorian's main attraction for many people will be the rooftop pools—one for adults, one for children. Summer rates are 614 drachmas ($17) single, 873 drachmas ($24) double; spring and fall rates are 15% less, winter rates 30% less.

A good bet (a very good bet) for anyone who plans to spend a lot of time in the Archaeological Museum is the **Hotel Marmara**, Halkokondyli Street (tel. 626-362). It's a few blocks from the museum, and a few blocks from Omonia Square, on an intersection that's marginally less hectic than the square. As its name implies, the Marmara has lots of marmara—marble in the lobby, in the bathrooms, in the bar. The restaurant, bar (TV), and lounges are spacious. The Marmara's 140 rooms go in high season for 526 drachmas ($15) single, 741 drachmas ($21) double; 25% less in winter.

Acadimias Street runs parallel to Venizelou, and about half-way along, just behind the University and National Library, the nine-story **Hotel Acadimos,** 58 Acadimias (tel. 3629-220), rises at the corner of Hippocrates Street. You can't ask for a more cultured spot than that. The hotel's 130 rooms have balconies, telephones, baths or showers, and many of them have fine views of the Acropolis or Lycabettus Mountain, but there's no air conditioning here. There's a cocktail bar and lounge on the first floor, and a restaurant where for 197 drachmas ($5.50) you can have a good lunch or dinner and watch the latter-day Aristotles ambling from library to class to shaded bench. Peak-season rates at the Acadimos are 442 drachmas ($12) for a single, 638 drachmas ($18) for doubles; only 10% less in winter.

The nine-story **Alfa Hotel** at 17 Halkokondyli Street, just off Omonia Square, is a class B hotel operated by the company that also owns the Deluxe King's Palace and Class A Esperia Palace; the Alfa's 100 rooms, each with private bath or shower and room phone, are available for 741 drachmas double, about $21. Sun terrace on the roof.

## Class C Hotels
## (from $10 to $15 double, peak season)

The official hotel guide to Athens includes more names in these two categories than in all the others put together. In all, there are over a hundred hotels in Athens offering rooms between $8 and $15 a night for doubles in peak season. This guide can't possibly review all of them, but in the following pages you'll find a selection of some of the best budget hotels in the city.

The six-year-old **Hermes Hotel,** 19 Apollonos (tel. 3235-514), has an entrance like an airline terminal, but its severe facade is softened by shrubbery draping over the balconies. It's a small hotel—only 45 rooms—all with balcony, phone, bath or shower. The rooms at the rear look on a school playground; the upper floors have views of the city, and in some cases the Acropolis. Dinner is 181 drachmas ($5), and there's also an à la carte menu with snacks and sandwiches. Room rates are 368 drachmas ($10) for a single, 460 drachmas ($13) for a double—all the rooms are actually double-size.

One major advantage of the **Royal Hotel,** 44 Mitropoleos (tel. 3234-220), is you don't have to take a coach tour to visit the cathedral. You just cross the street. The hotel's entrance faces a tiny square with a circular garden in the center and trees all around, a few shops, a cafe or two, and the curved back of the cathedral; and it's right next door to the bronze-faced headquarters of the Greek Shipowners' Association. The location is the best part of it. The hotel has a peculiarly Athenian facade, with marble on the street level, and tall narrow windows, very classically proportioned, going up four floors. There's a bright indoor cafe facing the street, and a mirrored lobby one floor up. The doubles with bath are spacious and liberally furnished—couch, chairs, dressing tables, large windows and good-size bathrooms; the singles are quite a bit smaller. There are telephones in every room. The Royal offers the same rates all year—doubles with bath are 497 drachmas ($13.50), doubles without bath are 468 drachmas ($12.50), including breakfast, and tax.

The Royal Hotel's neighbor, the **Imperial Hotel,** 46 Mitropoleos (tel. 3227-617), has a slightly Germanic facade—square cut with small windows. It doesn't have a lobby at the entrance, but when you go up one flight you'll find a pleasant sitting room and the manager, G. Klissouris, who speaks English, is anxious to please, and enjoys meeting all the Americans who stay in his hotel. The Imperial's rooms are simple, clean, and large, and all but two have shower or bath. All have a telephone, balcony, and central heating (but no air conditioning). The singles have double beds and tend to be roomier than most singles in this price range. There's free parking in the square across the street. The Imperial has no rear views—its balconies only look toward the cathedral and Acropolis. There are 21 rooms on five floors; rates are from 253 drachmas ($7) single, from 373 drachmas ($10.50) double.

Kolokotroni is the street that begins at the National Historical Museum and runs more or less parallel to Ermou and Mitropoleos. The **Hotel Carolina,** 55 Kolokotroni (tel. 3220-837) is about halfway along. It's one of those places you walk into and instantly feel right at home—or back in the dorm, because the

---

For people who want to be in the heart of things you can't be much closer to the heart of old Athens than the intersection of Iperidou and Asteriou streets in the Plaka. Here the three-year-old **Hotel Nefeli** squeezes 18 spic-and-span rooms into a three-story wedge, each of its chambers equipped with modern bathrooms, room phone, trim furniture. Nothing fancy, but comfortable and functional. The spacious, cool lobby is dominated by an orange plastic phone bubble, and there's a trim breakfast-room-lounge right on the corner. Obviously not the quietest spot in the city, and when the Plaka wakes up so will you, but here are modern rooms in a central location for only 508 drachmas double, or just over $14 for room, breakfast, and taxes. First choice in this category.

Carolina has the prices and atmosphere to attract droves of college kids. The Carolina is run by two Greek-American brothers who came over from Carolina a few years ago and since then they've activated and improved the hotel, which used to be an apartment building. Every room faces front, most of them with balconies. The best rooms are on the roof, but since this is the kind of hotel where you'll be constantly meeting new friends and dashing off to the Plaka, the view doesn't matter much. There's a small snackbar on the first floor, a few steps up from the lobby. The hotel has 35 rooms, eight baths; the rates are about 375 drachmas for a single with bath. Doubles without bath are about 380 drachmas (including as many hallway baths as you wish), and 465 drachmas with bath. Breakfast is around 42 drachmas. The fun is free. Tax and service included.

The **Philippos Hotel,** 3 Mitseon (tel. 9223-611), is something of an oddity—it's on the *other* side of the Acropolis, the side with the classic picture-postcard view. This is a residential district, except during the Athens Festival when it becomes a funnel for the crowds heading up the road to the Pnyx for the Son-et-Lumière show. If you're staying at the Philippos, you don't have to join the crowd, you simply step out onto your balcony and there's the whole show, right there.

The Philippos is a simple little hotel, only a few years old, and completely redecorated in 1971. You go up a few stairs to the tiny lobby and TV-fitted bar, where there always seem to be American college girls sitting around reading Aeschylus. The Philippos is another of those cozy, communal, everybody's-a-buddy places. In the rooms on the upper floors you'd better be—because each one can sleep five. The other rooms are slightly cramped, even when they're supposed to sleep two, but if you're in the first flush of Aeschylus you probably won't notice. The bathrooms are clean, tiled, and fitted with hand-showers. There are balconies in all the rooms, and on the upper floor they're as large as terraces. From these you can look up at one of the most sublime achievements of European civilization. The upper floors are perfect for young people and families, because they can all squeeze into one of the rooms for less than they'd pay for dinner in the restaurant downstairs. The Philippos' restaurant, incidentally, is a cheerful pseudo-taverna with stucco arches, chandeliers, and red, blue, white, green, and beige tablecloths and cushions—and air conditioning. The restaurant is open for lunch from 12:30 to 2:30, for dinner from 7:30 to 9:30, and either meal costs 158 drachmas ($4.40). However (and a surprise for a small budget hotel), you can phone down for sandwiches, snacks, or omelets *at any time of the day or night*. There's also a cozy, inexpensive little taverna around the corner on Areopagitou Street. You can sunbathe on the hotel's roof, and if you want to go sightseeing, you can catch the # 1 or # 5 bus two blocks away and take it to Constitution Square and Omonia Square. Rates are 368 drachmas ($10.25) single, 460 drachmas ($12.75) double in summer; 20% less in spring and fall, 40% less in winter.

The **Omonia Hotel** (Omonia Square, tel. 523-7211) has ten floors and 275 rooms, each of which has an iron balcony and picture windows which give the building an airy appearance. The lobby, one floor up above the entrance to the sunway, is surrounded by a bar cafe facing the square, with a restaurant at the rear. There's always plenty of activity around this friendly, spotless hotel; all rooms have private baths and showers, phones and comfortable furniture, and they're particularly spacious, especially the singles. Good value at 383 drachmas single ($11), 553 drachmas double ($15), both including breakfast.

The **Asty Hotel,** 2 Pireos (tel. 5230-424) is a slightly younger hotel than its competitor on the next block—the Omonia. It has 128 rooms, all with balconies, half of them facing the square with its fountains and greenery, clean and comfortable but rather "institutional." The Asty's restaurant, on the first floor overlooking the square, is, incidentally, one of the more popular eating places in the neighborhood. Rates: 375 drachmas ($10.50) single, 586 drachmas ($16) double.

The **Hotel Pythagorian,** 28 Aghiou Constantinou (tel. 5242-811/4), is another of those good-guy Class C hotels in the region of Omonia Square. The attractive entrance with square marble columns and vinyl "wood" paneling leads to a lobby and dining room and a white spiral stairway that goes up to a mezzanine lounge with green marble floor and overstuffed chairs. The 56 rooms, spread over seven floors and topped with a roofgarden, all have tiled bathroom with baths and bidets, rooms with typical lino-floor-plain-modern-furniture decor. Rooms at the front have balconies. In-season rates are 444 drachmas ($12.50) single, 590 drachmas ($16.50) double, with breakfast.

The street that runs from Omonia to Ermou is called Athinas, and halfway down it crosses Evripidou. Aghiou Demetriou is where the two streets meet. Okay? The **Hotel Kronos,** 18 Aghiou Demetriou (tel. 3211-601), is actually in a convenient location for either the hustle and bustle of Omonia or the hustle and bustle of the Plaka. It's a small modern hotel, in a small square with a church, trees, and grass. Most of the rooms have private baths or showers. Rooms with bath are 368 drachmas ($10.25) in a single and 460 drachmas ($12.75) in a double. Breakfast is 42 drachmas extra. Off-season rates are reduced by 20%.

Theater Square, unfortunately, no longer has a theater—it's now backstage Athens, a beehive of importers and exporters by day, and quiet as a church by night (but probably not for single ladies). The ten-year-old **Hotel Alkistis**, 18 Platio Theatrou (tel. 3219-811), has a sleek ten-story facade of glass, steel, and marble, 112 rooms and eight suites with motel-modern decor, private baths and showers, and telephones. Ninety-six of the rooms have balconies, and if you pick the right one, you'll have a fine view of the Acropolis. All the rooms and hallways are spotless and freshly painted; the comfortable, spacious lounge has TV and a bar and the roof garden boasts a panoramic view (there are tables and chairs, but no bar service so you have to bring up your own drinks). Manager "Papou" (or Grandfather) Georgiou claims to be an honorary citizen of New Mexico, Minnesota, and Oklahoma, although he has never set foot in the U.S., but he does host lots of young Americans each year—students who come to earn credits in Greece under the auspices of the American Institute of Foreign Studies. When you step into the Alkistis' two-story, marble lobby you may have trouble believing you're in a Class C hotel, but one look at the rates and you will be persuaded that this is another of the city's remarkable bargains. Summer rates are about 437 drachmas ($12) in a single, 583 drachmas ($16) in a double, including heating, service, and tax. These low rates are reduced by 10% in the off-season. *But get your reservations in early—the Alkistis is one of the most popular C class hotels in Athens.*

Dorou is one of the streets leading off Omonia Square, and it's a useful name to keep in mind if you want to avoid the frenzy of the square but still enjoy its budget prices. The **Hotel Alma**, 5 Dorou (tel. 5222-833), is a fairly modern, eight-story hotel with 64 rooms, all with telephones, some without private baths, most of them badly lit. If you can, try to get one of the six big rooms on the seventh floor, or one of the two on the eighth floor; they have spacious verandas where you can dine or sunbathe and enjoy penthouse living, Athens style. The first-floor cafeteria serves continental breakfast only (but it's closed from November through April); the reception area is cramped and grubby, but then the rates are only 343 drachmas ($9.50) for a double without bath.

The **Hotel Nestor,** 58 Konstantinou (tel. 535-576), has a rather olive-drab exterior but the 50 rooms themselves are bigger than usually found in this category, bright, with handsome furniture, with pastel-colored walls and balconies, all with bath or shower. There's an outdoor cafe, and a dining room enlivened with fresh flowers on every table. The friendly, 50-room, seven-story Nestor has been popular for years with Scandinavians: now it's the turn of the Americans. Singles are 368 drachmas ($10.25), and doubles are 449 drachmas ($12.50) in peak season.

Another gleaming, marble-facaded hotel with its front steps in the market is the **Omega Hotel,** 15 Aristoghitonos (tel. 3212-421). This one has a roomy, wood-paneled lobby, a pleasant lounge and coffee bar. Its 54 rooms have private bathrooms, but the furnishings are fairly basic. Hardly a steal at $10 single, $12.50 double for stays of three nights or longer.

Plateia Exarcheia is a charming triangular plaza lined with trees and cafes, with its apex at the **Hotel Exarcheion.** This Class C hotel, built in 1973, has 49 rooms (all with private bath or shower, most with balconies), and there's a splendid view across the city from the rooftop bar, six floors up. Double rooms are 430 drachmas ($12); some of the singles are oddly grouped in pairs and share a bathroom (what the management calls a "suite")—they cost 340 drachmas per person (less than $10). Breakfast is an additional 40 drachmas per person. If your first stop in Athens is the National Archaeological Museum, and you want to be in an area that's Athenian rather than touristy, then this is a good address to head for—55 Themistocleous (tel. 3601-256).

## Rock-Bottom Accommodations for Adventurers and Students

In a city like Athens, where $10 will set you up in a single room in a first-class hotel in the off-season, you hardly need to bother with the local rock-bottom prices. However, thousands of young (and some not so young) people arrive in Greece each year with minimal dollars in their pockets and backpacks on their shoulders, and Athenians seem to go out of their way to cater for them, providing dormitory accommodations, and in some cases allowing them to bunk down in their sleeping bags on the conveniently flat-roofed houses and hotels.

The **YWCA,** or **X.E.N.** as it's known in Greece, hardly deserves the title rock-bottom, because it's in a big, modern building that at first glance seems more like a first-class hotel, in a convenient location—at 11 Amerikis Street (tel. 3624-2011), just a couple of blocks from Syntagma and the American Express office. X.E.N. has a hairdressing salon and library, as well as kitchen and laundry facilities on every floor. Membership costs less than $5 a year for girls under 16, more for adults, but you don't have to be a member to stay there. Each room has beds, tables, chairs, marble floors; there's no air conditioning, but the sunless rooms at the rear are cool even at midday in midsummer. June through October, rates for stays of one to three nights are from 120 drachmas ($3.33) for a single without bath to 160 drachmas ($4.44) for a double room *with* bath. Drawbacks? The building closes at 1 a.m. (the Plaka is just getting under way at that time), and you can't have a shower between 3 and 5 in the afternoon—"the quiet hours."

The **Athens Youth Hostel** at 57 Kypselis Street (tel. 8225-860) charges about $1.50, with facilities for breakfast and light meals. It's open all year, but you need an International Youth Hostel Card (you can buy one on the spot for $10, and it's valid all over the world). There's another year-round hostel at 20 Kallipoleos Street (tel. 7664-889); again the charge is around $1.50, with breakfasts and light meals available.

**Cleo's Guest House** is a two-piece hostelry more or less in the Plaka, yet only a two-minute hike from Syntagma; the two addresses are 3 Patrou and 18 Apollonos streets, and prices are from $2.50 and up per person. Even closer to Syntagma, at 28 Nikis Street, the **Crystal House** offers dormitory accommodations in a remodelled 18th-century mansion complete with lounges and hot water. Rates are $3.50 per person in the dormitory, $1.50 for rooftop space. The **Phaedre Hotel** is a Class D establishment, but its rates are so reasonable it can reasonably be included in this category. Its location, at 16 Cherefontos Street (tel. 3238-461), belies the ominous overtones of its legendary namesake—a quiet little square facing the palm-filled courtyard of St. Katherine's Church, surrounded by neighborhood tavernas and narrow streets, one block from Filellinon Street, near the Monument to Lysicrates. The rooms are relatively big, but none of them have private bathrooms, just washbasins, with three toilets to every floor—but then consider this bargain rate: 274 drachmas double, or just $7.60 in summer. Hot showers are 20 drachmas, cold showers 10 drachmas.

# Chapter VI

# DINING OUT IN ATHENS

YOU MAY HAVE heard some people say Greek food is dull. Dull? Try this for starters: *caravides*—fried crayfish with Russian dressing; *koheli*—lobster, mussel, crab, shrimp, or red snapper baked in a shell with cognac; *moussaka*—chopped meat with eggplant, cheese, and bechamel sauce; *teropita*—those delicious little cheese puffs filled with feta; *yigantes*—white lima beans in tomato sauce; *dolmadakia*—vine leaves stuffed with meat, onions, and spices, and served with lemon sauce.

That's not a random selection from many menus. It's not even a random selection from one menu. It's only the start of one recent meal—which was concluded with mixed grill of lamb chop, veal, and kidney, tomato and spring onions, followed by a deep-fried fritter served in a hot sugar sauce, followed by apple spiced in honey.

So let's straighten out some of the facts about dining in Athens. Greek food is *not* dull. Maybe if you're staying there for a week or longer, your palate may lose its enthusiasm for more Greek food because so much of it is cooked in oil and flavored with lemon. But for the average visit of two or three days, you won't have time to sample all the dishes you're going to want to sample. If you do stay longer and you do want a change of pace, you can always go to one of the restaurants serving American food in its infinite variety—hamburger, club sandwich, and steak.

Most Greek restaurants also serve a few dishes which are popular in Greece but which are not Greek dishes. Most of the inexpensive restaurants feature spaghetti, cannelloni, wiener schnitzels, omelets, and steaks. Remember, Greeks have been entertaining tourists from other European countries for a long time now, and try to cater to them. There always has been a choice of French and Turkish eating places, but now Athens has acquired Chinese and Japanese restaurants, even an English pub.

The other rumor you hear about Greek food is that it contains some unsavory ingredients. This is sometimes true in the country, and in the lambing season partially true in Athens. If anyone ever asks you if you'd like to try *ameletita,* just smile and say no thank you. Even in Greek it means unmentionables. Plural. Or if someone suggests *kokoretsi,* decline. It's second cousin to a Scottish haggis and we all know what a yummy that is. And don't be surprised if you take your Greek date to a seafood restaurant over by Piraeus and she gobbles up the entire fish— head, eyes, and all. It's not that she's starving. It's simply the Greek custom. You don't have to follow suit.

If you're tentative about what you eat (and when you're traveling, changing time zones, and generally rushing around, you have every right to be), stick to basic dishes like roast lamb and veal. They're cooked on the spit, with only a whisper of spices.

Unfortunately, as you will see a few pages from now, inflation has been catching up with kitchens in Athens, and some of the basic Greek dishes are getting close to the point where they're not worth the price. Nevertheless, if you're on a tight budget your dollars will buy you more sustenance in Athens than in most European capitals. If you're really counting your leptas rather than drachmas, stick to restaurants *(Estiatorion)* rather than tavernas, to *ouzeri* rather than cafes.

## Types of Eating Places and Dining Tips

The one thing that Greece has that most countries don't have is **tavernas.** There probably was a time when a taverna was something quite distinct from a restaurant—and even more distinct from a nightclub. But that's no longer the case. A taverna can be a pub, a restaurant, a cafe, a nightclub, or a combination of all of them. Since many of them provide music, and are really for an evening on the town, you'll read about them later on in our chapter on nightlife.

The other unusual feature about Athenian eating places is the **Roof Garden.** Apparently the roofs of Greek houses used to be flat in order to collect rain water, which was then drained off and fed into a tank under the soil; when proper plumbing and water systems came along, people didn't need their roofs as dams, but they then discovered that they were refreshingly cool places to spend an evening. So they started turning them into gardens, or at least terraces. The idea spread to restaurants. Now many of the new hotels in Athens include a roof garden, and you should certainly plan to spend at least one evening up there. The basic, authentic roof gardens are on tavernas in the Plaka, and the ultimate roof garden is probably the King George Hotel's, which is half indoors, half outdoors.

Athens at midday in midsummer is often too hot for sitting down to a meal, and this has probably given rise to the city's varied types of snackbars—the Western-style snackbar, the tea and pastry shops, the fig-and-nut store, the pastry vendor, and the souvlaki shop. Keep these snackbars in mind if you're on a budget, or if you're having problems adjusting to the curious meal hours in Athens (a subject we'll come to in a minute).

## The Pastry Vendor

He's the local equivalent of the pretzel man. He sells two, sometimes three, items. First, there are rolls and hero-style breads, plus a bread known as *koulouri*—a large, thin bagel with sesame seed on top. It costs 4 drachmas—the perfect 10¢ snack. The pastries include plain *bourekia,* a sort of doughnut with sugar sprinkled on top. You can buy bourekia either in a "long-john" shape, or in a rounded shape with a small smidge of jelly in the middle. *Bougatsa* is a pastry pie with cream inside (or sometimes cheese or apple or spinach), and sprinkled with powdered sugar. Some pastry vendors also have ham sandwiches, or *piroski* (bread with sausage inside).

## Fig-and-Nut Shops

They sell figs, dates, prunes, walnuts, pistachios, almonds, honey, raisins, syrup, and so on. You buy by the drachma, and these goodies hit the spot if you're on a budget, or if it's a long time until your nine o'clock date.

## Picnics

What with all that sunshine and all those scented lemon trees, you may want to find a corner of some centuries-old agora and have a picnic. To stock up, visit a grocery store or the Pris-Unic-Marinopoulos supermarket. Start with some cheese. The main types are *graviera* (Greek-Swiss), *feta* (Greek goat cheese), *kefalotiri* (a yellow, salted cheese), *kasseri* (a hard yellow cheese), and *roquefort* (which in these parts is any kind of blue cheese). The olives are stored in large wooden barrels and aged for months. Order them by the drachma (4 drachmas is about as much as you'll need unless you're on an olive kick). Yoghurt is ladled from large vats and spread onto wax paper. Six drachmas' worth is probably your limit. You'll never taste fresher yoghurt than in Greece (try it served with honey for breakfast).

## Pastry Shops

The Greeks have sweet tooths. Shamelessly so. *Baklava* is a gooey goody made of layers of pastry, honey, nuts, pastry, honey, nuts, etc. *Kataifa* is equally gooey but filled with sweetened nuts and shredded wheat, and in its most glorious state, served with a mound of chantilly cream. *Galaktoboureko* is much simpler—a hollow pastry filled to overflowing with custard cream. Greek chocolate, like Greek olives, is bitter, and you can sample it in the form of layer cakes, tub cakes, or flaky mounds. Many pastry shops in Athens also sell coffee, so you can sit down and enjoy yourself right there and then—simply pointing to what you fancy.

## Cafes

As in most Mediterranean countries, people pop into cafes at the slightest opportunity. In winter, they'll have a quick espresso as a pick-me-up; in summer, something cooler. The cafe is an institution. Almost an epidemic—Constitution, or Syntagma, Square can seat 3,000 imbibers at one time. The cafe waiter is no less immaculately attired or competent than his counterpart in a real restaurant. Even the simplest order is attended to with style. Ask for a lemon juice and he'll bring you a tall glass with freshly pressed lemon juice, a carafe of water, and sugar on a silver tray—all for something like 75¢. And having paid your dues, you're free to sit in this informal "club" all afternoon watching the world go by, flirting, dozing, writing postcards. In Athens, as in other parts of Europe, it's perfectly proper to sit at an empty chair even when there are other people at the table.

## Refreshments

**Coffee.** Ordering a cup of coffee for the first time in Athens is almost as bewildering as trying to order a sandwich in New York if you're a stranger (white, wholewheat, rye, pumpernickel, toast, etc.) The list of coffees on cafe menus in Athens goes roughly as follows—espresso, cappucino, French, Viennese, Nescafé, Greek (which had been known as Turkish coffee until the troubles flared up in Cyprus in 1974). If you just say coffee, you get either Greek (if the waiter thinks you look Greek) or Nescafé (if he thinks you look American). What you probably want is, in fact, French. Nescafé is instant coffee brought to you with a cup and some hot water and you mix your own. Cappucino comes from those hissing Italian coffee machines, and is a combination of coffee and cocoa with a white froth on top, sometimes served with a pinch of nutmeg or cinnamon. Coffee for the Greeks comes in three degrees of sweetness: *metrio*— medium strong, medium sweet; *vari-glyko*—strong and sweet; *sketo*—sweet but without the froth. Most Greeks seem to drink it *metrios,* and that's the way you'll probably prefer it. Besides, it's the easiest to say.

**Wines and other liquid refreshments.** You can't *not* drink wine in the land of Bacchus. Most people think of *retsina* when they think of Greek wines, but there's more to it than that. Retsina is resinated wine. Originally the resin was added to preserve the wine, then everyone liked it so much that way the resin stayed there. However, it's an acquired taste. Most visitors prefer the regular Greek wines, from the bottle rather than the barrel. There are hundreds of them, some good, some okay, some yugggh. Order the following and you won't go far wrong:

*Reds:* Demestica or robust Castel Danielis, both from the Peloponnese; Caviros or Cellar from Attica (the closest thing to a local Athenian wine); Naoussa from Macedonia; or Chevalier de Rhodes from Rhodes. Of these, Demestica is the least expensive, Caviros the most expensive. Porto Carras is a sturdy wine from new vineyards associated with a new resort in the north.

*Whites:* Again, Demestica, Santa Helena, or the muscadet-like but light Santa Laura, all from the Peloponnese; Robola from Cephalonia; Pallini, or the pricy Cava Cambas and Elissar from Attica.

*Rosés:* Roditis, Cimarosa, King, Cellar. Be adventurous and ask for half a kilo (yes, wine is measured by the kilo) of the open wine if they have it. This will be the local wine—the white will probably be resinated, the red probably not. Although retsina is an acquired taste it's surprising how fast many foreigners do acquire the taste and at prices around 30 drachmas a kilo, who can blame them? Obviously you take pot-luck but the wine from Attica is usually good.

The main Greek apertif is *ouzo,* a clear anise drink which turns misty gray when you add water. *Mastic* is a thick white gum from a tree that grows only on the island of Ios—it's dropped into a glass of water still clinging to the spoon and it's stickier and sweeter than anything in the world.

Greek **beer** (usually Fix or Alpha) is so-so; the best brews are the Dutch Amstel, which is made locally, or the German Henninger, which is brewed in Crete. Beer is sold in two sizes—550 grams and 330 grams; remember to ask for a small beer (330 grams), about the size you're accustomed to back home.

## Water

Is one of the most refreshing drinks in Athens, and comes automatically to the table—even when you order coffee—but without ice. If you prefer bottled water, soda water is more reliable than the still variety. A popular Greek refresher is the lemonade—fresh lemon juice, the real kind, squeezed into a glass, and usually served with a separate glass of water so that you can mix to your own taste. You can spend an entire afternoon in a cafe nursing one lemon juice. Two other popular Greek refreshers, on sale almost everywhere: Coke and Pepsi.

## Dining Hours

To understand Athenian meal times, you have to understand Athenian office hours. Most people trudge into their offices at 8 or 8:15, work nonstop until one or two (unless, they're executives, in which case they nip out for a quick ouzo at noon), stop for lunch and a siesta until 4:30 or 5, then go back to the office until 8 or 8:30. Shops follow the same basic schedule. Thus, lunch is closer to two than noon, and nobody thinks of starting dinner before nine in the evening. If you have a date, arrange to meet for drinks at nine, then go on from there. If you're accustomed to eating earlier, you'll have problems. Most restaurants don't start serving dinner until nine, but a few (mostly in the budget category), which are probably accustomed to serving tourists from Northern Europe, will serve you a meal from six or seven on. Now you know why there are so many snackbars in Athens! (Memo to businessmen: In Athens you're more likely to be invited to a business *dinner* than a business lunch.)

## Prices

This is probably the most tempting part of the subject, despite inflation. You can go to the finest restaurant in Athens, pick out the most expensive dish, and still end up spending less than you would on a humdrum meal back home. Dinner in the Tudor Hall of the King George, one of the most beautiful restaurants in Greece, costs around $26 for two without drinks. The same meal in New York, without the view of the Acropolis, would come closer to $40. If you want to shoot the works, Athens is the place to shoot. If you have to survive on pennies a day, you needn't get skinny in Athens. There are plenty of restaurants in this guide where you can eat, and eat *well,* for under $5.

Restaurant prices, like hotel prices, are controlled by the government, specifically by an organization referred to on the menus as the Marketing Police. Each type of restaurant is fitted into a category and must supply meals within those limits. Individual items will vary on the à la carte menus of different restaurants, but all hotels within a given category must supply fixed meals at a fixed price.

## Column A and Column B

Most menus in Athens have two columns of prices. The first column is the price of the dish. The second is the price of the dish plus service—15%. You'll be charged the price in the second column, and we've no idea what will happen if you try to pay the price in the first column. Theoretically, it's probably a good idea to show customers how much they're tipping—except, as in the case of hotel service charges, people may still feel obliged to tip more. See below.

## Tipping

Despite the service charge, most people round out the figure on the bill and leave the change as a bonus tip. You don't have to, but all Greek restaurants, even the humblest, are swarming with busboys and assistant waiters who rely heavily on tips. If your busboy, or *miero,* is particularly attentive about getting rid of empty plates and so forth, tip him separately by placing a few coins *on the table,* not the saucer.

## Taxes

The government imposes something called a luxury tax on restaurants—anything from 3% to 17%, and some restaurants unsportingly add this tax to their clients' bills, which they're allowed to do. Usually 3%. In fancier places with music you may also find something called an entertainment tax listed on the menu; if you don't feel like paying it, don't go in.

Now for the restaurants themselves. What you will find in the

# Greek Menu Terms

*Hors d'oeuvres*

| | |
|---|---|
| Taramosalata | Fish roe with mayonnaise |
| Tiropita | Cheese pie |
| Spanakopita | Spinach pie |
| Melitzanosalata | Eggplant salad |
| Tomates yemistes me risi | Tomatoes stuffed with rice |
| Midia Fassolia salata | Dandelion salad |
| Piperies Yemistes | Stuffed green peppers |
| Tzatziki | Cucumber with yoghurt |

*Fish*

| | |
|---|---|
| Astakos (Ladolemono) | Lobster (with oil and lemon sauce) |
| Bakaliaro (Skordalia) | Cod (with garlic) |
| Barbounia (Skara) | Red mullet (grilled) |
| Caravides | Crayfish |
| Garides | Shrimp |
| Glossa (Tiganiti) | Sole (fried) |
| Kalamarakia (Tiganita) | Squid (fried) |
| Kalamarakia (Yemista) | Squid (stuffed) |
| Oktapodi | Octopus |
| Soupies Yemistes | Stuffed Cuttlefish |
| Tsipoura | Dorado |

*Meats*

| | |
|---|---|
| Arni souvla | Spit-roasted lamb |
| Arni Yiouvetsi | Lamb in tomato sauce |
| Arni avgolemono | Lamb with lemon sauce |
| Brizola moscharisi | Beef or veal steak |
| Brizola hirini | Pork steak or chop |
| Dolmadakia | Stuffed vine leaves |
| Keftedes | Fried meatballs |
| Kotopoulo souvla | Spit-roasted chicken |
| Kotopoulo yemisto | Stuffed chicken |
| Loukanika | Spiced sausages |
| Moussaka | Meat and eggplant (or potato) |
| Paidakia | Lamb chops |
| Pilafi, risi | Rice pilaff |
| Souvlaki | Lamb (sometimes veal) on the skewer |
| Youvarlakia | Boiled meat balls with rice |
| Yuvetsi | Lamb with noodles |

following pages is a listing of Athens dining spots arranged by type (Greek, steak houses, international) in the case of the moderately priced and expensive restaurants, followed by a roster of recommendations (restaurants, snackbars and cafes) where you can dine for $5 or less. Since you've come to Greece for local color, we'll begin with restaurants and tavernas which have a distinctive Greek flavor and ambience.

**THE TAVERNAS:** Nothing could be more Greek than the taverna. The simplest tavernas (and for many people, these are the most enjoyable) are plain rooms in nondescript buildings, or in patios and gardens under arbors and olive trees; furnishings usually consist of plain-jane wooden tables and chairs, the tables covered with white paper on which your waiter sets glasses of water. The kitchen is usually open to view, and the selection of food is either still in the pots or spread out in glass-enclosed showcases—diners simply walk over to the pots or display, size up the various dishes, then indicate to the waiter what they want. Simple—especially for foreigners who don't speak Greek. Menus follow the same basic pattern—that is, moussaka, dolmadakia, arni souvla, barbounia skara, and some regional variations of these basic dishes. In some tavernas, on the other hand, you have no choice, and it matters not whether you speak Greek or Swahili because waiters simply arrive at your table with platters of food, beginning perhaps with the selection of *mezedes,* or appetizers, mentioned at the start of this chapter. In Athens, the most famous of these fixed-menu tavernas is **Taverna Myrtia** at 35 Markou Moussourou-Mets, somewhere behind the Olympic Stadium (say, a $3 taxi ride from Syntagma); it's fairly typical of its kind, with rush-matting walls, beamed ceiling, a collection of island pottery and copper lamps, a few paintings. Myrtia also regales you with a strolling trio. It's the most expensive of the tavernas listed here, about $20 per person for a meal of innumerable courses (probably more food than you can manage) but it lends itself to convivial evenings: The tables are covered with jolly red cloths, and waiters squeeze and maneuver through the crammed tables with platefuls of tiripitae, beans plalci, artichokes, octopus, followed by shrimps, swordfish, quail, followed by liver, beef pie, lamb and pork in a wine sauce. Since it's an indoor taverna, Myrtia is closed in summer, and you must always call ahead for a reservation (719-198).

**Steki Tou Yianni** at 1 Trias Street (about five minutes from the National Archaeological Museum by taxi) sounds like a steak house but in fact the name translates as "Yianni's Lair." Like Myrtia, it's an excellent introduction to Greek food for those who feel they ought to try some traditional fare but may be nervous about doing so. Decor is basic Greek rustic: walls paneled to the waist with wood, the remainder with that basket-weave that's almost *de rigeur* in tavernas, and as you enter, you walk past a row of aging barrels filled with the house wines. From the maître to the micros, everybody speaks English—they're very friendly and the service is impeccable. The menu is in Greek but that's no problem if you sit back and enjoy the eight or so courses that are brought individually to your table. Typical dishes are squid in batter with a cocktail sauce, seafood pie served from an oyster shell, moussaka, tiropitakia with spiced sausage and beans, dolmades and, finally, stifado (or Greek stew). Followed by (if you can still cope) Greek desserts. Yianni's fine house wine comes from Attica, and is served in attractive earthenware jugs. Reckon on spending about 1,000 drachmas (about $28) for two with the house wine (more, if you order à la carte). Steki Tou Yiánni's is closed on Sundays and for about a month in summer. Reservations: 8212-953.

Many Athenians will tell you that the best unspoiled, untouristy taverna is **Xynou**, at 4 Angelou Geronta Street on a back street in the Plaka (it's near Plaka Square, just in case your cab driver has trouble finding it). It's basically a cluster of leafy courtyards with soft lights, murals of life in ancient Athens and a trio of balladeers singing gentle songs (which may occasionally be interspersed with ungentle sounds from the open-air movie next door). Xynou is where well-to-do Athenians dine (you'll see more jackets here than in most tavernas), but prices are still moderate: a good meal with wine should cost no more than $8 a head. Reservations: 3221-065. Open 8 p.m. to 2 a.m., closed Sundays.

The Hilton Hotel's award-winning **Taverna Ta Nissia**, big, beautiful and airy, is said to represent an island taverna, but surely a very classy taverna on a very classy island. The ceiling, 40-feet high, is redwood, the floor is marble, ditto the trout tank; decoration consists of lots of copperware, the table linen is persimmon, the china deep turquoise with brown and orange stripes, and the menus come in handwoven binders. That sort of place. The food doesn't let you down either, beginning with the ten-dish *mezedes* for just over $5. For the main dish you might want to sample the spit-roasted Olympia lamb with fresh mint and rice pilaf ($6) or *Gourounaki Souvlas,* which is roast suckling pig basted in its own juices, and served with crackling skin ($5.50). Desserts are prepared by an Austrian patisserie whose skills so impressed the Prime Minister of Greece that he went home with a "doggy bagful" of pastries. Reservations: 720-201. Open daily.

In Piraeus, **Taverna Vassilenas,** 72 Aerolikou Street, near the station is another of those spots where you just sit down and let the waiter bring you the meal course by course. It's a typical Greek meal, 18 courses (but small portions), and costs only $6 to $8 per person. For reservations, call 4612-457; closed Sundays.

Other tavernas worth bearing in mind (in most cases, less expensive than those above) are **Rodia** at 44 Aristipou Street (tel. 729-883) and **Rouga** at 7 Kapsali Street (tel. 727-934), both in the fashionable Kolonaki district; **Costiyannis,** near the National Archaeological Museum, which we'll mention in more detail in the section on under-$5 dining; and the selection of tavernas in the Plaka, listed under "Nightlife."

**OTHER TYPICALLY GREEK RESTAURANTS:** The following selection is similar in style and cuisine, but these are considered restaurants rather than tavernas.

**Gerofinikas,** at 10 Pindarou Street (between Syntagma and Kolonaki) is considered by many to be the finest of the Greek/Levantine restaurants, and it certainly is not the sort of place where you can expect to be seated without a half-hour wait if you forget to make a reservation. You enter it through a long, unprepossessing passageway that leads you into a surprisingly leafy indoor "courtyard," which is air-conditioned in summer; displays of Oriental desserts and great bowls of fresh fruit greet you at the door, and off to the left there's a big open kitchen with the day's dishes set out for your inspection—lamb fricassee, eggplant Beyendi, *doner kehap* (grilled veal) and *mouskari,* or veal with vegetables cooked in a paper bag. The succulent desserts include the syrupy sweet *ekmek kataif,* topped with chantilly in summer, with thick cream in winter. With prices of main dishes in the $4 to $5 range Gerofinikas is one of the best buys in town, but if you want to dine there you'd better call ahead for a reservation: 3636-710 or 3622-719. Daily 12:30 to midnight.

**Vladimiros,** at 12 Aristidemou Street (tel. 717-407) is a delightful restaurant on the way up to the Lycabettus funicular. It's an ideal spot for American visitors—a neighborhood restaurant catering to a local clientele who may want a change from their native moussaka, so without acting like a tourist you can enjoy beef, pork, lamb, and veal dishes cooked over charcoal and garnished in continental style: beef stroganoff, tournedos Captain Morgan, shrimps and, maybe best of all, paupiettes Vladimir (slices of beef layered with cheese) are each priced at 220 drachmas, or $6. Vladimiros is equally popular in summer for its garden beneath the pine trees of Lycabettus, in winter for its cozy rooms filled with paintings. This one is worth searching out—except when the piped music is overwhelming. Daily, from 8:30 p.m.

One of the brightest little restaurants in Athens is **Fatsio's,** 5 Efroniou, a few blocks from the Hilton and fewer still from the Caravel, where walls and ceilings are hand-painted in the style of Thessaly, with cornucopias and flowers in sunny blues, yellows, and reds. Even the linen napkins are sealed in clear plastic. The display of dishes includes baked veal with eggplant (110 drachmas, $3), baked swordfish (150 drachmas, $4), veal with tomato sauce (only 80 drachmas, $2.25). Reservations: 717-421.

The air-conditioned **Corfu** at 6 Kriezotou, just around the corner from the King's Palace Hotel, is classed as a "luxury" restaurant although the decor suggests something more modest. Likewise the food. As its name might lead you to expect, it features several Corfiote specialties, like beef "Pastitsada," which is boiled beef and spaghetti (150 drachmas) and sirloin of beef "Sofrito," which is sliced beef in a wine sauce with noticeable amounts of garlic (158 drachmas); the rest of the Corfu's menu ranges from moussaka at 81 drachmas to lobster at 406 drachmas. A place to drop into in a thunderstorm if you can't make it to one of the better spots near here; but if you want to call ahead for a reservation, the number is 3613-011. Open daily from noon to midnight.

**DINING AT THE TOP:** By any standard, the King George's **Tudor Hall** is one of the most striking restaurants anywhere. As you now know, if you read our chapter on hotels, the Tudor Hall is the top floor of the luxurious King George Hotel. The name gives you a clue to the decor. It's like a baronial hall in an old English stately home, the walls and ceiling entirely covered with dark, carved wood and hung with immense tapestries, sconces, and chandeliers. The tables are solid, polished oak, with brass table lamps, cut crystal stemware, and silver cutlery (unless you're at a state occasion, when the hotel will roll out its gold cutlery). It's a striking room, but there's another attraction to keep you from enjoying it throughout the meal—the view of the Acropolis. The view is undisturbed, because in summer one wall of the Tudor Hall disappears and the tables spread out across the big terrace; in winter, the terrace is enclosed in floor-to-ceiling glass. An annex room is almost entirely given over to a spit that seems large enough to roast the fatted calf. Your first choice from all the items on the menu will probably be something from the spit. The fixed-price dinner up here will cost you about $15, service included, but you can also choose from an à la carte menu and go higher or lower. Although the view far outshines the cuisine, you'd better call ahead for a reservation—3230-651.

You can get an even closer view of the Acropolis from the Roof Garden of the **Astor Hotel** (16 Karageorgi tis Servias, tel. 3224-971), one of the city's few year-round eyries (in winter it's enclosed in glass that doesn't block the view). This is another place for lingering. Once you get up there, order a bottle of Santa Elena or Cimarosa, and slowly scan the menu; you'll be reluctant to rush through your meal and get back down to earth literally and otherwise. Enjoy roast lamb, 110 drachmas ($3.05); shish kebab, 178 drachmas ($5); or the complete 198-drachmas ($5.50) dinner with moussaka or soup as a first course, roast lamb or chicken with rice, dessert, and/or feta cheese. If it's still too early to drag yourselves away, order some Greek coffee. Then follow it up with a Metaxa. Two people can still leave with change from $20.

Another popular spot for sky-high dining (highest in the city, in fact) is the **Dionysos Restaurant** on top of Mount Lycabettus (tel. 726-374 for reservations), with a menu similar to its namesake near the Acropolis—in other words, you can choose from a wide-ranging menu and enjoy a dinner for anywhere from $5 to $15 per person.

Farther down Mount Lycabettus, you can dine on the rooftop restaurant of the **St. George Lycabettus Hotel** (2 Klemenou Street, tel. 790-711). In summer you get a magnificent 360-degree view from the outdoor terrace, in winter you're tucked away snugly in the elegant Grill Room. In both cases, you're entertained by a combo for dancing. A la carte dinners here will average somewhere between $12 and $15.

Another relative newcomer to the high-rise dining scene is the **Tower Suite,** atop the tallest building in Athens, the 30-story

Tower of Athens (at the intersection of Vassilisis Sofias Avenue and Messogion, a few blocks past the Hilton, tel. 720-201). The inspiration here is Manhattan—soft lights, red drapes, brass fern planters, a three-way vista with a long bar facing west to the distant Acropolis. The food is international—steaks, veal piccata, filet of sole, for around $9 to $12 with an additional 20% tax for entertainment—two shows nightly on a small stage behind a marble pond.

**FRENCH AND CONTINENTAL RESTAURANTS:** The Balthazar (27 Tsocha Street at Vournazou Street near the American embassy, a $1 cab ride from Syntagma; tel. 644-12-15) is an imposing corner town house with a curving driveway, steps at the front, and a secluded garden for summer dining in the rear. The first things that greet you as you come in through the main door are crystal chandeliers, beautiful walnut paneling, lofty ceilings, and marble fireplaces. The three-story mansion was built at the turn of the century for a well-to-do Athenian family (not shipping—textiles), but in recent years it had served as government offices before falling into decay. It was rescued by a young economist consultant, Nikos Paleologos, who had his passport removed by the previous regime, so he had plenty of time on his hands to put the place in order. It took him 18 months; he imported a special craftsman from London to restore the decorative ceilings, decorated the walls with his private collection of original paintings of ships, and decked the windows with his private collection of antique glass bottles (some of them are real curios). The setting may be elegant, but the Balthazar is, in fact, fairly casual about its elegance: the waiters are in shirt sleeves, and Paleologos commutes from the kitchen to the tables in blue denims. The name, by the way, comes from a reference in *Cyrano de Bergerac*—faire un Balthazar, meaning have a feast or big meal—and that seems to be the clear intent of Nikos Paleologos and his wife. Their meals are hearty. Some suggestions from their varied menu: minute steaks with brandy and mushrooms for 190 drachmas ($5.43); sole Florentine, filets of sole with spinach, mushrooms and sauce for 140 drachmas ($4); roast veal stuffed with pistachios, 170 drachmas; escalopes of veal with asparagus, 190 drachmas; the daily Eastern curries served with homemade chutney, 170 drachmas ($4.85). For openers, try the spiced cheese log which is a blend of island cheeses and herbs—70 drachmas ($2). Dinner only, from 7:45 to 1 or 2 a.m.

Right behind the Hilton, on the corner of Hadjiyanni Mexi and Ventiri streets, the **Bagatelle** fills its wedge-shaped corner with a sidewalk terrace screened from the traffic by thick greenery. The terrace is for drinks only, and there's a second bar inside, adjoining a 20-table dining room, but the smart place to go in the evening is downstairs to the piano bar. A typical dinner here might consist of avocado vinaigrette (145 drachmas) or potage du jour (55 drachmas), filets of sole bonne femme (210 drachmas) or filet mignons in a tasty Madeira sauce (280 drachmas); with dessert and wine, your meal at Bagatelle will cost about $10 to $15 per person. Open to 1 a.m., closed Sundays.

The next restaurant is over on the far side of the Acropolis, near the Herod Atticus Theater and Philopappos Hill, with one of the best views of the Acropolis in the entire city. The **Dionysus** is difficult to fit into one category, since it's several restaurants in one: it serves Greek food and continental food (escalope Holstein, chicken Negresco, crêpes suzettes) in its glass-walled restaurant and terraced garden; and snacks in its vine-covered courtyard cafe, which is almost right opposite the main entrance to the Acropolis. Dinner in the restaurant will cost $8 to $10 a head; in the courtyard, there are tourist menus for under $8, and simple dishes like omelets, spaghetti, and sandwiches cost well under $5. With these prices, and this setting, Dionysus is a very popular place. For reservations call 913-778.

One of the newest continental restaurants in the city is **Maxim's**, in Kolonaki at 4 Milioui Street. Decor is Spanish-Mediterranean, with ladder-back cane chairs and red tile floors, white stucco arches, but the food is displayed Greek-style in refrigerated glass cabinets: roast lamb in spinach and lemon sauce, shrimp en brochette, roast veal, moussaka, delicious lobster salad. Budget $8 per person for lunch or dinner, without drinks. Reservations: 3615-803.

Some other restaurants featuring mainly French cuisine which have opened recently in Athens are **Cave Mirabelle** at 7 Leventi Street (tel. 743-333), **Prunier** at 63 Ipsilantou Street, near the Hilton (tel. 727-379) and **Skorpios** at 1 Everou Street (tel. 7796-805): the oldest French restaurant in town, **L'Abreuvoir** at 51 Xenokratous Street in Kolonaki (tel. 729-061) is still for many Athenians the best, but many visitors find it too stuffy and expensive.

If mention of French cuisine puts you in the mood for duckling à l'orange, you might consider taking a ten-minute, $2 cab ride over to Piraeus, specifically to the Castella peninsula. There you'll find the **Papakia** (tel. 476-180), at 8 Karageorgi tis Servias (make sure your cabby doesn't confuse it with the same street near Syntagma). Papakia is a big stone mansion on a bluff above the new beach and a floodlit mound of rocks, with a big terrace where you can sit and watch the schooners riding at anchor in Pasalimano (Pasha's Port). More important than the view is the international menu—from the duckling to squid to curried prawns to souvlaki. Add the wines from France, Germany, Greece, and Portugal, and you'll have a memorable meal. Dinner and wine here will run you $20 to $25 for two people.

## A Welcome Addition

Probably the most interesting restaurant to open in Athens in recent months is the new **G. B. Corner** in the prestigious Hotel Grande Bretagne, with one entrance in the glittering, elegant lobby, the other on Panepistimiou Avenue. The G. B. Corner has an Edwardian, masculine air, all dark wood and cut glass, brightened by clusters of globe lamps. The most surprising feature of this newcomer is its moderately priced menu (eggs Benedict or salads, for example, for $2 to $3.50) with its innovative dishes—including hamburger "Rossini" (that is, with pâté de foie gras and Madeira sauce) for 170 drachmas, about $4.75. A welcome addition to the Syntagma scene, a pleasant place to visit any time of the day or half the night (it's open until 3 a.m.) for a drink, a coffee, or a full meal.

**ITALIAN AND ORIENTAL RESTAURANTS:** Each year, Athens becomes a mite more cosmopolitan, and although you probably are not coming to the land of olives and feta cheese to eat pizza and tempura, you may like to know that they are available.

The smartest Italian restaurant in town is **Al Convento da Walter,** located in a modern apartment building, somewhere between the American and British Embassies, at the corner of Evzonon and Anapiron Polemon in Kolondci. The decor, in tones of mocca and coffee, is chic and modern (although the thickly upholstered modular sofa/chairs would probably be more appropriate in the lobby next door), and the fresh flowers and lemon-colored napery tell you that the dapper staff takes a pride in the place. Prices are moderate—peti di pollo al Marsala for 164 drachmas, filetto voronof (veal in a cognac and mustard sauce) for 224 drachmas; in other words, if you avoid pricey appetizers like prosciutto crudo (160 drachmas) and salame de Milano (152 drachmas), you can dine well for under $10. If even these prices are too lofty, Da Walter's **Pizzeria** annex is just around the corner. Open daily from 8 a.m. For reservations, call 748-726; taxi fare from Syntagma is about $1.

One of the most attractive Italian restaurants in town is the **Trattoria** in the Hilton, next to the stylish Taverna Ta Nissia. It can be noisy at dinner, but the prices compensate for the distraction—pizzas for 120 to 165 drachmas (say, $3 to $4.50), canneloni Rossini for 125 drachmas, spaghetti al pomodoro for 95 drachmas. Good value.

Tucked away in a narrow street (near Farmaki Square) in the Plaka is a Japanese restaurant, **Michiko**, 27 Kidathineou Street (tel. 220-380), in a Japanese courtyard, complete with fish pond, fountains, butterfly bridge, and kimono-clad waitresses. The 20-odd tables are distributed along flagstone paths, on two raised terraces beneath frilly red awnings; an elevated wooden platform serves as a bar in one corner; and the whole place is sheltered by a venerable tree and decorated with colored lanterns. Sukiyaki and tempura may not be what you've come to the Plaka to savor—they're not exactly bargains here—but they're there (at 300 and 140 drachmas respectively) if you feel like a change of pace from moussaka and eggplant some evening. Michiko also charges 10 drachmas (27¢) for cover and a 3% entertainment tax, although there was no entertainment the night we were there—unless they mean the fountains. (Open to midnight; closed Sundays.)

If you have an uncontrollable longing for the flavors of Canton and bamboo furniture, your best bet is probably **Mr. Yong's Chinese Restaurant** at 3 Lamahon, just off Nikis Street. Open daily until 1 a.m. Reservations: 3230-956.

**STEAK HOUSES:** The Steak Room, at 6 Aiginitou (between the Hilton and the American Embassy; tel. 717-445) is one of those restaurants you might want to try if you weary of moussakas and veal. Some people will tell you it serves the best steaks in Athens, prepared in the American manner and served with baked potato and sour cream or butter. The Steak Room's owner, Michael Papapanou, a Greek who spent ten years in Canada, gets his beef loins from the north of Greece, ages them, then cuts them right at the charcoal fire. For any cut (from porterhouse to filet steak), the price ranges from $6 to $8. His stint in Canada also taught Mr. Papapanou the mysteries of extra-dry Beefeater martinis and Irish coffee.

The Steak Room is so popular, by the way, it doubled in size a few years ago, and since then they've had to add yet another extension, called **The Annex,** also fully air-conditioned. The Steak Room is open seven days a week, from 6:30 p.m. to 1 a.m. for dinner. For reservations call 717-445.

The Steak Room claims to have been the first steak house in Athens, and if so, it started quite a trend. They're now springing up all over the place.

**Templars' Grill,** the steak house in the Royal Olympic Hotel (phone 9226-411 for reservations), is the most spectacular. It flies its Aberdeen Angus steaks in from Scotland and they're reputed to be the tenderest in town, prepared and grilled by a chef who spent several years in the States. Daily, from 8 to midnight. Prices for main courses are from $5 to $10.

**Flame Steak House** is only a few blocks from its rival The Steak House, at 9 Hadjiyanni Mexi, on the corner of Michalacupoulou, near the Hilton. Restaurateur Elias Dialektakos picked up the tricks of his trade in Chicago, then packed up some American-style light fixtures, amber glassware, and ashtrays, and returned to his homeland. His eight year-old eatery has knotty-pine paneling and bar, and comes equipped with air conditioning and taped stereo, hand-hammered copper plaques depicting Michelangelo paintings, all set off by burgundy rugs and gold tablecloths. Most dishes on the menu are charcoal-broiled —like filet mignon at $6.50, but there are also items like golden french-fried shrimps for under $5. One of the restaurant's nicest features is a roomy terrace for sidewalk dining, with an orange awning and trellised greenery to shut out the traffic. Every evening from 6 to 2 in the morning. Reservations: 738-540.

**The Stagecoach,** 6 Loukianou Street in Kolonaki, is located across the street from the residence of the British Ambassador, but when you push aside the swing doors it's instant Wild West, complete with long brass-railed bar, wooden booths, wooden gallery, waiters in pseudo-cowpoke garb. You'll find six cuts of steak on the menu here, from 250 drachmas to 520 drachmas (for that old ranch favorite—chateaubriand), as well as prime ribs, broiled jumbo shrimp and apple pie; the Stagecoach is air-conditioned, open for lunch from 12 to 4, dinner from 7 to 1 a.m., and the number for reservations is 743-955.

## Meals for Under $5
## Restaurants, Cafes, and Snackbars

Despite the steady rise of prices in Athens in the past few years, there are still many entries in this category. Some of those restaurants and tavernas mentioned above have a few items on their menus which could, with judicious selection, bring you a meal for under $5; conversely, some restaurants in this section list a few expensive dishes which *could* put your meal over the $5 figure. On the whole, however, you should have no problem keeping within your budget at any of the restaurants, cafes, and snackbars listed below. There's no need to detail the menus in each of these places: they all follow a basic pattern—moussakas, dolmadakia, keftedes and various lamb, veal and pork dishes in assorted Greek styles (such as those listed earlier in this chapter). Many of them also have a sprinkling of international dishes like omelets, spaghetti, schnitzels, escalopes and, of course, fish. In most cases, the waiter will offer you a menu in English.

**RESTAURANTS AROUND SYNTAGMA:** The air-conditioned, rustic-decorated **Delphi,** just off Syntagma at 13 Nikis (tel. 3234-869) has a wide-ranging menu with budget-priced omelet with sausage at 60 drachmas ($1.65) and shrimp with rice for 152 drachmas ($4.25), as well as a selection of dishes within that price range—rice with minced meat, veal with okra, moussaka, and a choice of unusual salads featuring squash, dandelion, beetroot, and cabbage. The Delphi is open daily from 11:30 a.m. to 1 a.m.

Just around the corner at 10 Exnofondos Street, the **Meteora's** white-jacketed waiters serve up all the usual budget dishes—plus a few specialties like octopus, stuffed eggplant with onions, pork chops with white wine sauce, zucchini salad. A three-course meal could leave you with change from your $5.

In a city where misspelled menus are two a drachma, **Sintrivani** at 5 Filellinon takes some kind of prize, for where else in Athens have you been offered "soup on the eyelid?" Nobody, to our knowledge, has actually partaken of this intriguing dish but if you're prepared to settle for lamb or swordfish kebabs for 73 drachmas then you won't be disappointed by Sintrivani tou Syntagmatos—"the fountain of Syntagma." Go upstairs in summer and you can dine in a very pleasant roof garden; service is friendly, and it's only a two-minute walk from the square.

One of the all-time favorites around here is **Restaurant Vassi-**

lis at 14a Voukourestiou, which will presumably become still more popular once Voukourestiou is transformed into a pedestrian mall. Here you can dine off moussaka, dolmadakia, omelets or spaghetti for around $2, with salad and bread. Another reason, besides low prices, for the Vassilis' popularity is that it serves lunch from noon to 4 and dinner from 7 to 11:30 (including Sunday), thus pleasing both the tourists and the Athenians.

Another restaurant in this basic Greek style, with similar prices and dishes, is the recently remodelled **Kentrikon**, which overflows into the arcade just off Kolokotroni Square, next to the National Historical Museum.

**SNACKBARS AROUND SYNTAGMA:** First, two with similar names: the **American Coffee Shop**, on the corner of Nikis and Karageorgi tis Servias streets, offers southern fried chicken for around $2, but you can pamper yourself with other nostalgic dishes for just over a dollar—fish and chips, char-broiled hamburgers, two eggs any style. Open from 7 a.m. to midnight. The American snackbar is located directly across from the post office at 3 Mitropoleos, and greets you with signs announcing the day's special—which is liable to be hamburger with french fries followed by apple pie, for around $3; inside, there are cozy booths where you can try the non-daily specials—breaded fish fry with french fries and salad, fried chicken, pancakes with syrup, or complete lunches and dinners for around 150 drachmas, ($4.50).

The **Elysee**, at 1 Mitropoleos Street, in an L-shaped corner arcade which has a row of tables and chairs, is a cool, shaded place to have a snack and still not shut yourself off from the excitement of the Square. The Elysee's prices and menu are similar to the American's. Now cross to the other side of Syntagma and walk a few doors down Stadiou Street to #7, where you'll find another arcade and the **Elite**; this is an attractive snackbar with tanks of tropical fish flanking the door, trim modern decor with dark walnut booths, and a welcoming burgundy-colored carpet. The usual menu, the usual prices.

The newest snackbar in this area is two blocks down Mitropoleos from Syntagma—the **Pam-Pam**, at #9, near the Greek Handicrafts Showroom; modern decor, regular tables and chairs at street level surrounded by showcases filled with tempting pastries and candies, a surprisingly comfortable split-level dining room upstairs, and a wide-ranging menu that includes something for everyone.

Two new snackbars which have opened in the streets to the west of Kolonaki Square: **Mövenpick,** at the corner of Akidimas and Amerikis streets, is a branch of the Swiss chain, serving a variety of light meals from donuts and pastries on up; **Spoonful Self-Service** at 29 Tsakaloff is a pleasantly modern cafeteria with free form tables and lots of mirrors, and a variety of Greek dishes for $2 and $3. It's open from noon to midnight.

## DINING AROUND OMONIA SQUARE: Over in the Omonia Square area, prices tend to be a few drachmas cheaper than around Syntagma. One of the busiest restaurants in this neighborhood is the **Ellinikon** at 3 Satovriandou, just off the square, with seating for 100 diners. This is a very Athenian establishment, not just for the cuisine: the waiters here act as subcontractors, buying food from the restaurant and selling it to the clients at a slight profit. (In restaurants of this type waiters may *buy* their position from outgoing waiters.) Even so, the prices are modest (chicken, moussaka and pastitsio, or spaghetti and meat pie, are around 50 to 70 drachmas), the personnel are friendly, the place clean and tidy. Closed on Sundays.

While you're in the square, you might also take a look at two hotel restaurants—those of the **Omonia** and **Asty;** both serve three-course lunch or dinner for $4.50 to $5.50.

The best of the snackbars in this neighborhood is probably the **Floca Self-Service,** two blocks from the square at 16 Emanuel Benaki Street. Since it's a member of the Floca chain, it's reliable, spotless, and good value: stuffed vine leaves for 36 drachmas, moussaka for 35 drachmas, roast chicken 60 drachmas—in other words, a meal for $2 or $3. The Floca is air-conditioned.

One block behind the National Archaeological Museum and popular with students and well-to-do Athenians as well as with visitors, **Taverna Costoyannis** serves consistently top-rank meals in a big, rambling, busy taverna at 37 Zaimi Street. Unlike other restaurants that remove only the roof in summer, Costoyannis discards its walls too, so you can dine virtually in a garden surrounded by whitewashed walls and luxuriant creepers. Costoyannis has a stunning selection of appetizers, with a special recommendation for shrimps with bacon (140 drachmas), tzatziki (33 drachmas), eggplant Imam (38 drachmas), and swordfish souvlaki (124 drachmas). Visit Costoyannis with a few friends, order half-a-dozen dishes and dip in. Call for a kilo of the house wine, called "brusco," and you'll still be amazed when

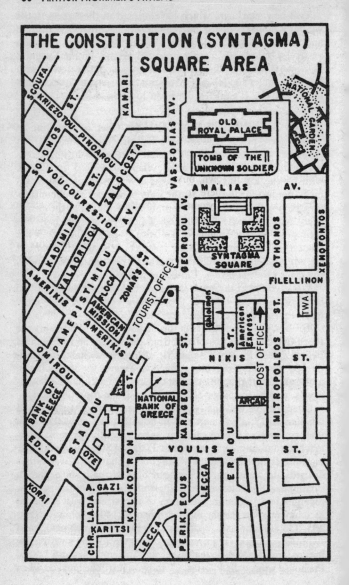

# THE CONSTITUTION (SYNTAGMA) SQUARE AREA

your bill comes—about 100 drachmas a head! Say, $3. If you want to splash out, or if you can squeeze in yet another dish, the grills, both meat and fish, are excellent. Costoyannis fills up from 9 on, so go early or reserve (tel. 8220-624) unless you don't mind waiting for a table. A taxi from Syntagma will cost another 30 to 35 drachmas each way. Costoyannis is closed for lunch and all day Sunday.

Another convenient spot in these parts is the two-floor **Cafe-Restaurant Chez Nous** at 53 Patission, across the avenue from the National Archaeological Museum; for 40 to 50 drachmas you can get stuffed peppers or meatballs; for approximately 75 and 85 drachmas you get yiouvetsi or moschari. Not the most interesting cafe in town, but it is clean and convenient.

One other spot where you can dine nostalgically or Greekly, in some style, is the **Byzantine Coffeeshop** in the Athens Hilton. This is a big circular arena beneath a dome with a corona of copper lamps; one wall is decorated with unusual mosaic panels of women in the costumes of Ancient Greece; the floors are marble, the tables are marble. Some coffeeshop. Hamburgers are 125 drachmas ($3.50), frankfurters on a bun, 75 drachmas ($2.05); apple pie, 65 drachmas ($1.80); one egg any style, 35 drachmas ($1); a BLT, 80 drachmas ($2.25). Greek specialties include moussaka, 85 drachmas ($2.35), and dolmadakia Avgolemono, 65 drachmas ($1.80). For a simple snack try the bourekakia—flaky pastry filled with cheese (three pieces for 45 drachmas). The Byzantine is open 24 hours a day.

**THE CONVIVIAL CAFES OF ATHENS:** The third type of eating place in this price group is the cafe. In some cases, the cafes are also snackbars; in some cases, they also have restaurants. They're listed here because their *main* role is as a cafe—a place where you can idle away hours over a coffee, lemon juice, Coke, or ice cream, or enjoy a light lunch of pan pie, cheese puffy, or sandwiches.

There are three main centers for cafes in Athens—Constitution Square (Syntagma), Kolonaki Square, and Fokionos Negri Street.

Syntagma is the largest, with 3,000 chairs (armchairs at that) deployed around its sidewalks and around the fountain in the center of the square. Two of the cafes are operated by the deluxe hotels **King George** and **Grande Bretagne.** The waiters in these two are impeccable but those from the King George have to cross from the square to the hotel to collect your order and it can be disconcerting to see your baklava floating on a tray through the traffic (they rarely lose either a baklava or a waiter). The Grand Bretagne has a convenient walkway under the street from the hotel's basement level. If you're gasping for a drink, go to a *red* chair in the square, and you will be served by the excellent Dionysus kitchen (and serving especially good pastries from its associated restaurants, Zonar's and Dionysus, two favorites in town).

---

### Kolonaki Square

Syntagma is where the tourist go, but **Kolonaki Square** is where the Athenians sip their coffee, and talk business or gossip. Kolonaki Square is only a few blocks from the National Gardens and Syntagma, just off Vassilissis Sofias. It's something of an oasis, with a grove of trees and a new fountain in the center and a cafe on every corner. Pick almost any cafe on Kolonaki Square. By day your choice is determined by the position of the sun; late at night the crowds drift toward the **Nouphara**, a three-part cafe that begins on the sidewalk at the corner and ends two doors down and one floor up.

---

For Americans, the most popular cafe is **Papaspyrou**, the one surrounding the American Express Office, on the west side of the square. Papaspyrou is at its busiest around 5 in the afternoon, when the mail arrives at American Express and the tables fill up with beaming or crestfallen faces, depending on the mailman. These cafes serve sandwiches (veal, ham, cheese—80¢ to $2.50), pastries (60¢ to $1), orange or lemon juice and tea or coffee (60¢).

**Phivos,** 2 Othonos, is the cafe with the blue awnings and green chairs at the corner of Syntagma and Filellinon. It bills itself as a patisserie/cafeteria/snackbar, so you can satisfy any degree of hunger here. But take a peek inside at the pies, pastries, baklavas, and chocolates, and you'll probably decide to settle for something light. And sweet. Pastries are 24 to 36 drachmas (65¢ to $1); coffee, 24 drachmas. Hot dishes, like hamburgers, dolmadakia, canneloni, and moussaka, are around $2.

A cafe where you can get an exceptionally good cup of coffee is the **Café Do Brasil** in the arcade that cuts the corner between Ermou and Stadiou. The Brazilian is part of a chain, with a stand-up counter downstairs and tables upstairs where executives look down on the tourists scurrying among the stores in the arcade. Coffee costs from 15 to 25 drachmas; sodas, 12 to 20 drachmas; pastries, 35 drachmas; and ice creams, 20 to 40 drachmas. There's also a special breakfast of toast, butter, jam, and coffee, or eggs, ham/bacon/or sausage for around $2.

Two of the most famous cafes in Athens are, in fact, on none of these squares, but on Panepistimion Avenue, two blocks from Constitution Square. **Zonar's** is the huge cafe on the corner with a row of red tables and chairs beneath a bright-red awning. The interior of Zonar's is an Expo for sweet tooths—with display cases piled high with candies, chocolates, pastries, baklavas, galaktoboureko, and bougatsas, as well as the classical pastries you'd find in Vienna or Munich. Even the decor carries through the theme—chocolate-brown walls, cream-colored ceilings, icy chandeliers, and marble-topped tables (although the management is whispering about redoing it). At the rear, a few steps lead up to the restaurant, and a few more lead down to the cozy American bar. You can have snacks here (sandwiches are 40 drachmas to 80 drachmas), but most people come to savor the pastries at 18 to 30 drachmas (50¢ to $1); and sip the espresso, cappucino, Viennese coffee, Nescafé, French coffee, and Greek coffees—from 23 drachmas to 29 drachmas. Zonar's is half a block of self-indulgence. Don't miss it.

**Floca's,** next door is a mini-Zonar's—kataifa, say, without the chantilly. But it's a delightful place nevertheless, with heaps of pastries, snacks, and coffees. Its menu also features a few spectacular ice cream dishes—Bé-Bé (parfait vanilla and strawberry ice cream, fruit salad, meringues, whipped cream, and biscuits), and Hippy (chocolate, pistachio, and mocha ice cream, meringue, chocolate sauce, whipped cream, cherries, and Hippy biscuits). Floca's confectionery counter looks like Christmas; if you're on a diet, stay outside on the terrace.

**Fokionos Negri,** our third cafe haunt, is over in Patission, the residential district beyond the National Archaeological Museum and slightly off the beaten track. But if you're spending more than a few days in Athens, and you want to get beneath the surface of Athenian life, hop into a taxi, or take either the #3 or #12 trolley bus, and ask the conductor to let you off at the stop nearest to Fokionos Negri. This street is sometimes called (but never by Athenians) the Via Veneto of Athens, and you'll soon see why. It's a broad, plaza-like street with trees, fountains, cafe tables, and umbrellas in the center, and cafes on the corners.

Some of these cafes are so popular they have two or three corners each. The remainder of the street is taken up by flower shops, beauty parlors, cosmetic shops, and other services pampering to the needs of Athenian society. Again, you can choose almost any cafe, but if you plan to sit indoors, try the **Oriental,** at #25 and #27, which is one of the most luxurious cafes ever. You don't sit at tables—you plop into armchairs and sofas, with your coffee, pastry, or ice cream laid out on coffee tables. Fokionos Negri also has some fine restaurants, among them **Taverna I Thraka,** where a Greek feast for two, with wine, will cost approximately $15 (the menu, by the way, is in Greek only); and **Paesano,** with the burning Olympic torch above the awning, for pizza.

**ALL-NIGHT CAFES AND SNACKBARS:** There's something magical about the Athenian air that makes you not want to go to bed, and if you feel like continuing through the night, there are several places where you can pass the time. On Kolonaki it's the **Nouphara;** on Constitution Square, it's **Alkyon** (tucked away in the corner of the square itself). After midnight the Hilton's **Byzantine Coffeeshop** fills up with journalists, artists, politicians, and visitors—and it never closes. Likewise, the **Night and Day** coffeeshop in the Hotel Caravel and the **Red House** in the Park Hotel.

**THE OUZERI OF ATHENS:** Here's an opportunity for some authentic local color: the ouzeri are traditional "pubs," neighborhood bars, where Athenians stop in at any time of the day for a quick refreshment of ouzo (the local aperitif with an anise base), whisky, or coffee. The decor is usually quite basic, the clientele is mostly male (although women are welcome to use them too), and most of them serve local snacks or sandwiches (meatballs, sausages, shrimps etc.). There are two close to Syntagma Square. If you walk to 10 Panepistimiou, then through to the end of the arcade with the Nikix & Takis shop you find yourself in a high-ceilinged but rather shabby bar called **Apotsos,** which may well be the oldest ouzeri in town; you sit at a small wobbly marble table, surrounded by walls plastered with antique metal signs advertising Huntley & Palmers Biscuits, Taylor Brothers Mustard, and Johnnie Walker Whisky, and order a beer or ouzo and any of the following: saganaki (delicious fried cheese), dolmades, their own sausage or meatballs. You'll be

.refreshing yourself here in the company of politicians and journalists; another favorite haunt of journalists is the ouzeri across the street, at #7 Panepistimiou—**Orfanides,** just around the corner from the G. B. Hotel, with a few tables on the sidewalk at the corner of Voukourestiou. **Athinaikon** at 8 Santaroza (near Omonia Square) is the gathering place for lawyers and judges (the law courts are nearby), and there's another ouzeri halfway up the hill to **Lykavittos,** which is a godsend for thirsty, camera-toting pilgrims. With the exception of the latter, these ouzeri tend to be less expensive than the regular cafes (lawyers and judges are no fools).

## RESTAURANTS OUTSIDE OF ATHENS: In summer, most
Athenians don't come into the center of town for dinner: they drive out to their favorite hideaways on the outskirts of town—in the countryside or by the sea. You might want to follow suit, in which case here are some tips on where to go.

### Kifissia
Kifissia is a village some ten miles from the city center, once primarily a resort, now both a resort and residential suburb, which in recent years has become a home away from home for many Americans who have come to live and work in Greece. It's not the sort of place you'd come to if you're in Athens for only a few days, but you may want to spend an hour or two here to cool off in summer, or stop off for a meal on your way to Delphi or other points in the hinterlands. You can get to Kifissia for 11 drachmas (about 30¢) on the subway from Omonia Square, or for about $7 by taxi; once there, take a 20-minute, 100-drachma ride around the town center in a horsedrawn carriage before or after your meal, or pay a brief visit to the **Soulandris Natural History Museum** and its displays on flowers and zoology.

Some of the most popular restaurants in Kifissia are the **Edelweiss, Apergi, Blue Pine Farm,** and **La Belle Hélène.** At the restaurant of the **Grand Chalet Hotel,** you can sit in the garden as you sip or dine and look across at the marble quarries on Mount Pentelicon. (You may have gathered from reading the chapter on hotels that the Greeks use marble the way Americans use Formica, much of it from Pentelicon; and in case you were thinking that by now the mountain must be a molehill, take a look across the valley—Pentelicon still stands.) These are all pleasant spots for a meal, but they are "international" rather than Greek in flavor; for more typically Greek settings go to Varsos or Taverna Moustakis.

**Varsos,** just off the main square, is a cavernous pastry shop that's been pleasuring sweet tooths for over a hundred years, where diners linger over kataifa, baklava, and that unique ice cream with a texture like Turkish delight known as kaimaki, 24 hours a day, 365 days a year.

**Taverna Moustakis** serves its Greek delicacies indoors in winter (in a cluster of wood-and-wicker rooms around an open kitchen where you can order your meal by pointing), in a tree-shaded courtyard in summer, serenaded by strolling bouzouki players. The Moustache is a popular spot with Kifissians, so call ahead for a reservation (and directions, if you're driving); the number is 8014-584.

## Mikrolimano

The other popular dining spot on Athens' outskirts is in the opposite direction, by the sea, but less than $3 away by taxi. Until a year or so ago it was known as Turkolimano ("Harbor of the Turks"), but in post-Cyprus Greece the signposts now direct you to Mikrolimano, "Little Harbor." Little *and* circular. It's a marina filled with sailboats from the seven seas, and crowned on the far hill by the ultrachic Royal Hellenic Yacht Club. The entire waterfront is ringed with seafood restaurants, each with its terrace set up beneath brightly colored awnings across the street by the edge of the quay. Some of these restaurants have no-nonsense, unadorned interiors; others (the newer ones) are interior decorated. A few of them have their own fishing boats, or their own sources of supply, and theoretically they should sell less expensive fish but it doesn't always work out that way as you'll discover on a stroll along the waterfront checking out prices.

When you visit Mikrolimano, here's the procedure: check out the restaurants and menus to see what the day's catch has been, and how much you'll have to pay. Next, find yourself a table across the street by the quayside, order an ouzo or a bottle of Demestica. Then go back to the restaurant, ask the waiter to open the icebox with the fish, and make your selection—*barbounia* (red mullet), *garides* (shrimp), *glossa* (sole), and so on. Have your waiter weigh the fish right there and then and tell you how much your choice will cost (the fish are usually sold by the kilo). Finally, tell him how you would like to have it cooked—

*skara* (grilled), or *tiganiti* (fried). Before returning to your waterfront table, select as an appetizer one of the Mikrolimano specialties—baked shrimp with tomatoes and feta cheese, or pikilea, a sort of seafood hors d'oeuvre (one portion is usually enough to appease two appetites until the main course is ready). Then you can settle back and spend the rest of the afternoon or evening sipping your wine, listening to the water lapping the hulls of the schooners and yawls. Afterward, get one of the weathered boatmen to row you around the harbor for half an hour or so (about 50 drachmas, say $1.50, for the boat, which will hold up to six passengers). You could almost be in Hydra or Mykonos or one of the other romantic Greek islands—yet you're only a $4 cab ride from your hotel.

Every Athenian has his favorite restaurant in Mikrolimano, although there is really only a marginal difference in prices (usually in the region of 350 drachmas a kilo for sole, 450 drachmas a kilo for red mullet)—which should work out at $7 to $9 a head per meal, without wine (prices used to be much lower, but fish are getting scarce and no one wants to go fishing any more, even in Greece). In summer, you may have little choice between one restaurant or another—you simply grab whatever table is available; if not, you should check out **Semiramis, Zefiros, Ta Prasina Trehantiria, Kokkini Varka,** the newish, three-story **Aglamer,** or, perhaps most famous of them all, **Canaris.**

## Zea Marina

If you go one bay beyond Mikrolimano you come to a larger but equally circular harbor known as Zea Marina, which is the part of Piraeus given over to pleasure boats rather than cruise

*Sounion, Temple of Poseidon*

ships; and if you're joining one of the Greek shipping tycoons for a cruise, chances are this is where you'll come to board his floating palace. Zea Marina is a pleasant spot to keep in mind on a stifling Athens day, when you want to get a breath of fresh air. Take the subway or bus to Piraeus and join the folks on a stroll around the promenade, stopping off now and again to admire a particularly handsome yacht, or taking a break in one of the cafes in the main square (there's usually music and dancing on weekends in summer). If you want to mingle with the owners of the yachts, have a drink in the **Landfall Bar** (at the far end, on the side farthest from Mikrolimano). If you're hungry, drop into one of the local tavernas for a meal (try **Tomandraki** or **Steki Toy Ianni** and you won't go far off course). Better still, buy a *penerli*—one of those inexpensive boat-shaped rolls filled with ham or eggs or meat—and sit by the edge of the marina dreaming of a Mediterranean cruise on the three-masted schooner *Creole*.

# Chapter VII

# NIGHTLIFE IN ATHENS

## Breaking Plates in the Greek Tradition

ATHENIANS DON'T paint the town red—they say "Let's go and break a few plates together!" It's an old Greek custom. When the audience is enjoying itself, it's expected to show its appreciation exuberantly. Greeks used to do this by smashing plates or glasses, or throwing flowers on the stage. The plate- and glass-smashing is now banned by the police, and the audiences started throwing flowers or plastic baubles instead; but you'll still find occasions when the music, the stars onstage, the stars above, and Dionysus combine to rouse the audience to smashing pitch. Just in case it happens some night when you're around, don't insist on a ringside table. Sit well back. (And don't break any plates because the taverna will charge a hefty premium for them.)

Athens itself is, of course, the greatest show of them all. The way to enjoy it is simply to go to the nearest cafe, find a table, and watch the performers—the lottery sellers, the sponge sellers, the souvlaki vendors, the taxi drivers, the stately old ladies all dressed up for a gala at the Grande Bretagne.

If you insist on paying for your entertainment, there are plenty of options open to you. Athens has a few ideas on nightlife you'll find nowhere else in Europe. Take your pick. You can watch ancient Greek drama in a theater dating from the time the plays were written. You can relive the history of the Acropolis in the awesome Son-et-Lumière, or Sound-and-Light, spectacle. You can sit on a roof garden beneath the floodlit Acropolis and watch a folklore show—or you can get up and dance a Zorba-like *syrtaki*. You can listen to a world-famous orchestra playing Beethoven in a 2,000-year-old amphitheater. And so the possibilities go on and on.

Whatever you decide to do, you'll soon discover one of the most appealing features of nightlife in Athens. Not only is it varied, not only is it unique, but it's priced so low you can enjoy almost everything it has to offer—even if you're on a tight budget. The only restraint on living it up right through the night is the thought that tomorrow you still have so many ancient wonders to see.

The entertainment pages of *Athens News, The Athenian, Athenscope,* and *The Week in Athens* are the best guides to local events in Athens, what's playing in theaters, concerts, operas, cinemas, nightclubs, tavernas, and restaurants.

## Sta Bouzoukia—
## (To the Bouzouki Clubs)

Long before the movies *Never on Sunday* and *Zorba the Greek* there was bouzouki. This six-stringed lute-like instrument was popular with *rebetes,* men who scratched out a living on the fringes of society in places like Piraeus, persecuted by the police for their crimes and drugs. Unsavory characters, indeed, but their music had an appeal that reached out and touched Greeks everywhere. No one know exactly when *rebetika*—the songs of the *rebetes*—began to be sung, but it was probably in the 1820s, around the time of Greek independence; they were played by the poor and the social outcasts, in bitter but stoical protest against the injustices of their lives—much like the early blues songs. With the songs came the dances: the *zebekiko,* an intensely individualistic dance which the *rebetis* performs for himself and not for the people around him; the *hasapiko,* another traditional *rebetic* dance for two or three men, no more, and again a private introverted dance. What you may recall from *Zorba the Greek* was *syrtaki,* which is a modified and faster version of the *hasapiko.*

Over the years bouzouki became fashionable with all strata of society, reaching its peak in the early 1950s. Then it declined, due mainly to commercialization; to make the instrument more versatile another pair of strings was added, then the instrument itself was electrified. Instead of just the traditional guitar for accompaniment, the sophisticated Athenians who went out for a night *sta bouzoukia* (to the bouzouki clubs) came to expect guitars and drums and piano, and possibly double bass and electric organ, besides a couple of bouzoukia. This is basically what you'll hear today when you go *sta bouzoukia;* the unamplified bouzouki has all but disappeared, and the districts where the *rebetes* themselves used to hang out have all been pulled down. However, you can still hear good modern bouzouki music in several taverns in Plaka, in downtown clubs in the winter months and in the seaside clubs in summer—places like **Delina** and **T'Asteria.** Another spot is **Harama** in Kesariani.

At some point during your visit, you should try to listen to this authentic Greek music. Even their pop tunes have retained that haunting, bittersweet quality. Their love songs are not so much about falling in love as being clobbered by love (some samples, roughly translated, from the current repertoire: "I hate my eyes since I've looked at you/you've made my eyes a little toy" . . . "Talk to me, talk to me/I've never kissed you/and I can only kiss you in my dreams" . . . "Believe that you met me some night in a dream/but for me it wasn't a dream"). Even when the songs are not about love, they're not exactly joyful jingles—"The worry beads broke/and fell on the ground/and all the men started to cry/the lamp has blown out/and the last ship has sunk. . . ." If you have active tear ducts, better take along plenty of Kleenex when you set off for a night on the town in Athens.

**IN THE PLAKA:** Take a few steps inside the Plaka and you'll quickly realize that pandemonium is indeed a Greek word. Until World War II there was only one taverna in the Plaka (it's still there) and the other buildings were private homes. Now every home seems to be a taverna and every other sidewalk and rooftop an extension of a taverna. Tavernas set up their tables in patios, on rooftops, even on the stepped streets climbing up the base of the rock. They compete not with dolmadakia and drachmas, but with noise. Most of the tavernas have music, which would be fine if they didn't also have amplifiers to blast out their sounds, reverberating through the alleyways and across the rooftops. Into the bargain, the Plaka has acquired a form of entertainment known as the open-air light show, which is a rooftop discotheque pounding kilowatt upon kilowatt of NOISE into the air.

Nevertheless, the Plaka is a unique experience, and if you're not in the mood for curling up with Aristotle it can be a lot of fun. Tremendous fun. If you don't want to get yourself involved in the raucousness, you can still find an occasional taverna without music in a quiet (well, relatively quiet) terrace or courtyard, with the music arriving distantly across the rooftops.

### Finding Your Way Around in the Plaka

Finding a particular club is not easy since most of the streets are identified in Greek only. However, you'll get there if you follow these basic directions. First, go to Cathedral Square. From the steps of the cathedral, turn left and follow the narrow street (Palieloghou Venizelou Street) past the Bayer and the BASF signs until you come to a modern white marble building on the corner; bear right, past the Stathis Greek Arts shop until you come to Adrianou Street, at right angles. Now go left on Adrianou, past a few gift shops until you come to a garden with palm trees. The street on your right is **Flessa Street,** and you'll know you're in Flessa because there are bright signs announcing discotheques and dancing bars, and, on the right, a building that looks something like a misfit from Kyoto, which is the Taverna Palia Athena. Continue up this street to the fork in the road and bear right. This puts you on **Lissiou Street,** which is where most of the action is—here and on **Mnisikleos Street,** which runs at right angles to it.

Coming from the Acropolis, follow the path past Areopagus, past the **Cafe-Bar Acropolis** (which has a magnificent view from its pathside terrace); there's an intersection on the left, but keep going along the path at the base of the hill, past an old church, then follow a curve to the left and down to a white wall; go right. From that point follow the noise, and from there you'll have to negotiate steps cluttered with tourists just listening to the music, tables filling up every inch of flat surface, waiters trying to get to the tables, people trying to get to the tables, people trying to get to the Acropolis, and occasionally someone trying to pinch a bottom. Once you're in the Plaka, how do you go about selecting a taverna?

### Picking a Place in the Plaka

On a busy weekend, the only valid piece of advice is: grab the first table you come to. There's really not so much difference in food or decor or service between one restaurant and another; if you can, get to the Plaka about half an hour before you're likely to feel ravenous, wander around and look the places over until you see something you fancy—in a patio, on the sidewalk, on steps, or on a rooftop (assuming you're visiting in summer). Within each category you have also a choice of noisy, *noisier,* NOISIEST.

Check out the prices, too, as you go along. Tavernas with

·music cost more than tavernas without music; tavernas with shows cost more than tavernas with only music. To give you some idea of what you can expect to pay, here is a sample of prices from **Taverna Kalokerinou** at 10 Kekropos Street (tel. 3232-054): moussaka, 160 drachmas; veal with eggplant, 200 drachmas; roast lamb, 200 drachmas; shrimps, 280 drachmas.' Appetizers cost anywhere from 60 to 100 drachmas; desserts, 80; a bottle of local wine will be 120 to 180 drachmas; and there's a cover charge of 30 drachmas. Work all that out and you'll find that an evening here, or in a similar taverna, will cost about $12 to $14 a head, with wine. This figure may be higher in other tavernas (prices in the Plaka, like the volume of the amplifiers, get higher and higher), depending on such variables as music tax, entertainment tax, show tax, and who is performing. *Prices in tavernas without shows are a few dollars less.*

Taverna Kalokerinou (above) is one of the most reliable of the tavernas with shows (with folk dancing and belly dancing and nonstop music from 9:30 for singing, dancing, or just plain finger-snapping and foot-tapping). The management here holds down the number of groups, so that couples and foursomes can get well-placed tables rather than being shoved into a corner. Like most other tavernas in these parts, the show is indoors in winter, on the roof in summer.

The corner of Lissiou Street and Mnisikleos Street is where you'll find one of the loudest concentrations of tavernas, one on each corner.

We'll start with the **Mostrou,** because it's the only one around that has its name in large English characters on a sign above the door. It's your landmark, as well as a potential destination. It's a big place with a roof garden for warm weather (the remainder of the year, you're in a semirustic room with a ceiling that looks like a TV studio with its complex of lights and spots for the floor show). The Mostrou show, indoors or outdoors, features a noisy modern band and vocalists for dancing, six dancers (in folk costume, but backed by an electric-organ/electric-guitar/electric-drums type of music), and the inevitable singer with handheld microphone who always manages to sound like Barbra Streisand doing an imitation of Judy Garland. The show is at its best when the dancers and band cut out the jazz and get down to some serious Greek dancing. Then you can't even catch the waiters' attention.

The Mostrou menu is probably one of the biggest in the Plaka, and there's a cover/bread/roll charge of 2 drachmas, and an "entertainment tax" of 7%. It's a bit more expensive than most (grilled swordfish 220 drachmas, chicken dishes 240 drachmas) —but then it has a bigger floor show than most. The music begins at 9:30, the show runs from 11 to 2, followed by more music. Closed on Monday.

Directly across the street, is another multifloored taverna with a roof garden—**Dionysus.** It's similar in atmosphere to Mostrou, prices are a few drachmas less, but here you have a chance to inspect what you're going to eat when you walk past the display case and kitchen at the entrance. Somehow, though, a less welcoming spot than Mostrou.

Across the street are two tavernas in the simple, peasant style, and consequently much cheaper. The one on the right as you face the steps that take you up the hill is the **Taverna Kritikou,** and you'll probably hear it before you see it. Its tables spread over the steps and through the doors to the dance floor, and if the only free table is at the rear, allow yourself three or four minutes to squeeze through. This was the first taverna in the Plaka, by the way. There's a minumum of decor here—a few murals in Plaka-primitive style and a less-than-classical arch of corrugated plastic above the band. It's a four-piece combo—with electric organ, guitar, drums, and bouzouki—but it gets the place going, encouraging a steady stream of men getting up to dance, egged on by the audience to perform wilder, more contorted leaps than their predecessors. Its attractive menu is decorated with paintings of the beast, fowl or fruit you're about to order—and the attractive prices include dolmades for 75 drachmas, chicken or squid for 110 drachmas, Cretan wine for 130 drachmas.

Again across the street—**Plakokiti Taverna O Fandis,** which translates as Jack's. This is another boisterous place that caters mainly to Athenians but welcomes out-of-towners. If anything, it's even more basic, more congested, and noisier than Kritikou, but it's spread out through three small rooms separated by arches and decorated on every inch of wall and pillar with the traditional Plaka Primitive murals. The band is raised to shoulder height, and the stamp-sized dance floor is half in one room, half in another. It's an infectious place, and most visitors probably wish they could do Greek dances. Some Americans actually try. To enjoy the fun you have to eat, but that's no strain on the budget. The Fandis has an inexpensive and varied menu: shrimp or octopus for less than $3; veal and potatoes and veal and onions for less than $2.50. Retsina costs about $2 a liter, and domestic charge white or red wine is $3 a liter. The cover is 2 drachmas, the service is brusque.

Now, follow the steps up the hill and continue up and up until you come to #4 Stratonos Street, where you'll find **Taverna Vlachou**—the Tavern of the Fool. You'll recognize it by the plaster drunk leaning on the lamppost at the door. The Vlachou has what appears to be a vacant floor on street level, so take the stairs up to the next floor, then another flight of iron stairs which you climb to get to the topmost floor, where you'll find an unrestricted view of the entire city. Movie companies have filmed panning shots of Athens from up here, and it's the view that makes the Vlachou worth the hike up the hill. It's a good thing you have such a spectacular view to keep you entertained while you're waiting for your waiter. Service isn't exactly coffeeshop sharp, partly because there are so many tables, but mainly because the kitchen is three floors down and the waiters have to walk up those narrow little stairways with every order. Try not to forget to order the salad—if the waiter has to make a special trip you won't be terribly popular. Veal in wine sauce with rice is 130 drachmas, grilled shrimps in oil and lemon sauce, 160 drachmas; wines average 125 drachmas to 150 drachmas a bottle.

## Some other Plaka tavernas

**Taverna Klimatiria** is located in a quiet corner on the outskirts of the Plaka, just under the Acropolis, at the corner of Thrassyvoulou and Klepsydras streets. Climb the steps into the taverna and you are in what appears to be a roughly decorated cellar with brick arches in the walls, the whole area crammed with tables, apart from the end where the musicians stand in a niche beneath one of the brick arches. Klimatiria has all the usual *mezedes* (from 43 to 91 drachmas) and a large selection of wines from all over Greece, from retsina at 78 drachmas to Robola at 278 drachmas; main courses are principally grills—shish kebab and veal chops at 128 drachmas, beef steak at 158 drachmas. In summer the roof comes off and the music (a couple of guitars, piano, and bouzouki) fills the air until about 2 a.m. A nice, friendly place, this one.

When you decide you've had enough of music while you eat, try a meal at **Café Restaurant Aerides** at 3 Markou Avriliou. This is on the edge of Plaka and in summer you eat on the pavement opposite the Tower of the Winds; from here you also have a glimpse of the Erechtheon up on the Acropolis, and hills away in the distance. They also have a raffia-and-greenery covered patio and a couple of rooms upstairs in an old Plaka house. You can get a three-course set meal for either 200 or 320 drachmas, or shrimps yiouvetsi at 145 drachmas and roast lamb with rice at 115 drachmas. Or, if you're really only here for the view, there's moussaka, dolmades, and stuffed tomatoes at 55 drachmas. Good selection of wines and several varieties come in half bottles. Service is courteous.

Head down Diogenou away from the Tower of the Winds and in 30 seconds you'll find yourself in a quiet, shady little square with tables and chairs under the trees, and **Taverna O Platanos** and a little *cafenion* facing each other. Another taverna without music for your battered eardrums, this is one of the oldest in Plaka and specializes in grills. Try a brizola moscharisi for 72 drachmas and a Greek salad at 30 drachmas; a perfectly acceptable kilo of open wine from the barrel is a mere 26 drachmas. Inside, the decoration is minimal, though the owners appear to be fixing it up at the moment. Lots of Greeks go there—perhaps they too like to get away from meat and music sometimes. When you've finished, slip over the square to the *cafenion*, have a cup of Greek coffee and ask for a backgammon set as you digest your brizola moscharisi. The official address for O Platanos is 4 Diogenou.

Tavernas, like everything else these days, have their ups and downs, and it might be wise to check with your hotel receptionist to see which are the brightest, liveliest places when you are in town. Here are two more names which usually crop up in most Athenians' lists of recommendations: **Palia Athena** (or Old Athens) at 4 Flessa Street (tel. 322-2000 or 323-8175), and **Taverna Erotokritos**, Erotokritou (tel. 322-2252), both noted for their floorshows.

When you walk around the Plaka looking for these places, you'll pass dozens of others, and if you see one that looks interesting, just drop in; the list above doesn't claim to be *the* top ten or whatever, but simply a sampling to let you know what to expect.

## Nightclubs by the Sea
## (and in Athens)

At midnight, when coaches turn into pumpkins, Athenians turn into swingers. Drop into any Athens nightclub just after dinner and you can almost certainly have a choice of ringside tables, overwhelming service, and a dance floor all to yourselves. At worst you may have to dodge a few tangoing tourists (until midnight, all the bands sound like Guy Lombardo). Come midnight, the whole atmosphere changes. The local swingers start filing in, the bouzoukis are plugged into their amplifiers, and the air fills with bittersweet Greek melodies. Everything keeps blasting away until three or four in the morning, or until the last plate has been thrown.

Before listing a few of the more popular clubs in Athens, here are some ground rules about nightclubbing in the city. You don't have to dress to the nines, but you'll find that most men wear jackets and ties. Most nightclubs don't have a separate minimum or cover charge. They usually incorporate it in the price of the first drink—somewhere in the region of 360 to 500 drachmas ($10 to $14), regardless of what you drink. Subsequent drinks are usually a bit costly as well. If you have dinner to while away the evening until midnight, your drinks will cost less, but, of course, you'll still end up paying at least $10 if you have Greek dishes, up to $20 if you order steaks. That's not unreasonable when you consider what you're getting in return—three, four, five, or six hours of entertainment, frequently with one of Greece's top singing stars, plus dancing.

Athens nightclubs set such a hot pace, the air conditioning can't keep up with them; so when the weather warms up the nightclubs pack up for the shore, and set up their music stands and stages all the way from Piraeus to Vouliagmeni. The night owls of Athens then scan the newspapers to find out where their favorite stars are singing and follow them. The actual club is relatively unimportant—it's the performers that count. If you plan to follow suit, here are some of the names to watch for— Marinella, Dalaras, Bithikotsis, Zambetas, Voskopoulos, Dionyssiou, Tsitsanis, and Kokotas. They're the ones who get the plates flying.

One of the newest and swankest of the shoreside nightclubs is **Delina,** in a dazzling year-round anchorage out near the airport. You enter it through a tunnel of aggressive multihued spotlights, which lead into a softly lit big circular bar; a concealed door then guides you into a vast area like a circus big top, so vast it could almost house the entire menagerie of Barnum & Bailey. The seaside end of this area is taken up by a large stage normally filled with a 22-piece (*twenty-two*) orchestra. The international floor shows are at 11 and 1. Minimum charge is 400 drachmas ($11), which is the cost of your first scotch and soda, but that will, if you wish, keep you going until the club closes at 5 a.m. Dinner will set you back about $20. A stunner of a nightspot.

Heading south along the coastal highway, there's the **Neraida** in Kalamaki (tel. 9813-850), possibly the loveliest setting, by the sea, beside a new marina. Minimum charge is around $10. **Fantasia,** by the beach, opposite the old airport, is the least sophisticated of the group, but currently one of the most popular. And the **Asteria,** at Glyfada Beach (tel. 8045-675), which is part of the hotel-bungalow complex, an attractive, modern, red-and-white taverna opening to the bay, the beach, and the sky, and worth the cab ride. These are not touristy spots (you'll rarely hear the theme music from *Never on Sunday* here), and all the songs are in Greek. But that's no problem. You don't have to understand them. You just have to cry. Now for some of the other nightclubs by the sea.

*Note:* None of these clubs is more than $3 by taxi from downtown Athens, and you can always get a taxi to bring you home in the wee hours.

Back to Athens, the two big nightclubs in *downtown* are the **Athinea** in its winter quarters at 6 Venizelou, and the **Copacabana,** which is just around the corner from the Stork, at 10 Othonos Street (the south side of Constitution Square). This Copa is a big place, with seating for 220, a six-piece orchestra, a juggler, exotic dancers, belly dancing (sort of), striptease (sort of), assorted singers, and a Greek folk troupe—all adding up to a show that lasts three hours somewhere between 11 p.m. and 6 a.m. A meal at the Copa (no relation to its New York namesake, by the way) will cost you from $15 a head, domestic wines about the same price per bottle (without dinner), and a full bottle of champagne or scotch (probably the best bet in the long run) costs $8 to $10.

Another strong recommendation is the **Supper Club** of the Hilton Hotel. It's something special—a nightclub 12 floors above Athens, plush, spacious, and stylish. The price of the floorshow, band, and dancing is included in the meal (say, médaillons de veau aux champignons for 320 drachmas, or $8.65). If you want to enjoy the show without dinner, come up after ten for a drink (first drink minimum charge 200 drachmas, or $5.40, or 300 drachmas, $8.10, on weekends). The Supper Club is on the left of the Hilton roof when you step off the elevator; if you walk along the terrace to the *other* end of the roof, you come to the Galaxy Bar's dance floor—indoor in winter, outdoor in summer. After 10 p.m., there's a minimum charge here of 200 drachmas

($5.40), thereafter 150 drachmas ($4.05) for every drink—a small price to pay for a unique experience. Just think, if you've come to Athens to see the Acropolis, all you have to do is come here to the Hilton rooftop, dance yourself skinny, and see the Acropolis without missing a beat.

## Discotheques

With all that lively Greek dancing going on around you there's not much need for discotheques. However, if your feet start to itch for the big beat, here are a few suggestions.

For a uniquely Athenian kind of discotheque, try the **Karyatis** at 11 Flessa, in the Plaka. It's a discotheque and light show with the sky as a backdrop because it's another of the Plaka's rooftop nighteries. It has no admission, no minimum, and no cover charges; drinks are 100 drachmas ($2.75). Couples only. There are two disc jockeys to keep things moving, and two "light showmen," to say nothing of the good old Acropolis up above. Open seven days a week from 8 p.m. to 5 a.m. Two other Plaka discos are **Mecca** at 9 Flessa (every evening from 8, drinks 120 drachmas) and **Pinocchio** at 117 Adrianon (8:30 p.m. to 3 a.m., entrance fee of 130 drachmas, normal drink prices).

The city's newest discotheque is in the **Tower of Athens,** but it's on the third rather than the 30th floor. It's a black-carpeted cave with crazy lights on the ceiling that flash on a checkerboard marble dance floor, and occasional tables that also turn out to be crazy lights that flash on the ceiling, or your face. Whisky, about $2.50; beer, $1.50, with a 22% tax. The address again: the corner of Vassilisis Sofias Avenue and Messogion, a few blocks beyond the Hilton (reservations: 706-111). The current favorite is the **Nine Muses,** at 43 Academias (reservations: 604-260), with colorful decor, lots of mirrors, and music from 9:30 on; in summer it moves to the Aster Palace in Vouliagmeni.

**Annabella** is the other "in" spot, patronized by chic Greeks as well as foreigners. It's at Aghios Kosmos in Glyfada (tel. 981-1124), situated on a promontory, with dancing on an open patio beside a pool in summer. In winter, the operation moves indoors where there is also a restaurant and boutique. Open every night from 10 p.m. on, all year; the first drink will cost you 230 drachmas, subsequent refreshments 150 drachmas.

Two hotel discos popular with Athenians as well as tourists are the **Galaxy Bar** of the Hilton Hotel (on the roof, from 10 p.m. to 3 a.m., with a great view of nighttime Athens) and the **Hori-**

zon Bar of the Caravel Hotel, again on the roof with dazzling views.

## Other Nightspots in Athens

**THE BOITE:** If you think the decor in a taverna is fairly basic, wait until you see a *boite*. The typical Athenian boite is small, crowded, smoky, and the seating may be "kindergarten" stools rather than chairs—but it can be a lot of fun. The boite is strictly for music—*rebetika*, folk songs, pop hits and, occasionally, resistance songs (although you may have trouble in determining what they're in resistance to). Performers are usually unknowns, but occasionally you may have an opportunity to hear one of Greece's more famous singers or composers. There are usually two shows nightly (the first one is never before 9), and the admission charge of 200-250 drachmas usually includes the first drink. Since the evenings can be long (you may have to sit through supporting acts until the star arrives) your best bet usually is to order a bottle of wine, and make it last the evening.

Some notable boites: **Skorpios** at 15 Kidhathineon in the Plaka, where you can hear the famous singer Hadziz (a great favorite with the ladies, as he has been for generations); **Skolion** at 10 Mnisikleos, also in the Plaka, which is run by a debonair young Greek Dino Constantinidos, patronized by his countrymen rather than by tourists, and offers piano, amplified bouzoukia, and dancing on a cramped patch of floor.

**LATE-NIGHT BARS:** No shortage of these in Athens, and you may have found your favorite nook on your first night in town. If not, here are some suggestions: **George's Bar** at 17 Voukourestiou, identified only by a large 17 on a door leading to a dimly lit basement which nevertheless has shelves crammed with paperbacks for its clientele of writers and other literati; **Larry's Bar,** near the top of Likavitou Street, is another favorite with the inveterate late-nighters in the Kolonaki district; **Spirit of 77,** 3 Kleomenous Street in Kolonaki, has quiet music, a winding-down sort of place where spirits other than those of 77 cost 50 to 100 drachmas; **Montparnasse** at 30 Haritos is yet another of Kolonaki's lounges, popular with writers and artists, and decorated with 1920s posters, glass-topped tables and overstuffed cushions in the shape of fruit. There are also, remember, the various late-night cafes mentioned in the previous chapter, and the popular **G B Corner** in the G B Hotel on Syntagma.

## Other Nighttime Activities

**MOVIES:** You probably didn't come to Athens to see a movie, but you may feel like one some evening as a balance to Aristophanes if you're going to be in town for several days. In any case, movie-going in Greece is like movie-going nowhere else; it's unusually inexpensive, and in summer it's particularly pleasant.

As soon as the weather gets warm, movies take place in open-air cinemas. Not drive-ins, but miniature stadiums with bleachers. You'll spot them at dozens of locations around town. Many of them show English-language films with Greek subtitles. You may have trouble deciphering their English titles, but if you peer at the stills you'll recognize old familiar faces like Frank Sinatra, Anthony Quinn, and John Wayne.

For the record, here's a list of movie houses in Athens that often show English-language films:

Aello, 140 Patission Street (tel. 8214-675)
Alex, 57 Papadiamantopoulou Street (tel. 7772-884)
Alexandra, 79 Patission Street (tel. 8219-298)
Alma, 46 Pipinou Street (tel. 8233-238)
Anessis, 14 Kifissias Avenue (tel. 7782-316)
Angela, 324 Patission Street (tel. 2282-121)
Apollon, 19 Stadiou Street (tel. 3236-811)
Argentina, 158 Alexandras Avenue (tel. 6424-892)
Astron, 37 Kifissias Avenue (tel. 6922-614)
Asty, 4 Korai Street (tel. 3221-925)
Attikon, 19 Stadiou Street (tel. 3228-821)
Danaos, 109 Kifissias Avenue (tel. 6922-655)
Galaxias, 6 Messoghion Avenue (tel. 7773-319)
Granada, 106 Alexandras Avenue (tel. 6463-685)
Go-Go, 300 Acharnon Street (tel. 859-700)
Elli, 64 Acadimias Street (tel. 3632-789)
Ilissia, 4 Papadiamantopoulos Street (tel. 716-317)
Kypselaki, 28 Zakynthou Street (tel. 8219-010)
Nirvana, 192 Alexandras Avenue (tel. 6469-398)
Odeon, 59 Messoghion Avenue (tel. 7786-024)
Opera, 57 Acadimias Street (tel. 3622-683)
Orpheus, 44 Stadiou Street (tel. 3232-062)
Pallas, 1 Voukourestiou Street (tel. 3224-434)
Petit Palais, 4 Rizari Street (tel. 7720-056)

Piccolo, 33 Syngrou Avenue (tel. 9221-956)
Plaza, 118 Kifissias Avenue (tel. 6921-667)
Rex, 48 Panepistimiou Street (tel. 3614-591)
Star, Ag. Constantinou Street (tel. 5225-801)
Trianon, 21 Kodriktonos Street (tel. 8215-469)

**DORA STRATOU DANCE THEATER:** The south side of the Acropolis can be a congested spot in summer. The crowd that's not heading for the Pnyx and the Son-et-Lumière show is probably on its way up the Hill of Philopappos following the sign for the Dora Stratou Dance Theater. The Dora Stratou Company is a group of folk dancers which was founded about 20 years ago and has earned a lot of bravos since then, both in Greece and on tours around the world, including the U.S.A. The show consists of a warm-up overture by the Zygia, a small orchestra made up of clarinet, violin, lute, santouri, and drums. The players are dressed in typical Greek native costumes—black waistcoats, mini-skirts, blouses, white stockings, and snub-nosed shoes. Like evzones in mufti. The dances and songs are dances and songs that Greeks have been dancing and singing for 2,500 years, and there's no finer place to watch them than under the feathery trees, on an Athenian hillside, a stone's throw from the Acropolis. You can almost see Pan and the nymphs dancing here. A typical program might include the Florina-Kratero from Macedonia, the Dodoni from Epirus, and the Ierissos from Chalkidiki.

You can get to the Dora Stratou Dance Theater by #16 bus from Constitution Square. The dances are performed every evening at 10:15 p.m., from May through October. On Wednesdays and Sundays there are "matinees" at 8:15 p.m. Admission prices range from 80 to 120 drachmas ($2.25 to $3.50), and your ticket reserves a specific seat in the amphitheater (real seats, not bleachers).

**CONCERTS AND OPERA:** Throughout the winter months, there are performances of opera by the **National Opera** (also known as the Olympia Theater, 59 Acadimias, tel. 3612-461; concerts by the **Athens State Orchestra** at the Kotopouli Theater (48 Venizelou, tel. 3614-592), and there are often recitals and chamber concerts at the **Gloria Theater** (7 Ippokratous, tel. 3626-702). Ticket prices range from 50 to 120 drachmas ($1.80 to $3.35), depending on the performers.

Nearby Piraeus has recently developed into a miniature cultural center, and you can sometimes take in concerts, operas, and recitals in that rejuvenated seaport.

The best place to find out about all these events is in the pages of *The Athenian, Athenscope,* or *Athens News,* or from the concierge at your hotel. He'll also tell you how to go about getting tickets, and in the better hotels he'll probably get them for you.

**SON-ET-LUMIÈRE:** If you arrive in Athens anytime between the beginning of April and the end of October, make a point of spending at least one evening watching the Sound and Light spectacle at the Acropolis. Son-et-Lumière involves batteries of lights—1,500 in all—which are flooded onto the Acropolis hill and the Parthenon in various combinations, to tie in with a commentary relating the history of the city. It's a stupendous show (with a pretentious commentary). It takes place every evening at 9:05 in English (at 9:55 if you want to hear it in French). Every evening, that is, except when the moon is full, because all 1,500 lights can't outshine it—and the Acropolis is then full of people.

To see the Sound and Light Show, you go to the small hill called Pnyx, which is on the south side of the Acropolis—the *far* side, if you're near Omonia or Constitution Squares. If you don't want to walk, take the #16 bus that goes along Dionysus Areopagitou, past the Acropolis, and get off one stop past the Herod Atticus Theater, where you'll find a sign that says Son-et-Lumière. (Or take a taxi—it should cost no more than 10 drachmas from either square.) From there, just follow the crowds. The 45-minute show costs 60 drachmas (half-price if you show a student card). If you don't want to spend even 60 drachmas, go to the Areopagus Hill; from that vantage point you can see the show, but you won't hear the commentary or the music.

The Son-et-Lumière show is part of a much more broadranging show—the Athens Festival.

**THE ATHENS FESTIVAL:** The Athens Festival takes place from mid-July to mid-September at the 1,800-year-old **Herod Atticus Theater,** on the slopes of the Acropolis. There you can sit on marble bleachers (now with free plastic cushions), beneath the stars, and watch some of the world's finest orchestras, musicians, singers, dancers, and actors in a setting unsurpassed anywhere in the world. The theater (sometimes known as the Odeon) was built by Herod Atticus as a memorial to his wife, Appia Annia

Regilla, so the architecture is Roman, not Greek. It holds 5,000, every seat has a perfect line of vision, and the acoustics are extraordinary. Even for a Chopin nocturne.

At the time of this writing the final program for 1979 has not been announced, but to give you an idea of the caliber of performers, recent visitors have included the Los Angeles Symphony Orchestra with Zubin Mehta; the American Ballet Theater with Natalia Makarova and Mikhail Baryshnikov; the Vienna State Opera and Philharmonic; and the Utah Symphony Orchestra with Maurice Abravanel; Béjart's 20th Century Ballet; the Royal Swedish Ballet; the Washington National Symphony; the Amsterdam Concertgebouw (with Bernhard Haitink conducting). When you add to that the splendor of the setting, the balmy night air, and the stroll back to the hotel or the Plaka, you have the ingredients for the evening of a lifetime. Here's your chance, for example, to see the National Theater, the Amphi-Theater, and the Art Theater perform plays by Euripides, Sophocles, Aristophanes, in an almost-authentic setting. It will be in Greek (you can buy a synopsis) but there's plenty to enjoy even if you don't understand the words. (However, if you don't want to wait for the last act, at least wait for an intermission before you get up and leave.)

Ticket prices for the Athens Festival range from as little as 50 drachmas to 500 drachmas. You can get details and tickets from the **Athens Festival Office** in the Spyrou Miliou Arcade at 4 Statiou Street, which is one block from Constitution Square (tel. 3221-459 and 3223-111, ext. 240). You can also get tickets from the box office at the Herod Atticus Theater (tel. 3232-771 and

*Theater of Herod Atticus below the Acropolis*

3223-111, ext. 137). English summaries of the Greek plays, at either location, are 50 drachmas.

**A NIGHT AT THE TABLES:** If nightclubbing is too tame, take a taxi to **Mount Parnes** and try your hand at blackjack or roulette. The casino on top of Mount Parnes is one of the largest in Europe (17,000 square feet of glitter and plush) with girl croupiers (some from England, most from Greece). About 1,500 gamblers a day make the trek up the hill to have their fling at blackjack, roulette, puto banco, baccarat, chemin de fer, boule, and craps. And it is a trek. Mount Parnes is an hour's drive from Athens; when you get there you can either drive all the way up the mountain, or you can take the *téléferique* from the base (35 drachmas each way, a five-minute ride, but it runs only every half hour or so).

The casino is open every day, except Tuesday, from 7 p.m. until 4 a.m. All you need to get in is a jacket and tie, passport, and 10 drachmas (and be prepared to fill out at least one form), but the casino is out of bounds to civil servants and bankers. If you discover that the goddess Tichi, the Greek's Lady Luck, isn't running with you, go to the grotto-like two-tiered circular nightclub and watch jugglers, equilibrists, and dancers. Admission to the nightclub is free, but the first drink is 180 drachmas ($5); subsequent drinks are 90 drachmas; dinner is 400 drachmas to 500 drachmas ($11 to $14).

**NIGHTTIME TOURS:** The simplest way to sample the nightlife of Athens is to take one of the special "Athens by Night" sightseeing tours. This kind of tour is more fun in Athens than in most cities because it usually includes a drive past the floodlit Acropolis, then along the edge of the sea to Castella in Piraeus, with refreshments in a typical taverna and dinner at a Greek nightclub, complete with floorshow and folk dancing. **American Express, CHAT,** and **Viking** operate these "Athens by Night" tours, and American Express also has an interesting "Theater Night" tour that takes you to performances of the Sound-and-Light Spectacle *and* the Greek dances at the Dora Stratou Theater. The "Theater Night" tour costs $13.50, including tickets but without dinner, and the "Athens by Night" tour costs $21 with dinner.

# Chapter VIII

# SIGHTSEEING IN ATHENS

IF YOU HAVE ONLY one day in Athens, your best bet is to take a guided sightseeing tour. But even if you're staying a few days and plan to do a lot of sightseeing, it's still a good idea to take the tour to get an idea of the lay of the land, and find out what really interests you. Then you can go back yourself and take in the spots you want to cover in depth.

Let's assume, however, that you plan to see the city on your own, and you've decided to begin with breakfast in **Syntagma,** or Constitution Square. The square itself is a sightseeing attraction (you've already read about its cafes). On the bottom side you have one of the highlights of the square as far as Americans are concerned—the office of **American Express,** usually surrounded by swarms of visitors, young and old, rich and poor, student and professor, booking trips to the islands, waiting for mail and/or money from home. The mail is delivered at 5 p.m., by the way, and this is the time to be there to meet old friends, catch up on gossip, make new friends, and sympathize with those who didn't get that check. The cafe on the corner, Papaspyrou, gets the brunt of the sorrow and elation. You have to move nimbly to get a table here.

However, the main sight of Syntagma is the former Royal Palace, now the **Parliament Building.** This is a large, squarish yellow building with a marble forecourt facing the square. Apparently, this site was chosen personally by young King Otto (the Bavarian who was put on the throne after the war with Turkey), and his site-selection technique was to hang pieces of meat in various parts of town and select the location where the maggots were slowest to develop. The main attraction here, apart from the constant arrival or departure of dark limousines, is the **Changing of the Guard.** This ceremony, complete with evzones and their pompoms, takes place every hour, 20 minutes before the hour, and on Sunday at 11, accompanied by its regimental band. If you get there late, you can always photograph the new evzone on duty at the **Tomb of the Unknown Soldier,** in front of the building.

You can spend whole days sitting in the cafes of Syntagma, enjoying the daily routine of the city—the crowds cramming into the offices in the morning; the lottery ticket sellers promising riches; the sponge sellers, more interested in sitting in the shade than selling a record number of sponges; the jet-setters dashing in and out of the King George and Grande Bretagne; the tourists checking into the airline offices, the limousines heading for Parliament, the Americans clustering around American Express; the shoppers disappearing into the arcades of Ermou and Karageorgi tis Servias streets; the crowds cramming out of their offices and cramming into the buses; young hippies; young blondes; young Greeks trying to pick up the blondes; young Greeks trying to pick up the hippies; the elderly gentlemen who've been congregating here through several reigns and regimes, as timeless as the Acropolis.

But sooner or later you'll want to leave the comfy cafe chairs and the shade of the awnings and go see the other sights of Athens, mainly the Acropolis. *Note:* In the following paragraphs, where mentioned, the winter period is from October 16 to March 31, summer from April 1 to October 15.

## Archaeological Sites

**THE ACROPOLIS:** "Future ages wonder . . . " and they admire, and huff and puff up the hill for a closer look. The Acropolis (meaning "upper city") is built on a rock 515 feet above sea level. The rock has been there, presumably, since the Creation; the walled fortress on top of it has been there for many millennia; but the Acropolis you see today, with its temples and its **Parthenon,** is a creation of the fifth century B.C. Let's simplify the upper city. The "Acropolis" is the entire plateau; it contains four ancient buildings, and one very discreet modern building which is the **Acropolis Museum.**

The first of these ancient structures is the **Propylaea,** an imposing entrance consisting of a central gateway with two wings (one of which was originally a picture gallery, the Pinacotheca). Just to the right of the Propylaea is a small temple known as **Athena Nike,** or Nike Apteros ("Winged Victory"). It was built in the fifth century B.C. to commemorate the victories of the

Greeks over the Persians, and its beautiful friezes portray scenes from that war.

The **Erechtheum** (pronounce it er-ek-the-*um* ), was begun in 421 B.C. and completed in 407 B.C., on the site of a temple to Erechtheus, a legendary king of Athens. In some ways this is the most hallowed spot up on the hill, because it is the spot where, so the legend says, Athena herself, the guardian of Athens, created the first olive tree. Legend also has it that the invading Persians destroyed this tree, but when they were driven off the tree miraculously grew again. It's a curious temple by Athenian standards: it's built on two levels, it's assymetrical, and its two porches have no relationship to each other. The smaller porch of the two is the famous one supported by the six **caryatids**, or stone maidens. During the Turkish occupation, the military governor housed his forty wives here.

But the crowning glory of the Acropolis is the great temple dedicated to the virgin goddess herself, the **Parthenon.** At one time the temple sheltered a gigantic statue of Athena, finished in ivory and gold, and its anterooms were stacked high with the treasures of the city. The Parthenon was built during the time of Pericles, between 447 and 432 B.C., and designed by what may have been the most successful architectural team of all time—Phidias, Ictinus, and Callicrates. They started out with a very uneven foundation, so that one end of the building rests on 35 feet of marble to bring it level with the rest of the structure; the temple lies east to west, with 17 columns on the north and south walls and eight columns on the other two sides.

But the numbers mean little compared to the grace and grandeur of the temple's lines. The Parthenon has no straight lines.

*The Acropolis*

Horizontal lines curve in the middle and the 50 columns bulge in the center then taper off toward the top. Traces of iron in the marble (from the hill of Pentelicon, on the edge of the city) give it a golden glow. In its youth, the Parthenon had statues and friezes and other decorations, but over the years they've been removed by various conquerors or explorers (the British Museum's famed Elgin Marbles come from the Parthenon). But long before Lord Elgin scrambled up the hill, the Parthenon had undergone various humiliations—for a thousand years it was a Christian church, then it became a Moslem mosque complete with minaret, and then a Turkish arsenal. It was hit by a Venetian shell during a siege in 1687, and that one hapless shell destroyed the interior and the roof of the temple. All the bits and pieces which were left lying around were put back into place during a restoration project that began in the 19th century and didn't end until 1930.

Take a breather now. What you see from up here (with the exception of the museum)—the Stoa, the Plaka, the Areopagus and Pnyx—was the extent of the city of Athens in its Golden Age. This was where it was all at. Pericles, the orator, aristocrat, general, and statesman, was the grand panjandrum. The plays of Euripides, Aeschylus, Aristophanes, and Sophocles were being premiered at the **Theater of Dionysus.** Philosophers and men of learning were gathering there and exchanging their wild ideas: Anaxagoras with his absurd theory that the universe was an organized system; Democritus mumbling about all matter being made up of atoms; Herodotus, the so-called father of history, researching his book on the Persian Wars. It must have been an extraordinary, exciting place.

Now for the rest of the Acropolis. The **Acropolis Museum** is a low structure tucked into the northern end of the plateau, hidden from the outside world. It was built in the last century to store the various statues and fragments of stone reliefs found on the surrounding hills—pediments, friezes, the *Moschophoros* (man with calf), *Athena Meditating,* and a collection of statues of women, known as "Korai" famous for their smiles which certainly make a change from Mona Lisa and her mystic smile). The museum helps you visualize how the buildings must have looked centuries ago.

The Acropolis is open Monday through Saturday from 7:30 a.m. to 7:30 p.m. (Sundays 10 a.m. to 6 p.m.) in summer, and from 9 a.m. to 5:30 p.m. (Sundays 10 a.m. to 4:30 p.m.) in winter. The Acropolis Museum's hours are the same as those of the

Acropolis, except that the museum is closed on Tuesdays (all year). Admission to the Acropolis is 50 drachmas, and another 50 drachmas gets you into the Acropolis Museum.

There's a lot to be said for spending a few days in Athens and doing nothing but looking at the Acropolis—from the Pnyx, from Dionysus Restaurant, from Philopappos Hill, during the Son-et-Lumière Show, from the Roof Garden of the Astor Hotel, from Lycabettus Hill, in the stark morning, at sunset, by moonlight. There's something so overwhelming, so commanding about the Acropolis that everything else becomes pallid by comparison.

However, it takes a lot of willpower to resist the other sights of Athens, so let's continue.

**THE AGORA:** We can still stay within the orbit of the Acropolis and feel its presence over our shoulders. The second most important corner of antiquity is the region around the Agora, at the base of the Acropolis on the northwest side. In Ancient Athens, the Parthenon was the center of religious life, but the Agora was where the business was done and the fun was found. Pericles' Aspasia probably headed right for this spot. One of the former arcades, the **Stoa of Attalos** has been rebuilt (by the efforts of the American School of Classical Studies), and now houses a museum filled with the bits and pieces found around the Agora, including models of the Acropolis and the Agora, which will help you understand both sites better—so go there first. Originally, the Stoa was the market, and housed some of the first government offices of a democracy. The dominant feature here, however, is the majestic **Temple of Hephaistos,** usually referred to as the "Theseion," or "Theseum." It may be even older than the Parthenon, and unquestionably it's the best preserved of all Greek Temples. The Ancient Agora Museum in the Stoa of Attalos, to use its full title, is open from 9 to 6 on weekdays, 10 to 6 on Sundays and holidays, throughout the year, and closed on Tuesdays. Admission is free on Sundays and Thursdays and 25 drachmas each for the site and the museum on other days.

Other sites in this neighborhood include the old **Dipylon Gate,** which used to be the first landmark on the road from Athens to Piraeus; the **Keramicos,** the cemetery of Ancient Athens where you can still see some old sculptured memorials and stelae in the graveyard itself, and funerary tablets and ceramics dating from the 11th century B.C. in the adjoining museum. The Keramicos

Archaeological Museum (to give it its formal title) is open from 9 to 4; Sundays and holidays, from 10 to 2; closed Tuesdays.

Still in this general region, but not in the Agora itself, you can visit the so-called **Tower of the Winds,** a clock built in the Roman period in the shape of an octagonal tower, with figures of the winds, a weather vane, and a unique hydraulic mechanism.

Farther to the east, between the Acropolis and the National Garden, is the **Temple of Olympian Zeus** (what a resounding name!), at the junction of two avenues—Amalias and Olgas—facing the southern entrance to the National Gardens. Begun in the sixth century B.C., the temple was built on a terrace 225 yards long, but today it's very much a ruin, and most impressive when it's floodlit in the evening. The best place to admire it from is not the site itself but from the lounge of the Royal Olympic Hotel, or the roof of the new Athens Gate Hotel. (The temple site is open from 7:30 a.m. to sunset in summer, from 9 a.m. to 5:30 p.m. in winter. Admission is 5 drachmas.) Nearby **Hadrian's Arch,** built by the Emperor Hadrian in the 2nd century B.C., marked the boundary between the ancient quarter of the city and the new Athens, or Adrianople as it was then called.

## The Museums

**NATIONAL ARCHAEOLOGICAL MUSEUM:** At 1 Tositsa Street (but the public entrance faces Patission Avenue). Don't rush in. Enjoy the setting first. From Patission you walk through a spacious garden with cafes beneath palm trees, up to a long, classical facade above a sweep of marble steps—usually crowded with footloose young travelers in search of a heritage, or a companion, and crowds of tourists pouring from sightseeing buses. It's not unusual for 8,000 people to visit this museum in one day.

Once in the exhibition rooms proper you're left with no doubt that here is the world's grandest collection of antiquities. Years after you've visited the National Archaeological Museum, its treasures will be imprinted on your mind. You need several hours, if not several days, to see everything here. Go on your own rather than on a tour, when you'll be whisked through so quickly you won't remember a thing; on the other hand, if you have time for several visits, it might be an idea to take a tour first time round, make a mental note of exhibits you want to see in a more leisurely manner, then return again on your own. At any rate, the Museum should be right after the Acropolis on your list of priorities—particularly if you intend to visit, or have just visited, other ancient sites in Greece.

All the treasures from Mycenae are here in Athens, and the distant site really comes alive before your eyes when you see the fantastic collection of objects discovered at the dig by the famous German archaeologist Schliemann. Note the magnificent beaten gold mask of a man with beard and moustache taken from the fifth Shaft Grave: Schliemann claimed, having removed the mask, to "have gazed upon the face of Agamemnon." The Mycenean Hall contains a staggering variety of finds: intricate gold and silver dagger blades, gold-leaf portrait masks, breastplates, swords, libation cups, and many representations of animals and birds—all dating from around 1550 B.C.

Contrast these objects of exquisite craftsmanship with the comparatively crude statues of the 7th and 6th centuries B.C.— the stiff, upright *Kouros* or youth is represented naked with one foot forward and the *Kore* or maiden is draped. Examples of this sculptural style have been found all over mainland Greece and the islands. Another remarkable category of exhibits (not grouped together) consists of bronzes, some of which have lain beneath the sea for the past two thousand years. Most famous of them is the statue of Poseidon, dating from 450 B.C. He stands poised to hurl his trident (which has long since disappeared), not far from the bronze head of Hermes (which was discovered at Piraeus) and the Horse and Jockey of Artemision.

If you're a lover of fine pottery, upstairs there's a huge and bedazzling collection of red and black figured bases of all shapes, from all periods. (The pieces you will see in the gift shops, with

*Erechtheum*

little metal tags attached, are hand-painted authenticated copies of these originals in the Museum.)

You should also visit the exhibition of the finds from Santorini (or Thira, as it has now been officially named), the frescoes alive with colorful representations of swallows, monkeys, dolphins, and elegant figures of youths and maidens. Thira/Santorini was an island civilization that flourished at the same time as the Minoan, back there in the second millenium B.C. The islanders built luxurious homes and decorated them with gorgeous murals and pottery. But one day, as legend has it, "Enkeladus in the bowels of the Earth was roused with undescribable fury" and the ensuing earthquake wiped out Thira (you'll read more about this in the chapter on the Greek Islands).

These paragraphs describe maybe one-millionth of this museum's treasures; unless you have time to pay several visits, confine your tour to a couple of halls, and within each focus on a couple of showcases—such as the displays of gold rings, bracelets, and seals. Otherwise you'll go daffy.

The museum's summer hours are: weekdays 7:30 to 7:30, and on Sundays and holidays 10 to 4:30; in winter, 10 to 4:30 weekdays, Sundays, and holidays. It is closed on Mondays throughout the year. Admission is 50 drachmas, except on Thursdays and Sundays when it's free (and when, of course, you'll have more competition for a close-up of Poseidon and Hermes).

There are three other museums adjoining the National Archaeological Museum, mostly of specialized interest—the **Epigraphical Collection** (inscribed monuments from all parts of Greece), the **Numismatic Collection,** and the **Display of Plaster Copies of Antiquities** (both for display and for sale). The hours are similar to the National Archaeological Museum and the same 50 drachma ticket will get you into all of them.

**BENAKI MUSEUM:** At 1 Odos Koumbari (corner of Vassilissis Sofias Avenue).

It is, of course, almost *de rigueur* to visit the National Archaeological Museum in Athens, and if you're a classical scholar you'll be excited by its thoroughness. If you're not, it may stagger you with its size. The Benaki, on the other hand, is a manageable museum. It's more human, which is probably how its founder, the late Anthony Emm. Beanki, would have liked it. This mansion was, in fact, his home, and most of the exhibits are part of his own collection, which his family turned over to the state after he died. Judging by the exhibits, Benaki must have been a man of wide-ranging interests, because here you'll find relics of the Greek War of Independence, ecclesiastical treasures, textiles, ceramics, glass, costumes, and furniture of Greek, Turkish, and Islamic craftsmanship.

The museum's on three floors, and the room arrangement is rather odd, so buy the 20-drachma condensed guidebook in English. Some highlights: the portable writing desk of Lord Byron; antique pistols and rifles impeccably decorated with silver and engravings; an intricately carved wooden door from Baghdad (ninth century); a virtually complete 17th-century reception room from Cairo with mosaic floor, fountain, basin, and tiled pilasters; a pair of early works by El Greco; some fascinating Coptic fabrics and embroidery; a whole roomful of Egyptian, Roman, Mycenean, and French silver and gold jewelry; one-third of the magnificent collection of Chinese art that once belonged to Georgiou Eumorphopoulos (the other two-thirds is in London)—Han, T'ang, Sung, Yuan, Ming, and Chin. There are also collections of household embroideries and festive costumes from the islands, golden embroidered coats from Epirus, liturgical seals, distaffs, and musical instruments. Be sure to visit the costume section in the basement to see the traditional designs that inspired the handwoven, hand-embroidered dresses you'll be looking at in the shops. And don't miss the incredibly carved wooden paneling from an 18th-century Macedonian mansion, or the bridal bed, a crib from Skyros, and the wooden hope chests.

The Benaki is well worth the short walk up from Syntagma, or down from Kolonaki Square. Open 8:30 to 2 and 4:30 to 7 daily, except Sunday afternoons and all day Tuesday. Admission is 40 drachmas, 20 drachmas for students.

**NATIONAL PICTURE GALLERY:** The **Ethniki Pinakothiki** and **Museum Alexandre Soutzos,** or National Gallery, is the gleaming new building opposite the Athens Hilton. The National Gallery was established in 1900; its new home was inaugurated, however, in May of 1976, and it's a beauty. The collection includes a Goya *(Fiesta),* Correggio *(Guardian Angel),* Poussin *(The Holy Family* and *St. Anne),* van Dyck *(Portrait of a Nobleman),* and half a dozen El Grecos. Unfortunately, they're not always on view. A large gallery is given over to temporary exhibits, and there's a sculpture garden at the rear. Open from 9 to

1 and 4 to 8 in summer, 9 to 4 in winter, 10 to 2 on Sundays and holidays, closed on Tuesdays. Admission is 20 drachmas (free on Sunday and Wednesday).

**BYZANTINE MUSEUM:** At 22 Vassilissis Sofias Avenue, the museum is at the far end of a pleasant courtyard lined with fountains and sculpture fragments, rather like a Florentine palazzo. It has two floors of mosaic fragments, altars, garments, archbishop's staffs, and Bibles. The descriptive signs are in French and Greek only. Open in winter, weekdays from 9 to 4, Sundays and holidays from 10 to 2, closed on Mondays. In summer, open weekdays 7:30 to 7:30; Sundays and holidays, 10 to 6. Admission 50 drachmas.

**MUSEUM OF GREEK FOLK ART:** At 17 Kydathineon Street, Plaka. Folk art here includes vestments, embroidery, wood carving, and silverware. Open daily from 9 to 1 in summer and from 10 to 2 in winter; closed Mondays. Admission free. The museum's collection of folk ceramics is displayed in a former mosque at 1 Areos Street, Monastiriki Square.

**NATIONAL HISTORICAL MUSEUM:** Kolokotroni Square. Modern history's equivalent of the National Archaeological Museum —the story of Greece from the Balkan Wars through more or less the present day. Open weekdays and Sundays from 9 to 1 throughout the year except for Mondays. Admission is 20 drachmas, 5 for students (free on Thursday).

**THE WAR MUSEUM OF GREECE** At 2 Rizari Street (corner of Leoforos Vasilissis Sefias). "War" in this fabled corner of the world means Achilles v. Hector, Neoptolemos v. Paris, Greek v. Persian, Alexander the Greek v. the rest, and continues all the way through recorded history to World War II and the Korea Campaign. The collection including Neolithic cudgels, obsidian hammers, Corinthian helmets, diagrams of ancient battlefields, paintings, uniforms, ship models, a glittering armory of swords and sabres, and, in the courtyard, an exhibition of howitzers, torpedos, and antique fighter planes. Refreshment corner in the basement. Open daily, except Monday, from 9 to 2; admission free.

There are various other museums in Athens dealing with specialized subjects such as anthropology and paleontology; if you're interested, check with the **National Tourist Organization of Greece** (see ABC chapter) for opening hours, prices of admission, and addresses.

**SOME NOTES ON MUSEUMS:** The following notes should be of interest to the serious museum-goer.

### Admission

Admission to all state museums is *free* on Thursdays and Sundays (but again, double-check). Naturally, this means that museums are busiest on those days, and if you want peace and quiet you'd better be prepared to pay some drachmas.

### Public Holidays

Museums and archaeological sites are closed on New Year's Day, March 25 (the National Holiday), Good Friday (until noon), Easter Sunday, and Christmas Day.

### Free Passes

People who can prove they belong to the following categories are allowed into museums free of charge: directors of studies and students of foreign archaeological schools; foreign archaeologists, architects, and artists on a study visit; foreign interpreters and guides; foreign professors of classical studies; foreign students of classical studies (high school or university level) *provided* they're accompanied by their professors. Foreign students of classical studies *not* accompanied by their professors will get a 50% reduction. To get your free pass you have to go to the office of the **Directorate of Antiquities and Restoration,** Department of Museums, 14 Aristidou Street (tel. 3243-056). The office is open Monday and Friday from 11 to 1 only. Take along your passport, one photograph, proof of who and what you are. On second thought, it might be easier just to pay.

### Season Tickets

A three-month season ticket to all museums and archaeological sites in Greece costs 250 drachmas ($7). You can get one from the **Archaeological Funds Department,** 17 Filellinon Street (tel. 3220-468). The office is open daily, except Sundays and holidays, from 7:30 to 2.

## Cameras

There are some curious rules here: a) if you pay the equivalent of the general admission charge you can take pictures, *provided* you don't use a tripod; b) you can use a tripod in museums if you pay a fee of 80 drachmas (for amateurs), or 120 drachmas (for professionals), extra if you're going to use electric current, and whether or not the object to be photographed will have to be removed from its case; c) you can use a tripod in archaeological sites if you pay a fee of 150 drachmas (amateurs) or 250 drachmas (professional) (*Note:* the Acropolis is classified as an archaeological site); d) if you're using a tripod you may not photograph "a person or persons together with an antique object."

## Minor Sights of Athens

Two of the more popular destinations for tour buses are the **Olympic Stadium** and the former **Royal Palace,** both within a couple of blocks of each other, beyond the National Gardens. The stadium was built on the site of the ancient Panathenaic Stadium, but this version was completely rebuilt in white marble for the first modern Olympic Games, in 1896. The Royal Palace was the home of King Constantine before he went into exile; it's a handsome, French-style chateau but you can't see much of it behind all the trees. Most people go there to see the evzones' changing-the-guard ceremony. Don't expect to see anything like the ceremony at Buckingham Palace. In fact, don't bother visiting the Royal Palace and the Stadium unless you have oodles of time.

Surrounding the Parliament Building, back at Syntagma, is the **National Garden** (often referred to as the Royal Garden). It's a formal garden, with a remarkable mixture of trees, lots of shady nooks, swan lakes, duck ponds, terrace cafes where orchestras play Viennese waltzes, and a beautiful palace-like building called the **Zappeion,** which is used occasionally for temporary exhibitions.

One place you should visit, though, even if only briefly, is the **Cathedral of Athens,** halfway between Syntagma and the Plaka, a red pile in Byzantine style, its interior draped with icons which in turn are draped with silver votive offerings like necklaces on an ample-bosomed dowager. The votive offerings are usually small effigies of people who have been blessed or cured by the particular saint. The cathedral genuinely *looks* like a place of worship, even to the black-garbed priests shuffling around in the rear.

The baby cathedral right next to it, the **Church of Aghios (or Saint) Eleftherios,** a tiny church dating from the 13th century, is as austere as the cathedral is ornate. This is a gem of Byzantine architecture, but it was built from marble and stone filched from pagan temples of the classical period. There are many of these venerable Byzantine churches around Athens. Your favorite will probably be the minuscule 11th-century **Church of Aghia Dynamis** (Divine Power), squatting in the middle of the sidewalk, beneath the arcade of the modern Ministry of Education, on Ermou Street.

## The View from the Top

Athens has a couple of vantage points, besides the Acropolis, from which you can get superb views of the city. **Lycabettus Hill** is really a limestone rock reaching almost 1,000 feet into the once-crystalline Athenian sky. In the evening, the top half is floodlit, and from the Acropolis it looks something like a giant soufflé. By day, it's a green-and-white hill topped by a tiny, glaringly white church, **Aghios Georgios.** It's a nagging challenge, and sooner or later you're going to want to climb it. Don't try to walk up (pilgrims used to, but it's an Everest for the faithless), and don't try to take a cab, because it only goes halfway and you still have quite a hike to get to the top. Take the two-minute funicular up the southeast flank. To get there follow the "télépherique" signs to the corner of Kleomenous and Ploutarchou Streets, between Kolonaki Square and the Athens Hilton. The fare is 20 drachmas round trip. The panorama from the top is priceless—all the way to Mount Parnes in the north, west to Piraeus and the Saronic Gulf, with the Acropolis sitting like a ruminative lion halfway to the sea. There's also a cafe/restaurant up there, which you've read about in the chapter on dining out.

**Philopappos Hill** is the big hill west of the entrance to the Acropolis. It gets its name from the monument to a versatile fellow who was a Syrian prince, Roman consul, and Athenian magistrate which was erected sometime between 114 A.D. and 116 A.D. On some maps you'll see a sign on the northwest flank saying *Prison of Socrates.* It's a cave, and maybe it was and maybe it wasn't the philosopher's prison.

Lower down this great outcropping of rock you come to the

hill known as the **Pnyx**, pronounced p-nicks. You may visit it some evening because it's now used as the auditorium for the Son-et-Lumière show, but you may not have time to reflect on what a hallowed spot this is. Free speech was born here. During the days of Pericles the Assembly met here; the Assembly, or Ecclesia, was nothing less than a quorum made up of as many of the city's 150,000 free citizens as felt like attending. The Ecclesia gathered here about 40 times a year, and listened to the great orators who addressed them from the speakers' podium (which you can still see). The amphitheater seated 18,000 and just to make sure it was well filled even when the Ecclesia was discussing something tedious, the police went around with ropes dipped in wet paint and herded the citizens up the hill to the Pynx. Some of the most fateful decisions in Athenian history were made right here, on this beautiful hillside; some of history's most rousing speeches were delivered right here on this speakers' podium.

Still another historic hill, to the northeast of the Pnyx, closer to the Acropolis, is the **Areopagus.** The name means the "hill of Mars," and according to legend this is where Ares (that is, Mars, the god of war) was tried for murdering one of Poseidon's sons. He was acquitted. So was Orestes, when he was tried here for murdering his mother. And it was probably on this hill, in the spring of 54 A.D., that Saint Paul delivered his sermon to the Athenians. Nowadays, when you walk past here on a soft Athenian evening the great hill is suffused with the silhouettes of young lovers and travelers.

How do you get to these hills? You can, of course, take a taxi, but to absorb the full significance of paths which have known the footfall of so many Olympian personalities you really have to walk. Slowly.

## Three Walking Tours of Athens

Athens isn't really such a big city, and most of the places you're likely to be visiting, at least by day, are grouped in clusters. Many of the clusters are within walking distance of each other. The best way to get around is undoubtedly to walk. For one thing you'll be able to experience the exotic sights, sounds, and smells of the city as you go along. You'll *feel* the city.

From Syntagma, the cathedral, the Plaka, the Temple of Olympian Zeus, the Benaki Museum, and the Byzantine Museum are all five to ten minutes on foot. Even the Acropolis is not insurmountable on foot.

However, strenuous walking is really only possible in the early morning, late afternoon, or evening. And you can't always plan things that neatly, especially if your visit is short. Fortunately, public transport is inexpensive (see Chapter IV for details on buses, taxis, etc.)

Anywhere you stroll in Athens you'll find the unusual, the exotic, the surprising, the ancient, or the elegant. The three tours below will give you some idea of the possibilities. The first tour is a general sightseeing tour, the second could be called a shopping tour, the third is a museums tour, but of course all three overlap. They all begin in Syntagma.

**TOUR A—THE SIGHTS:** From Syntagma, stroll down Mitropoleos Street (it's the one on the southwest corner) down past the shops to the cathedral and the Church of Aghios Eleftherios; when you leave the cathedral or the church, turn left, walk one block, then turn right onto Pandroussou Street and enjoy the Oriental bazaar atmosphere of its leather, antique, souvenir, and jewelry shops.

When you get to the square at the bottom of the street you're in Monastiriki; go left and you're at the **Library of Hadrian,** then round the curving street to the left until you come to the **Tower of the Winds** and the **Roman Agora.** Now walk down Pikilis Street and you're at the archaeological site with the **Stoa of Attalos,** the **Agora,** and the **Temple of Theseus.** From there you can walk up the hill to the Acropolis, or double back to the nearest taverna in the Plaka.

**TOUR B—SHOP-AND-STOP TOUR:** From Syntagma, leave by Mitropoleos Street; before you reach the cathedral, turn right and walk one block to Ermou Street, the main shopping street in this area. Continue up Ermou to Nikis, then turn left to Karageorgi tis Servias Street, go through the shopping arcade and into Stadiou Street, cross at the lights and walk up Amerikis Street to Venizelou Avenue, where you can stop for a coffee or lemon juice at Zonar's or Floca.

When you've built your strength up, continue up Amerikis Street to Akadimias Street, turn right and walk one block to Voukourestiou Street, then back to Venizelou Avenue. If you're bushed you can call it a day here and scramble over to Zonar's, or, better still, you can go left one block to Kriezotou, walk up the hill via Pindarou Street, to Tsakalof Street, then go right past the boutique shops there and so down the hill to the nearest cafe on Kolonaki Square.

Check this itinerary against the list of shops (see "Shopping in Athens"), and mark on this page which streets you really want to visit. That way you can probably shorten this tour. How long it takes depends on how much window shopping you do. It could last a whole day, in which case you'd have lunch in Zonar's or Floca, or one of the cafes on Kolonaki.

**TOUR C—MUSEUM TOUR:** From Syntagma, take Stadiou Street (between the tourist office and the King George Hotel) to the **Historical and Ethnological Museum.** From there, cross Stadiou, walk up Amerikis Street to Akadimias Street, where you turn right, then bear left at Kanari Street and walk the one block to Kolonaki Square. Leave Kolonaki Square in the bottom right-hand corner (Koumbari Street), and at the corner with Vassilissis Sofias Avenue you're at the **Benaki Museum.** When you leave the Benaki, continue up Vassilissis Sofias to #22, the **Byzantine Museum.** (If you're still feeling energetic after that, walk up the hill to the funicular and take a two-minute ride to the top of Lycabettus Hill, or walk back to Syntagma via the Parliament Building and the National Gardens.)

## Sightseeing Tours of Athens

One of the simplest, most relaxing ways to get around the sights of Athens, is to call one of the tour operators, make a reservation for the next morning, and have the bus come and pick you up at your hotel.

A company like **American Express** or **CHAT,** will pick you up in an air-conditioned coach, a comfortable 52-seater with a guide who'll speak English plus one other language. Both companies offer a choice of four or more sightseeing tours in Athens.

The **Morning Half-Day Tour** (9 a.m. to noon) includes the National Archaeological Museum (except on Mondays when they substitute the Benaki), National Library, University, Academy, Royal Palace, Stadium, Temple of Olympian Zeus, Hadrian's Arch, the cathedral, and Aghios Eleftherios.

The **Afternoon Half-Day Tour** (3:30 to 6:30 in summer) takes you via the House of Parliament, the Tomb of the Unknown

Soldier, Theater of Dionysus, Philoppapos Hill, Odeon of Herod Atticus, the Acropolis, Theseum, and the Agora.

The **Condensed Morning Tour** (9 to 1) follows the morning itinerary and adds a visit to the Acropolis.

Prices: half-day tours, $9; condensed tours, $11; full-day tours, $17.

The remaining tour is the **Athens By Night Tour,** which in Athens is more fun than usual because it includes a drive past the floodlit Acropolis, then along the edge of the sea to Castella (Piraeus), with refreshments at a taverna and dinner at a Greek nightclub (complete with dancing). During September, the tour may include a visit to the Wine Festival at Daphni instead of the drinks in a taverna. The tour lasts from 8:30 until 1, and costs $22.

An alternative evening choice is the Sound and Light spectacle (English language commentary) plus Greek folk dances. This tour, available nightly from May 1 to September (except when there is a full moon), lasts from 8:30 till midnight; the cost is $13.50.

# Chapter IX

# SHOPPING IN ATHENS

PEOPLE DON'T GO to Athens for a shopping spree as they might to London or Amsterdam or the Caribbean. But there are stores enough and temptations enough in Athens to lure you from ogling the antiquities, so be sure to bring along some spare cash for gifts and souvenirs—especially since there are so many attractive items which you can buy only in Greece.

What are the favorite buys in Athens? That's hard to pin down, but generally speaking Americans are impressed by the jewelry (especially gold items, and the reproductions of the patterns and designs of antiquity), flokati rugs, animal-skin rugs and bed covers, handwoven and hand-embroidered blouses and dresses, local pottery from the islands, tagaria (beach bags of cotton or wool), furs, and icons. There are many more, as you'll see when you wander around the streets of the city—or when you skim through the roundup below.

**WHEN, WHERE, AND HOW TO SHOP:** The stores in Athens open early, at 8 a.m. At 2 p.m. the doors are locked tight for siesta. They open again at 5 p.m., and close finally at 8:15 p.m. There are many exceptions to this rule, however. The stores are closed on Sundays, of course (also on Monday and Wednesday afternoons in summer), and on Saturdays they're open in the mornings only. Winter hours are slightly shorter. As for the kiosks and the Flea Market, they're nearly always open; and shops in the Plaka usually stay open late to catch the revelers. The main shopping centers in Athens are concentrated in the streets around Syntgama Square, around Kolokani Square, and the side streets between Stadiou and Panepistimiou, the two avenues that link Syntagma with Omonia Square. If you were to generalize, you might say that the gift and souvenir stores were more numerous around Syntagma; that the Athenians' everyday shopping was done around Stadiou (this is where some of the major department stores are to be found); and that cosmopolitan Athenians shopped in the streets between Syntagma and Kolonaki; but that is, of course, only a generalization and you'll find quality shops in the most unlikely neighborhoods.

Of course, the most interesting shopping streets can change from year to year: right now, for example, **Tsakalof Street** running off Kolonaki Square is turning out to be one of the most interesting shoppers' streets in Athens. At #42, the end farthest from Kolonaki Square and opposite the old Byzantine Church, **Market 42** is a town house containing six small boutiques offering clothes that try to be as trendy as the names—Toothpick, Lotus, Bombita and so on. If you don't find what you want, there's also a Coffee Bar to compensate you for the hike (if you can put up with the incessant music). A couple of doors down, **Kalimera** fills its windows with oddments—dolls, cushions, trinkets, gifts—in bright Christmassy colors. Heading towards Kolonaki Square, Tsakalof will unveil a steady procession of boutiques (for men and women), jewelry (Anemone at #24, Ritsi at #13), furniture and fabrics stores, pastry shops and restaurants. One of the nice things about Tsakalof is that it tends to be less frantic with traffic than some of its neighboring streets.

Traffic, in fact, is about to be banned from one of the city's most interesting shopping streets, **Voukourestiou** (two blocks from Syntagma, between Panepistimiou and Lycabettus), which is being transformed into a mall with flowers, fountains, and benches.

**BARGAINING:** Should you bargain in Athens? Before you run out and start haggling, be warned that not all the city's shopkeepers take kindly to it. You can tell by the look of the place whether you can or cannot. Save your bargaining for the streets, especially the Flea Market—but when you do it, do it with gusto. *Some rules:* Take your bargaining seriously—don't have the family gawking in the background. Totally disregard the vendor's first offer; reject out of hand his second. If you have a Greek friend, let him do the bargaining for you. And never rush. If you like something with a special passion, begin bargaining for the item next to it, then "settle" for the one you want. When in doubt, don't buy. It's cheaper next door.

**KIOSKS** If you can't find it anywhere else in Athens, you'll probably find it at one of the numerous sidewalk kiosks, a unique

Greek institution. They're open 18 hours a day, and sell an incredible assortment of goods: chocolates, magazines, newspapers, dolls, postage stamps, cigarettes, cakes, pharmaceuticals, chewing gum, films, pens, lightbulbs, detergents, cosmetics, books, and on and on and on (there's one that even stocks parakeets). And you can use their telephones for a couple of drachmas.

**ATHENS MARKETS:** Centering on Pandrossou Street, and spreading out to surrounding streets, the **Flea Market** is just what you'd expect it to be: a monumental assortment of cast-offs, some of it junk, the treasures or otherwise from the attics of Attica. You might like some of the brass and copper ornaments, jewelry, 1930 Victrolas, icons, lamps, woven bags, or old used clothing. A visit to the Flea Market can be quite exciting, especially if you try your hand at bargaining. Save this trip for a Sunday. (Other stores on Pandrossou Street sell new items, including handwoven blouses, kaftans, and a huge selection of bargain-priced leather sandals—Jackie Onassis buys hers here).

If the Flea Market should put you into a general market mood, then head as well for the **Meat Market,** at Eolou 81. A tiny entrance beckons the unsqueamish into a passageway of butchers' stalls, with red meat hanging everywhere. Twenty steps in, the passageway is transformed into a giant cross of stalls. The Fish Market is here, too.

On the other side of the Meat Market is **Sofokleous Street,** home to dozens of little cheese, olive, and grocery stores. Go there for a lunch of feta cheese, black/brown olives (they're loaded with vitamins A and C), a loaf of bread, and your choice of wine.

There is another, more "neighborly" flea market in Piraeus, **Ta Paliatzidika tou Pirea,** just off Ippodamias Square (near the subway terminal); good for copper and silver, pottery, lamps and hand-embroidered bedspreads, and so on.

In addition to these two flea markets there are several street markets (called *laiki*), following a tradition that dates back to the Middle Ages. Stalls are piled high with fruit and vegetables as well as clothing and country wares brought into town by itinerant merchants. These markets are held in different neighborhoods on different days (invariably from early morning until 2 p.m.); ask at the hotel reception desk for the day or location of the market nearest to your hotel.

## Handicraft Shops

-You'll find the handicraft/jewelry/souvenir/"Greek Art" type of shop everywhere in Greece, and it often doesn't make much difference exactly which one you step into. The prices and merchandise, all "typically Greek," are similar at most of them. In this section, however, the listing concentrates on shops selling handicrafts which are of better quality than the usual souvenir-type trinket.

Before you start racing from store to store, however, you might first take a look at what's available by stopping off at the permanent exhibition of **Greek Handicrafts** at 9 Mitropoleos Street, two blocks down from Syntagma. Here you'll find examples of ceramics from the islands, silverwork, hand-painted wooden utensils, leather desk accessories, embroidery, dolls, necklaces made from ahatis stone and various types of traditional rugs. If you have any questions about where to buy individual items, the staff will help you, although they're really there to help *commercial* clients since this is officially the National Organization of Hellenic Handicrafts, or Eommex.

The **National Welfare Organization** channels the work of poor families and schoolchildren from all over Greece; it supplies the designs (invariably adapted or copied from museum pieces) and the families do the rest. Their handiwork makes excellent gifts, easy to pack, easy to carry, easy on the wallet: a package of two embroidered linen guest towels for under $7, embroidered silk evening bags for $15 and up, sets of four napkins and placemats for $29, hand-embroidered tablemats for $83. These prices are about one-third less than you'd pay for the comparable articles in New York, and all profits go to charity. The N.W.O. has a shop at the Athens Hilton, a rug-and-carpet store at 24a Voukourestiou Street.

**Leshki** (19 Pindarou Street) is the kind of hole-in-the-wall shop you miss if you blink, but in fact it's worth a detour if you're interested in unusual leather wall plaques depicting characters from traditional Greek shadow theater (prices from 900 drachmas). Everything here is done by hand (two hands only—the proprietor's), ranging from hand-painted note cards (20 drachmas) to oxidized gold-and-silver necklaces in one-of-a-kind designs (1,400 drachmas to 6,000 drachmas).

**King's Shop,** Constitution Square. You've probably passed this shop a dozen times: it's located right next to American Express on Syntagma. Prices are on the high side here, but the merchandise is worth it—especially the Greek-style dresses (lin-

One of the most delightful handcraft shops in Athens is **To Anoyi** at 1 Sotiros, one floor up in a quaint little Plaka house with a bookbindery in the basement. When you climb the stairs to iconographer Katherine Apostolou's workshop you may find her painting to the strains of Mahler. Her dazzling display of crafts includes attractive enamel rings (100 drachmas), enamel ashtrays with delicate designs of boats and animals (100 to 180 drachmas), pottery from Volos, batiks, ikons, cotton scarves with traditional regional designs (130 to 260 drachmas), decorative wooden eggs in traditional designs (300 drachmas). Something here for every taste and every budget.

en with embroidery at the neck and/or sleeves), which can be made to order in two days' time. Other wares include gold and silver jewelry (you can spend as much as $1,500 if you feel like it), authentically reproduced ancient coins and icons, worry beads, antique braided handbags, tableware, stemware, costume jewelry, and unusual metal sculptures.

**Deros,** 4 Stadiou Street, is located in a large corner building, two floors of which are bulging with china, glassware, housewares, jewelry, and crystal chandeliers. You'll find the prices reasonable enough, especially for the porcelain statuettes.

Other handicraft and "Greek Art" shops include **Stathis** at 2 Palaealogou Venizelou Street (just off Cathedral Square); **Cleo's** in the Hilton arcade (bags, dresses, necklaces, bracelets, leather pitchers, rings); **Mati** at 20 Voukourestiou Street, where you can buy "mati" stones for keeping the evil eye away, as well as old monastery lamps, candlesticks, glass and silver, and all sorts of *unexpected* things; **Greek Corner,** (Sam Pessah and Son), 10 Karageorgi tis Servias Street, bursting with every sort of "authentica" available, including handwoven blouses and dresses from $10 to $250, as well as silver and gold jewelry.

**ADC,** short for Athens Design Center, is a small outlet for the works of a group of designers in ceramics, silver, and pottery. It's at 4 Valaoritou Street, and its displays include saucers, cups, plates, bowls, flowerpots, and ceramic sculptures. Unusual pottery pieces include turtle doves at half the price you'd pay in New York, spoons, dolls, and an interesting collection of unusual silver-and-bronze jewelry—rings from 500 drachmas, cufflinks from 1,200 drachmas, and necklaces up to 2,500 drachmas (about $70).

**Tanagrea,** 15 Mitropoleos, at the corner of Voulis and Mitropoleos Streets (near the little church in the middle of the sidewalk), sells "Les Faiences de la Grèce, all handmade items," in classic and contemporary designs from all the islands and areas of Greece.

**Cantoros,** at 28 Voukourestiou, specializes in ceramic lamps and ceramic bangles. It's an unusual shop and prices are reasonable.

**Pandora,** 12 Voukourestiou Street, is one of the more attractive shops selling artifacts, jewelry, and gifts; it's clean, well laid out and its owner, Mr. Sakellaridis, quite clearly takes pride in the place. Among the interesting items on sale here are silverplated and silver/gold-plated brooches from antique Creto-Mycenean and Byzantine original jewelry exhibited in various museums (from 390 to 55 drachmas); attractive gold-plated brass paperweights which are copies of old coins (270 drachmas); brass gold-plated paper clips and letter openers featuring the owl, symbol of Athens and wisdom (270 drachmas). Among Mr. Sakellaridis' strikingly original knick-knacks are superb heavy-sprung paper holders (almost like clothes pegs) made of gold-plated brass with engraved designs from Delphic friezes (from 270 drachmas). Pandora's artisans have also handcrafted gold-plated copper belts, necklaces, and bracelets, at prices ranging from 390 to 930 drachmas; these items will really upgrade your old black cocktail or evening dress and you'll feel quite stunning as well. Interesting rings range from 140 to 240 drachmas, cuff links in silver or silver with gold plating (some of Byzantine design) cost from 340 drachmas.

**Myconos** at 10 Mitropoleos Street is two floors of jewelry, glassware, woven bags, tiles, sports shirts, models of Mykonos caiques and terracotta wall plaques. Their own factory produces cotton caftan-like dresses with traditional Greek designs (from 800 to 1,000 drachmas); they also have some chunky modern silver bracelets priced between 1,000 and 1,500 drachmas, and their rugs featuring the famous Greek key design (black on red) are made from heavy wool but feel soft to the touch (prices from 7,000 to 8,000 drachmas).

**Museum Shops:** Greek arts and jewelry are also available in several museums, including the **National Archaeological Museum** (reproductions of vases, figures, and statues) and the **Bena-**

ki Museum (table linens, prints, matchbooks, etc.) Both of them, of course, also sell books, which are useful as souvenirs and gifts.

Dolls in Greek costume are one of the most popular souvenirs of a trip to Athens; you can buy them in most of the Greek Art and souvenir shops, or you can go direct to the factory and buy them for a few drachmas less. The place to go is Koumparoulis, at 2 Diogenou Street (near the Roman Agora and the Tower of the Winds), where you can watch Mrs. Koumparoulis make the dolls in her tiny workshop. The dolls are all dressed in exact copies of authentic Greek costumes, from all parts of Greece, and if they don't have the one you want on display, they will make it for you in 24 hours. Best of all, you get wholesale prices—evzones for 100 to 300 drachmas, dolls of all sizes from 150 to 700 drachmas. The firm will ship your dolls back to the States (delivery time is about 30 days), and they have now opened a branch in the new President Hotel on Kifissias Avenue.

## Jewelry

This is one of the most popular shopping items in Greece, and the range of merchandise ranges from souvenir trinkets based on ancient designs to chic avant garde creations in gold and precious stones.

Voukourestiou Street might be the place to begin your expedition, since the city's finest jewelers are located at the corner with Panepistimiou, and the new mall is lined with reliable shops.

Some of the most original and imaginative gold jewelry in the world is designed by Ilia Lalaounis and handcrafted by his artisans in a workshop in the shadow of the Acropolis. Lalaounis introduces two new collections a year (sometimes more when he receives a special commission from a sheikh or shah). A typical collection might include a dazzling array of gold necklaces, bracelets, and rings evolved from the shapes of aboriginal and prehistoric tools and statuettes, priced in the thousands of dollars. However, visit any of the Lalaounis stores and you'll find many items costing as little as $50. The main store is at 6 Panepistimiou, with branch boutiques in the lobby of the Hotel Grande Bretagne, the Athens Hilton, the Athens Tower, and on Corfu, Mykonos, and Rhodes.

Neck and neck, so to speak, with Lalaounis in quality and price is the second great name in Greek jewelry—Zolotas Chrysothiki at 10 Panepistimiou. On Voukourestiou Street itself you have Adler and Charles Pentherondakis at #13, Petradi at

#20 and **Petra Nova** at #19. The latter two feature petradi, or semiprecious stones (amethyst, tiger's eye, lapis, turquoise, and sodalite being the most popular here), set in imaginatively designed pins, necklaces, rings, earrings, pendants and what have you, at prices ranging from $20 to well over $100. Petradi has a particularly interesting selection of gift items, such as ashtrays of petrified coconut.

At 10 Nikis Street, **VIP** stocks Byzantine seals and brooches copied from originals in the National Archaeological Museum, mostly from the Mycenean and Alexander the Great periods, mostly priced above $100.

There are more museum-inspired designs as well as modern original designs at the family-run **Maria Trivizas** (herself an archaeologist) in a cubby-hole store at 17 Voulis Street; prices from a few dollars to $5,000, with a discount of 15% if you pay with cash or travelers checks.

There are also many jewelry stores in the streets running off Syntagma Square. At 4 Ermou Street, **Piocos** displays masses of silver items in a street-level shop and basement showroom, all fashioned by Piocos' own craftsmen and inspired by ancient, traditional and modern motifs.

**Gold Coin Jewelry,** 17 Stadiou Street, actually *sells you* money —a unique collection of unusual coins, some ancient.

If you admire the Lalaounis concepts but cannot afford the price of gold, visit a store called **The 4 Lamda** in the Athens Tower skyscraper. It's actually another branch of Lalaounis, with the same imagination and flare in design, but most of the items are crafted in silver, with scores of gifts in the $20 to $30 range, as well as more substantial items. Worth the taxi ride.

The new **President Hotel Furs and Jewel Shop** (in the hotel concourse, at 43 Kifissias Avenue) is run by Joseph Salvator Fleri, an affable Greek gentleman who served with a Scottish regiment in India in World War II; he'll guide you through the shop's small but select range of gold and silver bracelets, necklaces, and rings. The shop's moderately priced furs can be tailored to your size within hours. A sister store, **Mikinai,** is more conveniently located at 38 Mitropoleos Street, on the way to the Cathedral.

## Women's Fashions

This is a subject you have to look at from two angles: local designs and fabrics on the one hand, high-fashion and interna-

tional chic on the other. Sometimes they overlap, but in general
you will probably be interested in shopping only for local fashions—famous-designer clothes are even more over-priced than
normal, and the trendy gear here is still panting to catch up with
last year's trends in London, Paris, and New York.

Three young designers are still setting the pace in Athens'
fashion world these days, and all three of them turn enthusiasti-
cally to their Greek heritage for inspiration; yet they've all
managed to attract international attention since their designs
have been snapped up by various jet-set celebrities who shall go
nameless.

**Yannis Travassaros** has his boutique in the Athens Hilton. He
designs everything he sells, and in most cases he also weaves his
own fabrics, or trims coats or dresses with old embroidery and
authentic bibiles (needlework borders) from his own collection
of old Greek costumes. Most of his creations are for dressy
winter wear—pant suits, zigouni (sleeveless coats like the jackets
worn by Greek shepherds), evening coats, evening dresses. He
also has a sportswear boutique down by the Hilton pool. Some
prices: two-piece pant suits $120 to $300; dresses from $120; silk
blouses with embroidery from $100 to $250; zigounis $40 to
$1,000; patchwork vests $100 to $1,000; dresses made of
koukoulariko, a lovely raw silk made by the peasants of northern
Greece, $200 to $500. Travassaros also designs embroidered
handbags $75 to $100, handwoven braid belts with copies of
antique buckles ($50 to $85), and replicas of antique gold necklaces from $65 to $120. Alterations within three hours.

The other two hot-shot designers work as a team—**Nikos &
Takis**, two ex-painters who got fed up with people who expected
to bargain a $2,000 canvas down to $200, so they started design-
ing clothes. Their boutique is at 10 Panepistimiou Avenue, near
Syntagma Square (with branches at the Plaka in Athens, and in
Corfu, Delphi, and Rhodes). The Plaka boutique is in a 250-
year-old house at Eolou, near the big open square: The ground
floor is taken up by handicrafts; high fashion (and air conditioning) is upstairs. Again, the inspiration for the designs comes from
Greek and Byzantine costumes and decoration. A two-piece
coat-and-dress combination with Byzantine embroidery, pleated
panel down the back, costs from $400 to $500; pants suits are
about $225: evening dresses with embroidered necks and cuffs
start at $500. Nikos and Takis keep sizes 10, 12, and 14 in stock
but can usually run up other sizes, or make alterations, within

24 hours. Their favorite fabrics are cotton, wool, silk, mohair, and raw silk.

You'll find simpler items, like handwoven and hand-embroidered blouses and dresses at some of the handicraft "Greek Art" shops—such as **VIP** (10 Nikis Street), where you'll find a selection of all-wool, handwoven dresses from $100, and hand-painted silk dresses with matching stoles for $150.

**Lizard** (14 Kriezotou Street) and **Gianari Gallani Boutique** (on the corner of Kolonaki Square and Skoufa Street) both have elegant selections of leather goods—including shoes, belts, and jackets.

The **Hermes Gift Shop** at 25 Mitropoleos Street will make you up one of their lambswool jackets and coats, items unique to Greece, with an unusual flokati trim along the zipper and around the hems, in natural unbleached color, with or without hood. A hip-length jacket costs 1,440 drachmas ($40), knee-length coat 2,650 drachmas ($74), shepherd's jacket embroidered or trimmed 1,440 drachmas ($40). *Note:* These prices include shipping to the U.S.A. and insurance. Hermes also carries capes inspired by those of the evzones, or presidential guards, $55 in cape size, three-quarter and full-length just a few dollars more. The manager here, by the way, speaks a dozen languages.

## Men's Fashions

Again, the name designers are represented here, but the prices are outlandish, and since Greece is not noted for its own male fashion industry, the pickings are slim. If you want to look over suits, jackets, and shirts by Europe's top-flight designers (particularly Italian) the appropriate stores seem to be concentrated near the intersections of Acadimios Street with Pindarou Street, Voukourestiou Street and Amerikis Street. A few new mens' boutiques have now set up shop in Kolonaki, mainly along Tsakalof Street.

**Ascot,** at 29 Nikis Street (just off Syntagma Square) and 6 Kapsali Street (just off Kolonaki Square) features a wide selection of suits, sportcoats, slacks, shirts, sweaters, ties, and toiletries. It's the place to go if you find yourself short of a tie or shirt.

**Bouloubasakis Yannis** at Filellinon and Nikidimos streets also has a fine selection of menswear.

## Sandals

Head up Pandrossou Street from Monasteraki Square to #89,

and inside you'll find the "poet-sandalmaker" of Athens, **Stavros Melissinos.** Look in the dusty window and you'll see several yellowing newspaper articles about this remarkable man, in amongst the sandals, straps, and tools of the trade; inside the small shop, you'll find up to 30 different styles of sandals ranging in price from 200 drachmas (sizes 33-39) to 250 drachmas (sizes 40-45). If your feet are bigger or smaller, Melissinos will make you a special pair. He counts among his clients such exalted figures as Jackie Onassis and the Beatles and attributes to the former the fact that Pandrossou was not demolished several years ago. Melissinos is also a poet and philosopher. Framed certificates above his workbench testify that Harvard College Library and the Bodleian Library in Oxford, England have copies of his books in their collections. His *Persian Rubaiyat* (currently 50 drachmas and available from him) is in its fourth edition and on the curriculum of several colleges and universities in the U.S. An unaffected, gentle and friendly man, Melissinos will chat about his poetry to you while helping you choose your sandals. Genuine craftsmen are fairly rare these days, but a craftsman who is equally adept in two such different fields is rarer still—and a privilege to meet. His brother-in-law's workshop, **Tony's Sandals** at Adrianou 52 (on the far side of the Roman Agora), is the place to go when you want a comfortable pair of shoes or boots—casual style. A handmade pair of pale tan leather boots is currently 1,800 drachmas.

## Furs

A high priority on your fur stalking list should be **Voula Mitzakou** at 7 Mitropoleos, where the charming Mrs. Mitzakou herself runs the business her father founded over 75 years ago; her knowledgeable, England-trained assistant Stephanos will be happy to explain the entire process of making fur coats, and serious customers (with emphasis on the serious) will be treated to a tour of the workshops downstairs. (Mitzakou employs 25 people, each an expert in one specific stage of the process.) Mink jackets here will cost you anything from $650 to $2,300 (six different qualities of mink are involved), a full-length multicolored mink coat from $750, Persian lambs from $600 and Greek red fox jackets are $950. You can take your pick from 25 to 30 varieties of fur (from Greek wolf to French rabbit to sable) and get Mitzakou to design a coat specially for you (in which case you add a minimum of 10% to the off-the-peg prices). Mitzakou has full cold storage facilities, and exports fur coats to clients all over the world.

---

### Old Established Company

The fur stores listed above are fine for most people, but if you have a chauffeured limousine waiting for you at the airport to whisk you to a suite at the Grande Bretagne, then you'll probably be able to persuade someone to take you to a rather special place—**J.A. Sistovaris & Sons, Inc.,** at 14 Voulis Street (up one flight), 4 Ermou Street or 9 Venizelou. This old, established company, now in its fourth generation, uses only the finest quality furs (no slap-together remnants here) for the finest quality clientele. Expensive, naturally.

---

**George M. Trahos & Sons,** 7 Filellinon Street (tel. 3228-256). Everyone refers to it as the Fur House, so the Fur House it is. It's been in business for over 100 years, and it has its own expert fitters. What you buy here may be influenced by the time of year. Whatever you want in the way of furs, you'll find it at the Fur House. Pick your favorite fur—Persian lamb, natural Greek stone marten, autumn haze natural mink, tourmaline natural mink, palamino mink. Indian lamb is particularly popular because it combines lightness with warmth. Pick your favorite style—full-length, three-quarter-length, cape-stole, bolero jacket, and straight stole.

You'll have a choice of 500 coats, stoles, jackets, hats, and scarves—and prices that will make you feel soft and snuggly. A white Persian lamb full-length coat with lapel collar costs $295; an Indian lamb full-length coat costs $275; a natural ranch mink full-length coat with top-quality let-out skins costs $1,500. But you'd better go see them with your own eyes, even if you end up buying only a Persian lamb cape for $95 or mink hat for $40. Styles for men here, too, and, if you produce this book, you will receive a 30% discount.

### Antiques, Music, Art

**Antiqua,** 4 Amalias. This is a proper, elegant antique shop owned by a man who both knows and loves his wares. John Yannoukos, an English-speaking Greek who seems always to be polishing his treasures, has filled his store to the brim with clocks, jewelry, paintings, ancient Greek votive dishes, ivory statues, icons, Chinese vases and carvings, French and Venetian furnishings, and then some. The shop is a bit off Syntagma, and the prices range from $3.50 to $5,000. Mr. Yannoukos has a second antiques gallery at 2 Messoghion Street, Athens Tower.

**Tassos Th. Zoumboulakis,** 7 Kriezotou Street (tel. 3634-454) and 20 Kolonaki Square (tel. 3608-278). Mr. Zoumboulakis has appropriately situated his art and antique gallery close to the posh hotels of Syntagma Square—around the corner and seven doors up on the left from the King's Palace Hotel. Founded at the beginning of the century, the gallery (it's air-conditioned, by the way) collaborates with several of the finest art dealers in Europe and the United States, so it's not restricted to works by Greek artists. Nevertheless, those are the ones that will probably interest you most, and here you'll find a selection of the works of Greek artists who are known only within their homeland, and others who have earned reputations abroad. Among them are Tsazouchis, Chryssa, Matta, Alan Davie, and Fassianos. Also occasional works by Calder, Max Ernst, Rauschenberg, Magritte, and other contemporary artists.

On a recent visit, we saw a variety of graphics (lithographs, silkscreens, posters), multiples, and editions from well-known Greek and foreign artists. Prices start at about $6 for posters and go up to $2,000 for a Miro litho.

The splendid antique collection includes 19th-century silver candelabra, water jugs, candlesticks, commodes, and original icons (which you can admire but can't buy because the Greek government won't allow you to take them out of the country). Mr. Zoumboulakis also specializes in Greek folk art and the jewelry of Greek national costumes (brooches, pendants, rings, and things from $20 to $300), as well as embroideries from the native dresses (mostly 17th, 18th, and 19th century) of Attica, Crete, Naxos, Rhodes, and Patmos (they make exquisite wall hangings, but you'd better talk directly to Mr. Zoumboulakis about prices).

**C. Haritakis Antiques,** 7 Valaoritou Street (tel. 3621-254), has a fine collection of silverware, copperware, furniture, prints, porcelain, and icons. Branch at the Caravel Hotel.

**Les Amis du Livres,** in a short passageway at 9 Valaoritou, is everything its name promises to lovers of books—rare books, prints, engravings of Greek scenes. Open 8 a.m. to 2:30 p.m. on Monday, Wednesday, and Saturday; 8:30 a.m. to 1:30 p.m. and 4:30 to 8 p.m. on Tuesday, Thursday, and Friday.

**Collector,** in the lobby of the Hilton Hotel, is an antique shop specializing in pewter, brass, copper, and wrought iron—a 150-year-old gunpowder holder in handhammered pewter with silver plating, old copper cooking molds starting at $50, belt fasteners in brass or silver from $133 to $200, antique rings from $30 to $50, new ceramic necklaces in earthy colors $15 to $20.

**Gallerie Antiqua,** Queen Sophias and Messiogiou 2 (tel. 7705-881), is an elegant shop housing the works of noteworthy Greek and foreign painters, exquisite art objects, and furniture of high quality and good taste. Near the American Embassy.

## Rugs

Here's a quick briefing on Greek carpets: There are three basic types: **Mistra** (known also by its Persian name of **Sparta**) has 75,000 to 80,000 knots to the square meter, and costs $133 to $200 a square meter; **Delphi (Slezuk** in Persian) has 100,000 knots per square meter and costs about $250 to $283 a square meter; **Troja** (or **Siraz** in Persian) has 200,000 knots per square meter, and costs from $5,500 to $7,326 for 11 square meters (all prices approximate). While you're thinking dollars, it costs $3 per kilo (up to 45 kilos) to ship your carpet back to the States by air, and there are, more or less, four kilos to the square meter.

There's a bewildering choice of designs and colors—Horassa, **Hamadan, the Lobanof** with its playful lions, Greek designs from the Acropolis, blue-and-yellow Byzantine designs, the Sykrion (based on motifs taken from a village cemetery near Corinth), the Greek classical designs with their stark blues and whites and subtle flecks of ochre, some Oriental designs which look like woolen Jackson Pollocks (and beautiful enough to hang on a wall). The showroom also has a collection of "New Greek" patterns—flowers and whorls and flourishes that look as though they'll fly out of the borders the minute you step on them.

Two stores with good selections of rugs and carpets are **Arts and Crafts,** on the corner of Voukourestiou and Valaoritou Streets, and **N. Rossopoulos & Co.,** at 18 Panepistimiou; the main enclave of carpet stores is on Patission Avenue, beyond the National Archaeological Museum.

Flokati rugs are one of the most popular purchases for visitors to Greece, and most visitors flock to the flokati showroom of Chris Karamichos, **Karamichos-Flokati,** one floor up at 3 Mitropoleos. These flokatis come from the city of Trikala in central Greece, not far from Delphi, where the Karamichos family has been producing them for 400 years. Chris Karamichos, however, was trained as an engineer, and was sent on a five-year scholarship to study at Arizona University in Tucson, Trikala's sister city. He returned home with an engineering degree, but when he saw flokati again, through new eyes, he decided that what he really wanted to do was export Greek flokati rugs to the rest of the world. His friends thought he had become "a crazy American," but he persisted, and that's how the products of an unheard-of town in Greece have found their way into stores across the U.S. and around the world. All his flokati is made from a combination of wools from Greece (for wear) and New Zealand (for softness); the fibers are softened under a fresh spring waterfall in Trikala; then handwoven to make a thick, closely woven pile. In his showroom you'll find flokatis in natural tones, kaleidoscope patterns of plain colors, as well as rugs in multicolored patterns (zigzag, diamonds, and a tweed mix called flokomix). Prices range from $38 for a 2 x 5-foot rug in natural colors to $972 for a special very heavy multicolor, 9 x 12-foot rug especially woven by the Karamichos sisters. Postal expenses add on another $5 to $30, *but you're still getting a bargain by U.S. prices.* Karamachis-Flokati offers a money-back guarantee, and if you want to check out the quality before you come over, their rugs are on display at the Handicrafts Center in New York and in the Chicago Museum of Science and Technology.

Another highly regarded flokati dealer is **A. Kokkinos,** also at 3 Mitropoleos Street.

## Miscellaneous

If you didn't pack adequate shoes for clambering over all those ruins and archaeological sites, try **Mouriades** at 4 Stadiou Street, which most people consider the best shoe shop in the city (prices from $35, including some Bally models). On the other hand, if you've ruined your most stylish pair sightseeing you may be able to find a replacement at the **Charles Jourdan/Petrides** shop at 10 Ermou Street (where prices are fairly close to what you'd pay in Paris—and they have American-size lasts to boot).

When you want to bone up on your Greek history and need **English-language books** and paperbacks, go to the **American Bookstore** at 23 Amerikis Street, **Pantelides** at 11 Amerikis, **Eleftheroudakis** at 4 Nikis Street (round the corner from Syntagma and the best bookshop in town), or the bookstand in the **Athens Hilton** (which is open around the clock). Newspapers you can buy almost anywhere, especially at the ubiquitous kiosks.

**Peau d'Ange** (Angel Skin), at 21F Voukourestiou Street, has an extraordinary collection of small leather goods—wallets, picture frames, purses, bags, desk sets, diaries, and calendars—in unusual designs. A good spot for gifts.

*Argaliou* means loom and *Brailas* is the name of a family that looms, so **Argaliou Brailas,** at 7 Filellinon Street, is the place to head for top-quality handwoven silks. *Even the threads are handspun.* Priced by the yard (30″ widths)—$35. Handwoven wool is $26. Made-up items include handwoven capes for $48, and reversible handwoven handbags with shoulder straps (handcrocheted finish) for $7. They'll also make up anything for you, carefully tailored, within three to five days.

**Worry beads** are another popular souvenir. The komboloia, as they're called in Greek, are Greece's answer to tranquilizers, but try twiddling them yourself and you may find they have just the opposite effect—it's not as easy as it looks. Fortunately, they don't cost a fortune. You'll find selections in most "Greek Art" shops, a particularly large selection in the **Bead Shop** on the way up Palaealozon Venizelon.

**Sponges** might seem an unlikely purchase, but they're on sale on street corners all over the city. These are natural sponges fetched out of the nearby sea by hardy divers. They come in all sizes, from 15 drachmas all the way up to somewhere around 500 drachmas—but you'd pay three times the amount back home.

## Department Stores and Supermarkets

The three major emporia (at least, those that come closest to the American concept of a department store) are the **Athenee,** halfway along Stadiou Street; #33-35 to be precise; **Lambropouli** at Aiolou and Lykourgou Streets; and **Minion** at 13-15 Patission Street, near the National Archaeological Museum. The **Pris-Unic-Marinopoulou** stores are a combination department store and supermarket, where you can pick up some useful inexpensive items and the makings of a great picnic; these stores are identified by a large orange M, and the closest one to Syntagma is at 9 Kanaris Street, just off Kolonaki Square.

# Chapter X

# THE ABC'S OF ATHENS

THIS CHAPTER will serve as a reference guide to all the essential miscellany of travel in a strange city. These are the simple things you don't think about back home that can become major when you're away; buying stamps, finding an all-night drugstore, changing money, getting the news. So here is an alphabetical listing covering emergencies, and also some of those "uncategorizable" items we couldn't slip in elsewhere.

**AIRPORTS:** Note—there are two airport terminals in Athens. If you're flying a foreign airline, you'll arrive and depart from **Hellinikon East Terminal,** which is for international flights. If you fly anywhere via Olympic Airways, internationally or to the islands or some other city in Greece, you'll leave from the **West Terminal.** Make sure you tell your driver which one you want. There is also a shuttle service between the East Airport and West Airport, from 8 to 8 every hour on the hour. It's a ten-minute drive.

**AIRPORT BUS:** There's airport bus service to and from Amalia Avenue, near the corner of Syntagma. Buses leave every 20 minutes; the fare is 27 drachmas each way; there is no charge for luggage. But if you're not on a tight budget, the taxi fare is around $5 or $6, including luggage, direct from your hotel to the airport. Olympic Airlines buses leave from the Olympic downtown terminal at Syngrou 96 and go direct to the West Terminal at Hellinikon. 20 minutes, 27 drachmas.

**AIRPORT INFORMATION:** East Airport, tel. 979-9466; Olympic Airways only, tel. 9811-211; international flights other than Olympic, tel. 97-991.

**AMERICAN EMBASSY:** 91 Vassilissis Sophias Avenue (tel. 712951).

**AMERICAN EXPRESS:** Constitution Square (Travel Division, tel. 3244-975; Banking Division, tel. 3234-781. For changing money, buying travelers checks, making travel arrangements, booking sightseeing and escorted tours, receiving mail, meeting people.

**BABYSITTING:** Ask your hotel concierge.

**BANKS:** Open weekdays from 8 a.m. to 1 p.m., except for American Express which is also open from 5 to 7 p.m., and the National Bank of Greece which has 12-hour service seven days a week, from 8 a.m. to 8 p.m., both on Syntagma. There are Athens branches of a number of American and Canadian banks: Chase Manhattan, First National Bank of Chicago, Bank of Nova Scotia, Continental Illinois National Bank, Bank of America, and First National City Bank.

**BEAUTY PARLORS:** No problem. They're all over the place, and most of them are good. You'll probably feel most comfortable, however, in one of the hotel beauty parlors which cater to an international clientele **Try Costi and Taki** at the Hilton—in 1978 $9 for a haircut and $11 for a shampoo and set, prices for which they anticipate a 10 to 20% rise for summer 1979; **"George"** in the Grande Bretagne which charges around $7.35; or **Angelos** at 2 Amalia Avenue, 17 Omirou or 14 Kolonaki Square (about $18 for a haircut, shampoo, and blow-dry); or **Alkis and Takis,** in a palatial pink salon at the Hotel Caravel (tel. 738-503), charging 280 drachmas ($7.75) for shampoo and set. For men, a haircut will cost about $2 to $4.

**BUSES:** Remember to reverse your normal procedure: enter from the rear and exit from the front. Fares run up to 10 drachmas depending on distance. Service begins at 5 a.m. and ends at 1 a.m. On trolleybuses #7 and #12, you enter from the front and pay the exact fare. In general, cabs are a better value unless you have time to spare.

**BUSINESS HOURS:** Athenians have a six-day work week. In winter, the hours are 8:30 a.m. to 1:30 p.m., then from 4:30 to 7:30 p.m. (although most offices will close at 1:30 on Saturdays); in summer, June through October, the hours are 8 a.m. to 1:30 p.m., then 5 to 8 p.m. All government offices (and many private companies) work from 8:30 a.m. to 2:30 p.m. in winter, 7:30 a.m. to 1:30 p.m. in summer, and in fact there's a movement afoot to make those the standard hours for everyone to avoid the extra lunchtime traffic rushes. Stores follow roughly the nongovernment hours, but close on Saturday afternoons all year round (except for grocers barbers, and hairdressers which close on Wednesday afternoons). However, these figures are liable to vary with the day of the week, so call ahead for specific hours.

**BUSINESS ORGANIZATIONS:** Athens Cosmopolitan-Lions Club (tel. 601-311); **Propeller Club,** 194 Syngrou (tel. 951-3111); **Rotary Club,** 3 Kriezotou Street (tel. 623-150); **American Hellenic Chamber of Commerce,** 17 Valaoritou Street (tel. 636-407).

**CAMPING:** Inquire at **National Tourist Organization** (see below). There are a dozen sites in and around Athens, and more than 100 throughout Greece.

**CANADIAN EMBASSY:** 4 Ioannou Gennadiou Street (tel. 739511-19).

*Country Street Vendor*

**CAR RENTALS:** For full information, see Chapter on "Touring the Hinterlands."

**CASINOS:** There are casinos at Mount Parnes (just north of Athens), and on the islands of Corfu (Casino Achillion Palace) and Rhodes (Casino de Rhodes). Roulette, baccarat, chemin-defer, blackjack and slot machines.

**CHURCH SERVICES:** The main churches are St. Dennis Roman Catholic Church, on the corner of Panepistimiou Avenue and Omirou Street; St. Paul's Anglican Church, Filellinon Street; St. Andrew's American Church (interdenominational), 66 Sina Street; the Synagogue, 6 Melidoni Street.

**CIGARETTES:** A pack of American regulars costs around $1.50 —filters and king-size about $1.65. Greek filter cigarettes, on the other hand, are only 50¢ for 20.

**CLIMATE:** Summers are dry and hot, hovering about 80°F. It's cooler, of course, along the coasts and in the mountains to the north. In winter, the temperature can go down to 40° in some areas (Athens has a low of about 45° in January), and occasional rain can also be expected from October through April. But the sun shines 300 days a year.

**CLOTHING:** Specifically, sightseeing garb. For hiking up steep hills and steps (of which there are countless thousands in Greece), women will probably be happier in slacks rather than skirts (which can be too revealing). If you're planning to visit one of the sites where donkeys are the standard method of conveyance, slacks are again recommended to avoid a case of donkey chafe on your knees. For churches, women are expected to wear neck-to-knee clothing. Heavy shoes are essential for all ancient sites—and not such a bad idea for some sidewalks in Athens.

**CREDIT CARDS:** Diners Club, Visa, and American Express are honored throughout Greece. Decals identify cooperating merchants, but verify beforehand that the contracts are still in existence.

**CURRENCY:** The drachma, divided into 100 lepta, is worth 2.75 U.S. cents. 36 drachmas equal, more or less, one dollar. Coins come in 1-, 2-, 5-, 10-, and 20-drachma pieces, and a 50-lepta piece (10- and 20-lepta pieces are rarely used). Bills are the blue 50-drachma note, the red 100-drachma note, the green 500-drachma note, and the brown 1,000-drachma note.

**CURRENT:** Talk to your concierge before using any U.S. appliances. You will probably need anywhere from one to three adapters, which he should have on hand. However, in Athens and most of the mainland the current is 220 volts, A.C. The Hilton outlet is a law unto itself and requires the hotel's adapters (and transformers, available at no extra charge). Top hotels also have a 115V outlet for shavers.

**CUSTOMS:** U.S. nationals may travel freely anywhere in Greece for up to two months. On entering the country, you may bring 750 drachmas, and on leaving you may take 750 drachmas plus up to $500 in any foreign currency. However, there is no restriction on the number or value of travelers checks on either entry or exit. Be very careful about antiques you may have bought. The laws protecting Greek antiquities are very strict and none may be taken out of the country without prior special permission from the **Greek Archaeological Society** at 14 Aristidou Street, Athens.

**DOCUMENTS:** All you need (as an American or Canadian citizen) is a valid passport. Customs and passport control are fairly quick on arrival; the latter can slow you down on departure—so leave yourself a few extra minutes. Your arrival automatically gives you permission to stay two months; if you want to stay longer, you have to apply for a special permit.

**DRINKING WATER:** Safe to drink in urban hotels and restaurants, but beware of country restaurants. There, get bottled mineral water, and make sure the cap is tightly fixed.

**DRIVING:** The **International Drivers' License** is recommended, but not usually required. For information, contact the **Automobile and Touring Club of Greece (ELPA)**, Tower of Athens, 2-4 Mesogion Street, Athens.

**DRUGSTORES:** In an emergency, dial 107 for all-night service.

**ELEVATORS:** Greek elevators are reliable, but they don't operate on the same principles as in the U.S. Except in modern places, such as the Hilton, doors don't open automatically; you have to watch for the elevator arriving at your floor and then quickly pull the door open before someone else presses a button on another floor and the elevator shoots off. Others signal their arrival with a "ping." Also, in many cases the button doesn't register the floor you want until *after* the door is closed tight; so you may have to press your number a second time after the door has closed. Some elevator floors seem to fall out from under you when you step onto them; don't be alarmed, they're simply registering the weight.

**EMERGENCIES:** For all kinds of emergencies, dial 107 for an English-speaking operator; dial 171 for the tourist police; 104 for help with your car; 199 for the fire department; 712-951 for the American Embassy and 739-511 for the Canadian Embassy.

**FILM:** Expensive. Bring supplies with you.

**GUIDES:** If you want to hire your personal guide, the rates are around 600 drachmas (about $15) for a half-day in town, 900 to 1,000 drachmas for a full day plus 100 drachmas for meals. Mrs. Lela Cassavetty is a guide who knows her antiquities as well as her Athens (she took the astronauts around); her number is 710-318. Lena Galanaki, who shows visiting VIPs and American tour groups around, is also up-to-date on restaurants and nightlife; telephone 739-342. Otherwise call the association of tour guides at 3229-705.

**HOLIDAYS:** Most shops are closed on the following days—New Year's Day, January 6, March 25 (National Day), Shrove Monday, Good Friday, Easter Sunday and Monday, August 15, October 28, Christmas Day, December 26.

**HOSTELS:** There are two types: youth and student. In Greece, call or apply to the **Greek Youth Hostels Association,** 4 Dragatsaniou Street, Athens (tel. 3234-107/3237-590).

**LAUNDERETTE:** The self-service launderette Maytag is three blocks back from Acadimias and at the crossroads of Didotou 46 and Zoodochou Pigis. The proprietor speaks some English and while you're waiting for the machines to finish spinning, you can have a coffee or beer next door. The machine wash costs 60 drachmas, the dryer is 10 or 20 drachmas. For 100 drachmas you can get a service wash that includes the soap.

**LIQUOR:** You can buy it by the bottle, or take your own bottle to the grocery store and get a refill—the cost depends on the amount. Famous brands of scotch whisky cost about 500 to 1,000 drachmas, but you can also buy bottles at supermarkets for around 350-400 drachmas (say $10).

**LUGGAGE:** Pacific Ltd., a travel agency at 26 Nikis Street and the *East* Terminal at the airport, will store excess luggage while you tour the hinterlands or islands. Weekly rate: 70 drachmas per piece: Call 3236-851 for more details.

**MASSAGE, SAUNA:** The Hilton's resident masseuse charges $6 for massage, $4 for sauna. Call 720-201, ext. 381, from 9 a.m. to 7:30 p.m.

**MEDICAL ATTENTION:** For doctors and dentists trained in the U.S. or fluent in English, contact the Tourist Police or the Hospital (Dial 100 for both), the American Embassy (712-951), or the State Hospital of Athens (7778-901). The Athens emergency medical and ambulance service is 522-5555 (English spoken).

**MEDICINES AND TOILETRIES:** American brands are available in most pharmacy-type stores in Athens and other major tourist centers. But at a price. Bring your own supplies in the interests of economy. European brands are usually less expensive—but reliable. For names of all-night pharmacies, dial 107.

**MONEY CHANGING:** Best bets are the 8 a.m. to 8 p.m., seven days a week service of the National Bank of Greece, 2 Karageorgi tis Servias, right on Syntagma (the tourist office is in the same building), and the General Hellenic Bank, also on Syntagma.

**NAMES, SPELLINGS:** You'd think that after all these centuries they'd at least know the names of their streets. But no, as you've already learned, several places and streets in Athens have one or more names, and in most cases each name has one or more spelling. Thus Syntagma Square, also Constitution Square; Venizelou Avenue, also Panepistimou Avenue; Octovriou, also Patissiou; Mitropoleos, Metropoleos Street. Outside of Athens, the situation becomes even more confused. So you may have to check every street, restaurant, and town on your maps twice.

**NATIONAL TOURIST ORGANIZATION:** Information office is at 2 Karageorgi tis Servias Street, Athens (tel. 3222-545), right on Syntagma in the National Bank of Greece. In the U.S.A., it's at 645 Fifth Avenue, New York, NY 10022 and 627 West Sixth Street, Los Angeles, CA 90017 and 168 North Michigan Avenue, Chicago, IL 60601; in Canada, at 2 Place Ville Marie, Montreal, PQ H3B2C9.

**NEWSPAPERS:** English-language newspapers and magazines can be bought throughout Athens. Check with your kiosk around 6 p.m. for that day's edition of the *International Herald Tribune;* British papers arrive around 8 p.m. *The Athens News,* the *Athenian Monthly,* and the *Athens Post* are local papers serving the English and American communities, and are worthwhile for concert and theater listings.

**POLICE:** For emergencies only, dial 100 on the telephone. The tourist police will handle your travel-connected problems. The address is 7 Syngrou, Athens (office number: 9239-224 or 9236-968; add the area code 021 if you're calling from outside Athens). Dial 171 for Tourist Police Information in five languages, 24 hours a day.

**POSTAGE:** An air-mail postcard to the U.S. costs 7 drachmas; a letter, 11 drachmas per 10 grams weight. Don't even consider surface mail: it could take up to two months. The central post office is on **Kotzia Square** at 100 Eolou Street (opposite Omonia Square). There are branches at 4 Stadiou Street (only for parcel post, and located in the Spyromilios Arcade), in the lower level of the subway station at Omonia Square, on Syntagma Square at the corner of Mitropoleos Street (open to midnight), and in the main lobby of the Athens Hilton Hotel. There is also a Central Philatelic Service of the Hellenic Post Office on the first floor above the Central Post Office of Athens at 100 Aeolou Street, open in the morning, in order to serve better the requirements of stamp collectors.

**PRICES:** As we've noted elsewhere in this guide, prices are liable to change. Probably up. It's nobody's fault, it's just the way the world is these days. So please, *please* check the rates of hotels, tours, and meals with your travel agent.

**RADIO AND TV:** The American Armed Forces Radio provides 17 hours of programming each day, including music, hourly newscasts, and excellent sports reporting. For a touch of home, Walter Cronkite, Ray Scherer, and Howard Cosell are regulars. Hotel television usually costs a minumum of 50 drachmas additional per night, but features lots of English and American programs and old movies.

**SECRETARIAL SERVICE:** There's an efficient, multilingual secretarial service in the **Athens Hilton.** They'll arrange contacts with local businessmen, fix you up with stenographers and interpreters, handle mail and phone messages, set up appointments. Call Elly Economopoulo-Hadziotis or the appointment secretary at 720-201.

**SHOESHINE:** Shoeshine boys wait on the sidewalks at the thoroughfares with heaviest traffic. Cost is 5 drachmas (including tip) and the quality is excellent. For 7 drachmas you can flop down in one of the four stools of the shoeshine parlor on Filellinon Street, opposite the TWA office. Many hotels have free service.

**SIESTA:** They take it seriously in Athens, to the point where the police announce official siesta hours each spring (usually 1:30 to 5) and will take appropriate action against anyone disturbing the Athenians' postlunch bliss. For the tourist, siesta can be a nuisance—cutting into one's sightseeing time. If you don't want to take a nap yourself, here are some suggestions for whiling away the midafternoon hours: find a table under a tree in a cafe and sip a lemonade or ouzo; take a stroll among the pine trees in the

National Garden; feed the swans; wander along Panderossou Street and rummage for $1 bottle openers, cotton blouses, or leather sandals (a few of these Flea Market stores stay open through the siesta for the benefit of tourists); explore the Acropolis (it's a good time to have the place to yourself, if you can stand the heat). Whatever you do, though, don't cause a disturbance. (In case you were considering telephoning some Greek friends, don't—it's considered the height of bad manners to call people during the siesta.)

**SPORTS:** Most people don't go to Athens for a sporting vacation, so we won't deal with sports at length here. However, sports facilities are available—deep-sea fishing, freshwater fishing, underwater fishing, waterskiing, golf, tennis, hunting, and, of course, sailing (you can charter boats with or without a crew). For information on all of these sports, get in touch with the National Tourist Organization of Greece (see above); your hotel concierge may also be able to set up a visit to a private golf or tennis club.

**STUDENT DISCOUNTS:** Valid student identification will get you discounts; to 50% on state railway travel; at a number of lodging spots (see Hostels, above); to the Son-et-Lumière shows; at the Herod Atticus theater; on Island Tours; on bus and train travel to the rest of Europe; at theaters; at all antiquity sites; in some restaurants; at a number of museums and other entertainment facilities. Two important addresses are: the **Vikings Travel Bureau,** 3 Filellinon Street, Athens (tel. 3229-383), and **Lotus Student Travel,** 7 Filellinon Street (tel. 3221-680) for information on special travel rates.

**SUNBATHING:** The Greek sun is hot and piercing. If you overdo it and catch a burn, rub on—**yoghurt.**

**SWIMMING:** Your best bet is to head directly for the Apollo Coast and establish a base of operations there. Smart Athenians *never* swim in the Saronic Gulf this side of Vouliagmeni because of the pollution (remember, Piraeus is a very busy port); moreover, at Glyfada and Vouliagmeni you have the problem of aircraft noise. The place Athenians head for is **Varkiza,** which is about an hour by bus from the city (it leaves from Leoforos

Olgas, near the Zappeion, but you may be able to join another couple and share a taxi inexpensively). At all the beaches along the shore where you pay an admission fee you will find changing facilities and showers, and the beaches themselves are cleaned every morning; most of them also have snackbars and/or restaurants. Rates range from 12 drachmas near the airport to 90 drachmas at the deluxe Astir Palace Hotel; Varkiza is in the middle range and costs less than $1.

**TAXIS:** The rates are 10 drachmas to begin, then 8.50 drachmas per kilometer within the Athens/Piraeus area. Extras are 5 drachmas for every piece of baggage, 5 drachmas for any ride between midnight and 7 a.m. There is an additional charge of 5 drachmas when going to or from the airport or harbor. Theoretically, there are taxi stations on or near every major square, but that doesn't necessarily mean there are any taxis at the stations. There is no telephone service for radio-controlled cabs (you have to go all the way up to a limousine for that kind of service); a new law allows would-be passengers to flag down taxis which already have passengers and share the trip if they are going in the same general direction. This is intended to spread the taxis around, but in practice it makes a taxi more difficult to find than ever. Athenians have more money these days, and one of the ways they spend it is by taking taxis instead of buses. There's no easy answer, other than appearing on the doorstep of a deluxe hotel and tipping the doorman handsomely.

**TELEGRAMS:** The office at 85 Patission Street, Athens, is open 24 hours a day. Another at 15 Stadiou Street has hours from 7 a.m. to midnight. There's also an office in the Athens Hilton. Daily rates to the U.S. are around 15 drachmas per word. Evening rates are half-price.

**TELEPHONES:** A call to New York costs $12 for three minutes. You can place calls from 85 Patission Street, open 24 hours a day, or dial 161 from any telephone to get the long-distance operator. Public telephones are attached to the sides of kiosks. The cost is 2 drachmas, and you pay the kiosk owner. Phone booths with blue trim are for Athens calls only, with orange trim for calls outside of Athens; in either case, before dialing, the appropriate coin must be inserted. (Athens is in the process of changing its six-digit telephone system into a seven-digit system.

If you dial the six-digit number and get no answer, call the operator for help.)

## TELEPHONE SERVICE FROM GREECE TO U.S.A. (mainland):
**Via the operator:** Station calls (first three minutes) 270 drachmas; personal calls (first three minutes) 480 drachmas; each additional minute for personal and station calls 90 drachmas. The total amount of the call is subject to 8% tax.

**Automatic service:** From public telephone offices and coin-boxes 108 drachmas per minute. From subscriber's line 90 drachmas per minute, plus 8% tax.

You can place telephone calls at OTE offices—85 Patission Street open 24 hours a day, Omonia Square open 24 hours a day, 15 Stadiou Street open from 8 a.m. to midnight etc.; or dial 161 from any telephone to get the long-distance operator. When you want to communicate by I.D.D.D. system you have to dial the International prefix (00) then U.S.A. country code (L) and then the national number.

Please note that when dialing, all digits should be dialed without any pause and there is no special signal between groups of digits.

**TIME:** Athens time is Greenwich Mean Time plus two hours, Eastern Standard Time plus seven hours.

**TIPPING:** Porters at the airport and train station receive a fee of 10 drachmas per bag minimum. Taxi drivers expect you to round off the meter in their favor. Leave chambermaids 10 drachmas for an average stay of two or three days. Tour guides expect $1 or up, but *never* coins, although the tourist authorities say they don't have to be tipped at all. Theater ushers traditionally get 1 or 2 drachmas for showing you to your seat. Barbers get from 20% to 30%; public room attendants get 5 to 10 drachmas; hatcheck girls get 5 to 10 drachmas; busboys in restaurants get the loose change.

**TOILETS:** Most public toilets have symbols on the doors that quite clearly distinguish between the sexes. In case they don't, however, and instead have the appropriate words in Greek, remember—the Greek word for men has six letters, the word for women has eight.

**TOURIST POLICE:** Dial 171 for information (hotels, shops, sports, nightclubs, etc.) in five languages, 24 hours a day.

**TOURS:** A great variety of organized tours is offered, from sightseeing in Athens and environs to complete tours of the Greek mainland, to air tours and cruises to the many islands. Tour operators are listed below:

American Express, Constitution Square (tel. 3230-603)
Vikings Tours, 3 Filellinon Street (tel. 3229-383)
Key Tours, 2 Ermou Street (tel. 3232-520)
CHAT Tours, 4 Stadiou Street (tel. 3223-137)
Lotus Tours, 7 Filellinon Street (tel. 3225-408)
G.O. Tours Ltd., 1 Asklipiou Street (tel. 3627-300)
Host Hellas Ltd., 3 Filellinon Street (tel. 3227-025)

# Chapter XI

# ATHENS BY THE SEA

## Piraeus, Glyfada, Vouliagmeni, Sounion

THE ACROPOLIS is five miles from the sea, and in the days of Pericles it was quite a hike across the countryside to reach Phaleron Bay. Now it's a short bus ride, and the suburbs of Athens reach all the way to the edge of the sea. But the entire coast—from Piraeus in the north all the way south past the airport to Glyfada, and even as far as Lagonissi—is virtually an extension of Athens. In summer, the downtown nightclubs move out there, Athenians go to the seaside for dinner, wealthy Athenians flock out to the luxury hotels and beach houses—and stay put until September.

So, you're not really seeing Athens until you see something of its seaside satellites. In fact, if you're planning to be in these parts in midsummer you might even consider checking into a hotel by the sea and making your sightseeing excursions into town from there. Glyfada is only 20 minutes by car from downtown Athens; Vouliagmeni is 45 minutes; Piraeus, about 15 minutes.

### Piraeus—Even on Sunday

The port of Piraeus is about six miles from Syntagma. In 461 B.C. Themistocles linked the two cities by his "Long Walls," but now they're intertwined by their spawling suburbs.

Two outstanding events have taken place in the history of Piraeus. Themistocles chose the site as the home port for the Athenian fleet he was about to build—the "wooden walls" predicted by the oracle. After the Peloponnesian Wars it slumped back again to a fishing village, and when Greece became independent and Athens became the capital in the 19th century, Piraeus was a ragtag hamlet on the edge of the water.

After the turn of the century it slowly emerged as one of the major ports of the Mediterranean, thus preparing it for its second outstanding event—when Melina Mercouri made a movie called *Never on Sunday,* which has since introduced the waterfront of Piraeus and its boisterous bars to the whole world. The waterfront still looks like the movie here and there, but Piraeus has blossomed in recent years and on your way to or from your cruise ship you may want to spend an hour or two among its flower-decked boulevards and terrace cafes.

The dedicated archaeologist can find many remnants of antiquity here, including traces of the Long Walls (the subway track follows roughly the same route). The city's museums of archaeology and naval history are worth peeking into.

In the past few years, the city's gung-ho council has pushed ahead a rejuvenation program that included new beaches, new beach facilities, the big new marina at Zea, and a new open-air theater (the Skilitsion) up in the hills above the harbor, where you can see an extraordinary variety of entertainment (including a recent Berlin Ice Theater production of Franz Lehar's *The Merry Widow*). The Piraeus Municipal Theater on Korai Square, is an impressive building, in neoclassic style, where you can occasionally catch a production of Verdi's *Aida* or some other spectacular opera.

Around the bay from the docks, past Freatis, you come to the harbor of **Zea,** now officially known as **Passalimano** (but you'll probably find that most people still refer to it as Zea). You may be coming here at some point to catch a small ferry to some of the islands, but, if not, come anyway and take a look at the luxury yachts and three-masted schooners and other toys of the Mediterranean jet-set. There's a new, completely equipped mari-

*Port of Athens, Piraeus*

na here with restaurants, hairdressers, ship brokers, ship chandlers, and other appurtenances of seagoing.

On the opposite side of the bay is the hilly peninsula known as **Castella** (which was the site of ancient Munichia and another acropolis). It's mostly residential (very desirable, with views over the harbor and the Royal Hellenic Yacht Club next door), and there are several good restaurants and cafes up here.

And from here you can climb the 165 steps up to the Skilitsion Theater (the name, by the way, has nothing to do with its altitude or the sky, it's in honor of a former mayor).

Round another bend and you're into another bay and a circular harbor bobbing with more yachts and sailboats, the entire waterfront ringed with blue, yellow, and red awnings of the restaurants across the street. This is **Mikrolimano.** In the morning, it's a typical little fishing village, with the fishermen mending their nets and drying them in the sun; in the evening, it's Athens' dining hall. It's one of the most romantic places for dining out along the entire coast (yet only 20 minutes by car from Syntagma, and less by subway from Omonia Square to the Neon Phaleron or New Faliron, stop). There are tables all along the waterfront, their matching restaurants across the street. After dinner you can take a half-hour trip around the harbor with a gnarled old Greek seafarer in his caique. Around midnight you still won't want to head back into town, so take your car or a taxi further down the coast to one of the night clubs by the sea.

**SOUTH FROM PIRAEUS:** The next spot along the shore, known by the tourist authorities as the Apollo Coast, is **Faliron,** which away back used to be *the* harbor of Athens; then comes **Kalamaki,** which is a continuation of the nightclubs, restaurants, and tavernas of Old Faliron. The blue #1 bus, marked Edem, will take you from Syntagma to Faliron, and any bus marked Aghios Cosmas will take you to Kalamaki, both for less than $1.

**Aghios Cosmas** is a new beach development and sports center —two soccer fields, eight basketball courts, eight volleyball courts, two tennis courts, and a beach for 3,000 bathers.

## Glyfada

Glyfada is the first of the big resorts, and it's only ten miles from Athens (you can catch a bus from Vassilissis Olgas Avenue, and the fare is 12 drs). The main road to Sounion passes through the center of town, but turn off at the big green nightclub,

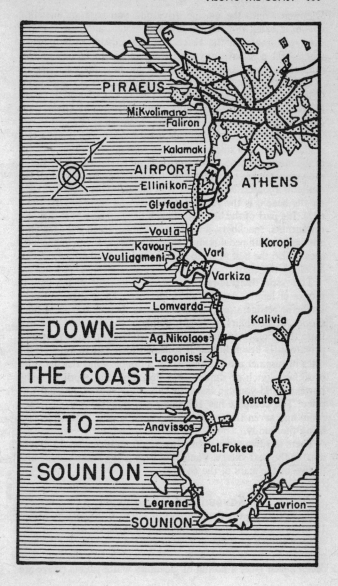

Dionysios, onto the marine drive and you pass an unending stream of cafes, restaurants, tavernas, hotels, and marinas. The cafe/restaurants on the beach side are mostly modern places where you can have anything from pizzas to freshly caught mullet, and your dinner bill needn't go above $8.

One of the most famous restaurants along here is **Psaropoulos** (telephone for a reservation—8945-677), popular with prime ministers and high society, but rather expensive by Greek standards—say, $10 and up per person, with wine.

All the way at the end of this marine drive, you'll come to a restaurant on both sides of the street, with tables right at the edge of the marina. This is **Antonopoulos** (tel. 8945-636). An order of prawns here (big ones, but only three of them) costs about $2; mullet is about $1.50. Right next to it, behind the trees and right on the beach, is the **Asteria** nightclub and taverna (tel. 8945-675). It's part of the big Astir Beach development that includes restaurants, snackbars, a bookstore, public beach (60 drachmas admission) with pedalos and canoes (50 drachmas an hour). This area is also the best place to stay in Glyfada, and one of the best all along the coast.

The **Astir Bungalows** curve around one side of the bay, in groves of lemon, orange, and pine trees. The bungalows have kitchens, refrigerators, showers, closets, beach towels, 24-hour service, beach chairs, patios for dining or sunning, and all a step from the cool, clear water. In other words, you have your own private little beach house. It's classed as a deluxe hotel so the rates in summer are $70 to $90 for a double—but that includes breakfast, lunch or dinner, and tips. Come in April or May, however, and you can have the same room for almost half the price. The complex has 100 one-room bunaglows, seven two-room and seven three-room bungalows, so it's a great place to bring the family.

There are two more public beaches (entrance fee—15 drachmas) in the next village, **Voula,** but keep going another five miles to two of the stars of the coast. . .

## Kavouri and Vouliagmeni

These two are the liveliest and loveliest of the resorts within 15 miles and a 12-drachma bus fare of Athens.

They're on a cape covered with pine trees, separating the bay, one half facing the ocean, the other half facing the bay. The ocean beach faces a flotilla of gleaming white yachts (there are still more of them tucked away in a marina farther down the cape); the restaurants are stacked above the beaches with terraces overlooking the sea, and new hotels and apartments are stacked up behind the restaurants. There are so many new hotels going up there's no point in saying which is the best place to stay.

Except for the **Astir Palace Hotel.** One of the great resort hotels of Europe. A true Shangri-La. The playground of the shipping tycoons. The Astir Palace Hotel has 147 rooms and 34 penthouse suites, all beautifully furnished, a palatial glass-and-marble lobby, an enormous terrace overlooking the hotel's private cove and its 77 secluded bungalows (where the wealthiest of the wealthy Athenians idle away their summers), shaded by trees and cooled by terraced lawns. In summer (May through September), a one-room suite (with bedside buttons to summon your groom or your maid, switch on the Don't Disturb sign, and dim the lights) for two costs from $175 to $235 with breakfast and dinner; a regular deluxe room is $110, half-pension, for two, and a one-room bungalow for two is $135, half-pension. But in April and October you have the accommodations for 20% to 25% less, and from November through March for 45% to 50% less, and the luxury remains, the armies of servants are still there, and even if it's too cold to swim it's perfect for playing tennis and hiking on the cape. If you can't afford it, or, more likely, if you can't get a reservation, at least treat yourself to lunch or dinner 485 drachmas—$15) in one of the Astir Palace's three first-rate restaurants. This is certainly class, Greek style.

In the same deluxe league but newer, the **Apollon Palace Hotel** towers nine stories above the beach at Kavouri, just beyond Vougliameni. Its 284 guest rooms are decorated in Scandinavia modern, with air conditioning, marble bathrooms, and balconies overlooking the bay; sporting facilities include *five* swimming pools (including one indoors), gymnasium, sauna, bowling alley, and tennis court. The dining room service is luxurious, the cheerful coffeeshop is open around the clock, and if you want to go into Athens, the private air-conditioned motorcoach makes the 20-minute trip six times a day, free of charge. Rates are 1,886 drachmas for a single, 2,357 drachmas for a double, in-season; 1,012 drachmas for a single or 1,256 drachmas for a double, in winter.

**SOUTH TO SOUNION:** But the best is yet to come. From Vouliagmeni to Cape Sounion (about 40 miles from Athens) the coastline twists and turns around beaches and rocky coves; a beautiful scenic highway winds alongside, sometimes by the edge of the sea, sometimes up on the cliffs. This is the true Apollo Coast. And from the point of view of sunning and swimming, it's worth the extra miles and minutes from Athens, because here you'll find less pollution (not that there's much to begin with) and less noise from the aircraft landing at Ellinikon Airport. Try, for example, the town of **Varkiza,** where the beach has small bungalows rentable by the day (300 drachmas, no reservations required), and a good, inexpensive, self-service cafeteria. For a hotel, try the 32-room Class B **Varkiza.**

South of Varkiza there are half a dozen small towns, most of them being spruced up and "resortified," and you now have a choice of about a dozen hotels in these parts. The most popular of these towns is **Lagonissi,** 25 miles from Athens, where you'll find one of the complete tourist villages set up in recent years by the Greek government—hotels, bungalows, chapel, kindergarten, tavernas, open-air cinema, sauna, beauty parlor, shopping center, beaches, tennis courts—all carefully landscaped to disguise any hint of concrete overkill. You can sunbathe here on any of five beaches, waterski, and snorkel in the clearest of waters. The rate structure needs a computer to figure out the variations for the complex's 99 rooms, 15 suites, and 243 bungalows (in three sizes). In summer you're obliged to take halfboard, which will set you back $58 or thereabouts in a double room or bungalow; from November through mid-March, rates are about 30% less. *Note:* There's a free, direct service by private coach between Athens and Lagonissi (a taxi or limousine, on the other hand, will cost you about $20).

Another up-and-coming resort along this stretch is **Anavyssos,** where the B Class Eden Beach Hotel has practically taken over the town (265 rooms, 506 beds); but your final goal is **Cape Sounion,** specifically, the romantic **Temple of Poseidon,** perched on top of the cliff.

## Cape Sounion

You get your first glimpse of the temple from the coastal road, several twists and bays before you actually get to the cape. First you see it, then you don't. Finally you're there. The temple was built in 444 B.C., probably by the architect who designed the Temple of Theseus in Athens, and only 15 of its original 34 Doric columns remain. But it's still one of the most dramatic sights of

Greece. Lord Byron was so carried away by it that he carved his initials on one of the columns; you try that today and *you'll* be carried away. After you've tramped around this sea-girt acropolis, go down to the bay for a swim (the beach is nothing special but the water and the view are), or lunch at one of the waterfront tavernas. If you decide to stay overnight, you have a choice of three Class A hotels in Sounion: the 90-room **Belvedere Park** (896 drachmas, or $25, for two with half-board), the 45-room **Egeon** (931 drachmas, or $26, for two with half-board) and the 64-bungalow **Cape Sounion Beach Hotel** (1,091 drachmas, or $31, for two with half-board); the largest resort in the area is the Class B **Sun Hotel and Bungalows** with beds for over 500 guests (818 drachmas, or $23, for two with half-board).

*Note:* There's an alternative, picturesque route back to Athens from Sounion, following the valleys and wine villages of the interior. It's a tough decision which to take—coastal or inland. Bets are you'll want to enjoy the constantly changing shore, the sparkling water that changes from deep blue to turquoise from bay to bay, the islands and sailboats and fishing boats along the way. In any case, most people want to stay at Sounion until the sun sets beside the Temple of Poseidon, so you may be driving back in the dark anyway. In which case, stop off at the Astir Palace in Vouliagmeni for dinner, or one of the fine seafood restaurants and beachside tavernas along the coast if you're less than impeccably dressed.

# Chapter XII

# DAY TRIPS FROM ATHENS

YOU'LL BE AMAZED how many trips to how many historic sites you can make from Athens. Many of them can be completed in one day—there and back. To get some idea of the choices you have, skim through the catalog of the CHAT tour people: half-day tours to Cape Sounion and the Temple of Poseidon, half-day tours to Ancient Corinth and the Corinth Canal, half-day tours to Attica and Marathon, one-day tours to Mycenae, Nauplia, Epidaurus, Thebes, and Delphi. You can even make one-day mini-odysseys to the Greek islands—and still be back in Athens in time for a night on the Plaka.

You've already read about Cape Sounion and the Apollo Coast in the preceding chapter. Now here's a quick briefing on some of the other sights.

## Daphni

Daphni is so close to Athens (five miles) it doesn't really merit a tour on its own, but it's often included in the itineraries of other tours, especially during the **Wine Festival** held every summer (July through September). You pay the small admission charge (50 drachmas), then sample as many local wines as you can handle. With a deal like that, your best idea is to take the special bus, rather than go by car (the bus fare is only 5 drachmas, and the bus leaves from Koumoundouros Square).

The other attraction in Daphni, year-round, is the medieval monastery dedicated to the **Dormition of the Virgin Mary**. It was built on the site of an earlier temple, in a grove of laurel trees, dedicated to the laurel-bearing god Apollo. The present church, which dates from the 11th century, is noted for its inlaid mosaics on a golden background, and for its cloisters, cells, and sarcophagi. Open daily in summer from 7:30 a.m. to sunset; in winter, from 9 a.m. to sunset; Sundays and holidays throughout the year, from 10 to 1 and 2:30 to sunset. Admission is 5 drachmas.

# Delphi

The famous city of the oracle is in that richly historical part of Greece known as Boeotia. Thermopylae and Thebes are not far off. Delphi itself is 110 miles from Athens, and the combination of ruggedly grand scenery and the haunting quality of the ruins makes it one of the most dramatic sights in all of Greece.

For centuries, the story of Delphi was the story of Mediteranean politics. Hardly a decision was reached without consulting the oracles at the Apollon Temple. Evidently, the mountain exuded strange fumes (now considered water vapors or carbon monoxide), which puts shepherds and peasant women into trances and led to prophetic pronouncements. In the magnificent setting of Mount Parnassos, with eagles soaring from peak to peak, it was easy to believe that here you stood in the presence of the gods.

Initially the name of the site was Pytho, and the Earth Mother known for her prophetic powers lived here. Later, seafarers from Knossos introduced the cult of Apollo Delphinius. The story starts with Apollo disguising himself as a dolphin. He jumps into the water and captures a Cretan ship, returning both booty and prisoners to Delphi. The prisoners become "priests" in his sanctuary and Delphi's reputation for wisdom and prophecy is consolidated.

Nearby personages came to consult with the gods. And, as was the custom, they brought gifts. From the eighth to the fourth centuries B.C., before an envious Nero looted the temples after Rome's conquest, the gift-giving and advice-seeking rose to such proportions that Delphi became a huge complex of treasuries and temples, all laden with works of art and riches.

Today, Delphi consists mainly of a theater, a sanctuary, an athletic area surrounded by a wall, and an excellent museum. But it is more than a ruins-cum-museum site: it is a total environment. Start your exploration from the main road, which leads both to the town and the ruins. Gaze toward the ruins, noting the distant views, the colors (especially at sunset and sunrise), the sheer valley below. Then amble through the ruins, starting with the **Marmaria** and the **Castalian Spring**, both of which are located below the main road. The ancient Greeks regarded

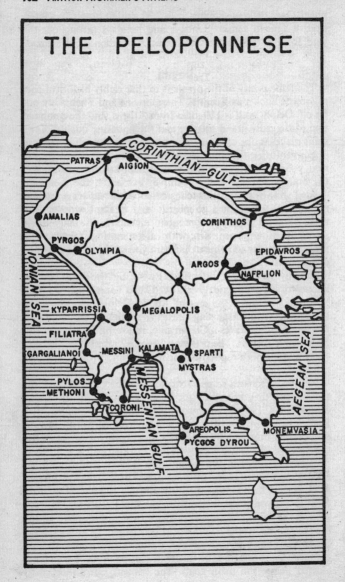

# THE PELOPONNESE

springs as a gift of the gods. Steps leading to the water can be seen carved into the solid rock surface. Then walk up the hill, beyond the road, onto the main site.

The **Sacred Way** is a path leading from the entrance to the stadium. Follow it as it zigs and zags between half-columns, perches, stones, and the **Treasury of the Athenians.** The Treasury is easy to recognize: it is almost completely reconstructed, using the original blocks of Parian marble. Look for the inscription written on the marble: "The Athenians dedicate to Apollo the Persian spoils from the Battle of Marathon."

At the top of the ruins site is the **theater,** built for an audience of 5,000, a model of engineering and aesthetic brilliance; and farther up the hill, there is a fifth-century stadium almost 200 yards long.

Returning from the ruins to town, stop at the **museum** near the entrance to the site and go immediately to the *Charioteer,* the famous bronze sculpture from the fifth century B.C., and one of the great masterpieces of Greek art. The museum's art pieces are mainly from the Mycenean period (1600 B.C. to 1100 B.C.). Note particularly the Roman *Statue of Antinous,* a column of *Acanthus Dancing Girls,* and the *Wingless Sphinx of the Naxians,* a characteristic work of the sixth century B.C.

For at least six centuries, Delphi's priests held most of the known world in thrall. Their ambiguous interpretations of the unintelligible ramblings from the "oracle" changed the course of history many times—and brought riches and incalculable power to a canny bunch of priests in a tiny mountainous village.

How it all began doesn't appear to be on record, but from the seventh century B.C. onward, the god known as Phoebus Apollo was heard to be speaking through the mouth of an old woman known as the Pythia, and what she said, after being placed into neat hexameters by the priest-interpreters, made kings tremble and emperors lose their sleep.

Ordinary people consulted the oracle, too, of course; the gods were willing to answer the question of anybody who brought money. More often than not, important people brought silver, gold, precious stones, and other gifts, and Delphi soon built up considerable treasure.

There was a set routine for the Pythia to follow on pronouncement days (which at first took place only during February, the month of Apollo's birthday), and it was strictly adhered to by one Pythia after another through the centuries.

First, the woman had to fast for three days and then, on the set day, bathe in the nearby Castalian Spring, burn laurel leaves at the altar, drink some water, and take up her place beside the copper-and-gold tripod which was set up over the fissure in the ground from which came "intoxicating vapors." Working her way into a trance she would then mumble garbled replies to questions asked of her. Sometimes the questions concerned banal personal problems and sometimes they concerned matters of state. But all got answers, usually so cryptic that they could be construed to mean anything at all, and seekers invariably went away happy.

A king, who was told that if he crossed a certain river a great empire would be destroyed, was chagrined to discover that the empire was his own. A man who came to ask about his stammer was instructed to go live in another country. The Roman emperor Nero was warned to "beware 73"—and died well before he reached that age at the hands of Galvus, who was 73.

Naturally there were some skeptics, among them Aesop, but the Delphi city fathers had providentially anticipated that by instituting formal trials for those they charged with sacrilege, and the sentence was usually to be tossed off a high cliff onto the jagged rocks below.

That well-known heretic Socrates may well have been thinking about Delphi when he announced that "the augur should be under the authority of the general and not the general under the authority of the augur."

This advice should have been taken to heart in 480 B.C., when Xerxes prepared to invade Greece with the combination of a massive army and fleet of ships. Athenians consulted the Delphic Oracle to find out what to do. They were told:

> Wretches why sit ye here? Fly, fly to the ends of creation.
> Nay, not alone shall ye suffer, full many a town shall be leveled;
> Many a shrine of the gods will he give to fiery destruction
> Get ye away from the Temple and brood on the doom that awaits you.

Athens, and most of Greece, was naturally in a panic. The message, for once, hardly seemed ambiguous, and some were ready to take it at face value and flee in panic. But wiser counsels prevailed and the Athenians and their Spartan allies held the northern passes until Themistocles built up the navy (here the Delphic Oracle redeemed itself somewhat with a prediction that the city would be saved by its "wooden walls") and eventually repelled the invasion attempt.

Delphi never entirely recovered from this erroneous taking of sides, however, and although the world rallied with contributions after an earthquake almost destroyed the town in 373 B.C., the oracle's influence continued to decline.

But worse was to come. In 356 B.C., a band of Phocians from the west suddenly invaded the town and captured the shrine along with all its wealth. For a time they terrorized their neighbors by raising an army of mercenaries paid with their newfound treasure, but eventually the shrine was restored to the priests to continue their prognostications for three centuries more.

The coming of the Christian era was the beginning of the end, and in 381 A.D. the emperor Theodosius outlawed "paganism" and Delphi passed into history.

**HOW TO GET TO DELPHI:** The simplest way is to take a one-day coach tour, in air-conditioned comfort, with a guide to explain the ruins and sights along the way. Both **American Express** and CHAT operate one-day tours (8:15 a.m. to 7:15 p.m.), costing $26 including lunch, admission fee, and a visit to the nearby monastery of Ossios Lucas. CHAT also has a two-day tour, much better if you can afford the time, because this way you can spend more time among the magnificent ruins and see them (and photograph them) at sunrise or sunset; this full 48-hour tour costs $62 in first-class hotels, $50 in tourist-class hotels, both with full board. And if you have five days, Viking will take you on a leisurely tour of Delphi and the Peloponnese for as little as $100 (departures every Thursday November to March and Tuesdays and Saturdays April to October). The cheapest way to reach Delphi is by regular bus service—only 400 drachmas ($10) round trip, with a choice of five departures daily from the bus terminal on Liossion Street, a three-hour trip each way. The most convenient way to get to Delphi is undoubtedly to rent a car and drive; for the first third of the trip you'll be driving on the relatively fast but tricky Athens-Thessalonika National Highway, then after an hour you turn off at the Delphi sign and start heading up into the mountains (where the roads are being improved enormously). This is a tough trip, and you should either leave very early in the morning to get to the site before the museum closes for siesta, or arrive in time for a leisurely lunch, an afternoon visit to the ruins and the museum, lingering there through sunset, then facing the after-dark drive back to Athens (allow four hours in this case). Better still, stay the night in Delphi and drive back next day, stopping at the quaint hilltop town of Arahova and the monastery of Ossios Lucas along the way.

**HOTELS IN DELPHI:** For a tiny town (population 800), **Delphi** certainly offers visitors a vast selection of accommodations, but then it's had a long time to practice being a host. The main street alone has over a dozen hotels, most of them inexpensive; those on the left side as you walk into the town are the most interesting, because they're perched on the edge of a cliff looking all the way across the plain to the Gulf of Corinth. Try the **Iniochos** (Class D, 15 rooms with private baths) or **Hermes** (Class C) for reliable accommodations under $14 double. The **Castalia,** also on the cliff side of the street, is an elderly Class B hotel with a large dining terrace overlooking the valley. The three most interesting hotels in Delphi are the 61-room **Vouzas** (closest to the ruins), a Class A hotel built in tiers *down* the side of the cliff; the 44-room Class A **Xenia,** and above all, literally and otherwise, the beautiful 185-room **Amalia,** a spacious affair of granite, marble, polished wood, modern and comfortable furniture, and well-equipped guest rooms that rent for $38 for a double per night. The Amalia, Delphi, Vouzas, and Castalia all have attractive dining rooms (the Amalia most of all), but you'll probably want to sample one of Delphi's tavernas with large, sometimes wind-swept terraces, overlooking the gulf and the plain (all that greenery you see down there, by the way, is the topside of something like three million olive trees); you can dine on these terraces for less than $5.

## Marathon

This, of course, is where the famous battle was fought in 490 B.C., when the Athenians trounced the Persians and the messenger ran the 27 miles back to the city, gasped out the news of victory, and flopped down dead. The site of the battle is now marked by a barrow in which the Greek soldiers were buried, and a white marble column. Buses leave Athens (from the terminal at 29 Mavromateon Street) to the Marathon battlefield approximately every half hour—one hour and $1 each way.

*The next batch of destinations are all on the peninsula known as the Peloponnese ("the land of Pelops"), the almost-island chunk of land that makes up the southwestern corner of Greece. It's a region of mountain scenery highlighted by an incredible collection of ancient monuments and brightened by flashes of beach and sea.*

## Corinth

The first town you come to in the Peloponnese is the city of Corinth, or rather the **Corinth Canal**. This channel, 3½ miles long and 75 feet wide, makes the peninsula an island, and chops 185 miles from the voyage between Italy and Piraeus. It was built between 1882 and 1893, but it was originally conceived way back in the days of Nero and Hadrian. In fact, Nero got so far as to dig the first shovelful—with a golden spade. But it didn't get much beyond Nero's first shovelful, and shipowners had to continue hauling their ships overland, over the *diolkos,* a stonepaved track, traces of which you can still see here and there.

This suited the Corinthians fine, because they supplied the hauling power and collected the fees. They also collected tolls on all cargos heading between the peninsula and the mainland, and between the Gulf of Corinth and the Saronic Gulf. Their wealth made them self-indulgent, and at one point the city could boast a thousand "sacred prostitutes" who plied their trade in the name and to the honor of Aphrodite. No wonder Saint Paul came along and gave the Corinthians a tongue-lashing. The tribune where he delivered his sermon is still there in Ancient Corinth. (There are now two Corinths. The new city was destroyed by an earthquake in 1928 and an even newer one was built after that. Its main interest for visitors is as a base for excursions to the fascinating surroundings.) The more fascinating of the two is **Ancient Corinth**. It too was completely destroyed—by the Romans in 146 B.C.—and most of what you see today dates from 44 B.C. when Caesar set up a colony there. The principal sites are the sixth-century Temple of Apollo, Saint Paul's tribune, the agora, and the Pirene fountain.

The **Acrocorinth** is a citadel towering over the town. This was originally the site of the Temple of Aphrodite. The citadel was built by the Byzantines, and at various states subtracted from or added to by Crusaders, Venetians, and Turks. Today you get a great view from the top. Don't try driving up the tortuous road; treat yourself to a $6 cab ride.

**HOW TO GET TO CORINTH:** The full-day sightseeing tours leave Athens at 8 a.m. and return at 8 p.m., after stops also at Mycenae and Epidaurus, and costs $23 without lunch, $27 with. You can also get there by diesel train, rail, or bus from Athens (check with your hotel concierge for times and fares); or in roughly 1½ hours by car, on the National Highway.

**HOTELS:** The new **King Saron** (156 Class A rooms) at Isthmia, the **Kalamaki Beach** (Class B, 66 rooms), and the 48-room Class B **Almyri Beach** at Almyri are all a short drive from the center of town; downtown, the Class B **Kypselos** has 18 rooms, all with private bath and larger-than-usual beds, for 430 drachmas double, about $12.

## Nauplia (Nafplion)

Depending on your first impression, Nauplia is either a holiday resort, or a medieval fortress town, or a picturesque little town by the sea. A closer look tells you it's all three. Nauplia was also at one time the capital of Greece, right after its liberation from the Turks. The tiny island fortress, **Bourtzi**, in the bay, was built by the Venetians; the **Acronafplia** citadel towering over the town's south side was built on the site of the ancient acropolis; and the town's third fortress, **Palamidi**, is actually seven fortresses in one, built by the Franks, with a winding stairway of

*Greek fishing boats*

857 steps leading from one to the other. (It will take you 20 minutes to climb them on foot.)

Nauplia is linked to Athens by an hourly bus service; the organized sightseeing tour will be described below because it also includes the next few towns on our list. If you decide to stay overnight in Nauplia, you'll find a good selection of Class B and Class C hotels, the newest one being the 120-room, Class C **Plaka**; there's also a 58-room Class A **Xenia**. At the latter, room rates run from 820 drachmas ($22.75) with half-board for a single, to 1,287 drachmas ($35.75) for a double with half-board (breakfast plus lunch or dinner). All rooms have private bath or shower, and overlook the sea.

## Epidaurus

This town, 20 miles from Nauplia, but on the Saronica Gulf, is famed for two things. In the sixth century it was a place of pilgrimage, a sort of Lourdes, where sick people journeyed to find a cure in the **sanctuary of Asclepius,** the god of healing. There was more than faith involved, however, and you can still see inscriptions of prescriptions in the sanctuary, and in the nearby **museum,** as well as the votive offerings brought by the people who had been cured. (*Note:* There's a whole room of the National Archaeological Museum in Athens devoted to friezes and statues on this subject—always with an oversized god-doctor seated nonchalantly at his desk, while Hygeia his nurse collects the loot from the patients, who are usually depicted as small and humble. Sound familiar?)

Other sights at Epidaurus include the **Greek Bath** (where the sick washed themselves), the **Abaton** (the so-called portico of incubation), where the sick slept on beds waiting for an apparition of the god who would cure them in their sleep, the **Roman bath, the stadium,** and **the museum** (admission 10 drachmas, free on Sundays and Thursdays).

You can get to Epidaurus by regular bus service from Athens via Nauplia, about $5 one way. During the festival, there's a special pullman bus service from Athens direct to Epidaurus on days of the performance only (but you'd better have your hotel concierge make a reservation in advance).

Nauplia and Epidaurus are the sort of places where you may also want to stay over (although, theoretically, we're talking here about one-day trips). Your best bet in Epidaurus is probably the 24-room Class B **Xenia**, with 24 bungalows from $20 with pri-

The other great sight of Epidaurus is the ancient **theater** with its circular "orchestra" and 50 tiers for 14,000 spectators. It was built in the fourth century B.C. by Polycleitus the Younger who ought to be around today to teach acoustics to his successors: despite its size and its age, the acoustics of Epidaurus are so perfect you can hear the performers' gowns trailing across the stage. Fortunately, you can still enjoy the benefits of these acoustics, because performances are given here every summer during the **Epidaurus Festival** (it's in June and July, and the National Tourist Office can give you details of dates and plays).

vate bath. In Nauplia, there are two Xenias—the deluxe **Xenia Palace,** in the battlements above the town, where the 54 bungalows rent for 2,000 drachmas ($55) for two with half-board (which is compulsory all year); and the Class A 58-room **Xenia** in town, where the rates are 1,538 drachmas ($43) for two, again with obligatory half-board. Another popular hotel in Nauplia is the 51-room Class A **Amphitryon,** with rates just a few drachmas less than the Xenia. There are, in addition, some dozen hotels in Class C and Class D, where rooms cost from as little as $6.

## Mycenae

Identified on some maps and guides as Mikine. Either way it's the mountain palace-fortress of Agamemnon, "lord of the many islands and all of Argos" (this part of the Peloponnese, including Nauplia and Epidaurus, is in a region known as the Argolis). This is the place that gave its name to an entire civilization that was cock-of-the-walk in the 14th century B.C., although some of the archaeological digs have uncovered evidence that the area was inhabited as early as 3,000 B.C. What you see here today are the impressive entrance (the **Lion Gate**), and the remains of granaries, reservoirs, and the **shaft graves** that sheltered the golden treasures of Mycenean art. (Homer's "Golden Mycenae") for all those thousands of years, before they were carted off to the National Archaeological Museum in Athens. Just outside the fortress walls, you can see nine **beehive tombs,** one of which is thought to be the tomb of Clytemnestra (who, you'll remember, bumped off her husband, Agamemnon, before she in turn was disposed of by her son, Orestes); one of the others is probably the tomb of Agamemnon himself. (Admission to the site is 10 drachmas).

**HOW TO GET TO MYCENAE:** Take the regular bus from Athens to Nauplia and get off at Argos, where you catch a local bus to Mycenae; there's also a train service from Athens to Fichtia, a couple of miles by bus from the ruins.

Corinth, Mycenae, Nauplia, and Epidaurus are included in a one-day (a one-crowded-day) sightseeing tour by CHAT from Athens, leaving at 8:15 a.m. and returning at 7:15 p.m. It's $23, including lunch at Nauplia.

There you have a cluster of some of the most famous spots in history, and we've only covered one small corner of the Peloponnese. But you'll learn about Arcadia, Sparta, and Olympia in a later chapter, since they are too far from Athens to be accessible on one-day trips.

## The $25 Mini-Odyssey

Everybody wants to see the Greek Islands, but not everyone has the time to be away from Athens for a few days. No problem. You just take the subway down to Piraeus, hop on a ferry, and sail across to an island with pine-clad hills, valleys of vineyards and pistachio trees, and a ruined temple overlooking a bay; or an island with a harbor ringed by restaurants and surrounded by a hillside of small palazzos; or an island with no cars where the only way to get around is by horse-drawn carriage or the back

*Kaisariani Church (ancient church near Athens)*

of a donkey. Better, call CHAT, Viking Tours, or American Express or some other tour operator, have them pick you up at your hotel, drive you to Piraeus—and leave everything else to them.

"Everything else" will add up to a memorable day that's part Mediterranean cruise exploration, part sightseeing, part sunning, and wholly relaxing. Say you decide to take the cruise—a bus will collect you, transfer you to a second bus and drive you down to Zea (the new marina round the bend from the main docks in Piraeus), where you'll board your cruise ship and head out of the harbor past the private yachts and the three-masted schooners waiting patiently for busy shipping tycoons to come and take them out for a sail.

There are currently three ships operating this three-island cruise—the m.v. *Meltemi,* the *Saronic Star,* both thousand-ton vessels, and the larger, 3,000-ton *Hermes,* which also has cabins you can rent by the day. Both the *Saronic Star* and the *Hermes* have swimming pools, and all three have plenty of deck space for sunning, as well as dining salons, lounges, bars, hostesses, and boutiques for souvenirs and film.

Your first port of call, 1¼ hours out, is the island of **Aegina.** This is the closest island to Athens, and consequently one of the busiest on weekends. Aegina is a mountainous little island, with a precipitious town perched above the dock, one white sunglazed street with a few cafes, a bakery shop, a souvenir shop or two, and a movie house.

You can go to the beach here, or you can join a tour up through the pistachio plantations and vineyards to the **Temple of Aphaea,** "a very ancient local deity," with a hexastyle Doric temple built of local limestone. Back on board it's time to have lunch (a simple tray-lunch). An hour later you come to one of the most interesting parts of the cruise as the ship squeezes through the Strait of Poros.

**Poros** is a conical island with a tiny village (also called Poros) that's a classic of its kind—a jumble of whitewashed buildings piled above the harbor, which is also the roadway which is also the sidewalk which is also the plaza, and is totally hidden under a mass of awnings and cafe tables that come right down to the edge of the water. Unfortunately, the *Meltemi* doesn't stop here, so you mark Poros down in your diary as one of those places you have to come back to some day.

Next stop is **Hydra,** a bleak, rocky, undulating island, until you get into the harbor which you immediately recognize from a thousand photographs. It's unique. The *Meltemi* sails right into this small bowl-like haven, almost right into the nearest cafe, next to the fishing boats and the tiny ferries that shuttle cargo and people back and forth to the Peloponnese. Hydra had its heyday in the time of Napoleon, when more than 30,000 people lived here; now the population is down to 2,382 and most of them are the artists or writers or gallivanting jet-setters. The town is different from any other in these parts because it's terraced with a type of house, or rather mansion, known as the Hydriot palazzo, dating from the 18th century. It's one of the prettiest harbors you'll find anywhere, complete with a cathedral, belfry, the School for Training Merchant Navy Officers, and dozens of stores selling souvenirs and some of the niftiest handcraft bargains in the islands. You have an hour and a half here, so you can either flop into one of the cafes and admire the harbor, or wander round to the rocky cove on the other side of the bay and join the artists, writers, and jet-setters in the unbelievably clear rock-bound sea.

By the time you sail for home the sun is low in the sky and glistening on the sea, and you can enjoy a comfortable cocktail on deck; by the time you get to Piraeus and the waiting buses, the sun has settled behind the mountains of the Peloponnese. You've cruised on the Mediterranean, you've seen three islands, and you've probably had a swim in the "Med." Not a bad day for $25. (The sightseeing trip on Aegina costs an extra $3.)

If you don't feel like following an organized itinerary, you can easily get to any of these islands by ferryboat. That way you get to go ashore at Poros too, and you'll also be able to visit the fourth and farthest island of the group, **Spetsai** (the one with no cars), and maybe catch a glimpse of Spetsopoula, the private island of Stavros Niarchos, the *other* shipping tycoon. There's plenty to see on all of these islands—ruined temples, monasteries, picturesque fishing villages with almost as many tavernas as houses; but most people come over to find a secluded stretch of beach (and there are hundreds of those).

## Ferry Services from Piraeus

| To | # of departures | | -One-way fares | |
|---|---|---|---|---|
| | Weekdays | Weekends | 1st class | 3rd class |
| Aegina | 24 | 30 | 105 drs | 78 drs |
| Poros | 8 | 8 | 128 drs | 101 drs |
| Hydra | 3 | 3 | 172 drs | 127 drs |
| Spetsai | 3 | 3 | 221 drs | 167 drs |

## Flying Dolphins

During the summer months (and on calm days in spring and fall) you also have the choice of a hydrofoil trip to these islands aboard the *Flying Dolphin I* or *Flying Dolphin II* of Ceres Flying Hydroways. They're Russian-built hydrofoils; they tend to be noisy, there's no deck space on top and no air conditioning below, the fares are almost double, and the ride can be unpleasant on choppy seas. Nevertheless, the hydrofoils do get you to the islands quickly (just two hours all the way to Spetsai), so they're popular with Athenians. The Flying Dolphins now also serve four locations on the Peloponnese coast (Porto Heli, Leonidion, Nauplia, Monemvassia), getting you there in much less time than by car (but if the sea is rough you may prefer the traffic jams). For full details of all schedules to these islands, check with the reception desk of your hotel, or with the National Tourist Organization information services at Syntagma; don't be discouraged if they hedge their answers, because the published schedules don't always tally with reality. In addition, double check your ticket as soon as you pay for it, to make sure it's for the correct shipping company and correct vessel and correct destination; mistakes have been made, and it's usually impossible to have your money refunded. But don't let these words of caution dissuade you—your trip to the Saronic islands çan be one of the highlights of your vacation.

*Chapter XIII*

# TOURING THE HINTERLANDS

BACK IN Chapter III you read a basic outline of what constitutes the nation known as Greece; now we'll fill in some of the details of the country beyond Athens. You can get to most parts of mainland Greece relatively easily and relatively quickly from Athens by car, bus, train, or plane, and there's certainly plenty to see once you get out there. In fact, there may be too much, and you may find it almost impossible to decide how to fit everything into one short vacation.

## The Western Peloponnese

In the chapter on one-day trips from Athens you read about the highlights of the eastern part of this peninsula (Epidaurus, Mycenae, and Corinth); the *Western* Peloponnese is a shade too far to be tackled on a one-day round trip—yet the chances are that you will want to visit Sparta, Olympia, and the district known as Arcadia, where Pan and the nymphs frolicked.

**Arcadia** is a region of rugged mountains rising to 3,500 feet or thereabouts, with many pleasant drives along winding roads through ancient villages and fir forests. Two of the most interesting towns in the Western Peloponnese are **Sparta,** which was the seat of the great military power that battled Athens in the Peloponnesian Wars, although not much remains of its former glory; and **Mistras** (or Mystra), where there is more to see—scores of Byzantine monasteries, palaces, and citadels in an extraordinary setting.

The main goal of visitors to this part of Greece is **Olympia,** where you can still see traces of the stadium where the first Olympics were held. Olympia was dedicated to Zeus, and at its peak was an impressive collection of temples, altars, statues, and treasuries. It survived for over ten centuries, until 426 A.D. when Theodosius II commanded that the temples be destroyed. The games, which were also in honor of Zeus, were held for the first time in 776 B.C., and then every fourth year thereafter, from June until September. They were heralded each time by messengers setting off in every direction to announce the start of the sacred truce, during which all warfare and squabbling among the city-states had to be suspended: for four months, the gods and heroes and everyone else in the neighborhood concentrated on running, wrestling, chariot races, horse races, the pentathlon, and, eventually, artistic and literary contests. The names of the victors in each contest were recorded alongside the date of each Olympic Games. You can still see traces of the stadium and temples, the monuments and statues, and the starting block for twenty runners. The **museum** of Olympia houses many intriguing finds unearthed during excavations, but its most famous exhibit is the famed *Hermes* of Praxiteles, standing nobly in a room all by itself.

There are other virtually unknown spots you might want to include on a tour of the Western Peloponnese: **Kyllini**, set among forests of wild oak and eucalyptus, was famous for centuries as a spa and is currently one of the largest holiday complexes in the Peloponnese; **Pylos**, built in tiers at the southern end of the Bay of Navarino, is a historic town in its own right but it is also close to the more famous ruins of the **Palace of Nestor** and the two formidable Venetian fortresses at **Methani** and **Koroni.**

## Central Greece

Take the National Highway from Athens to the north and you come to the regions known as Boeotia, Thessaly, and Epirus, none of which means a great deal to the average visitor until they discover that these are the lands of Delphi (which you read about in an earlier chapter), Thermopylae, Meteora, Ioannina, and Messolonghi, all names ringing with myth and history.

North of Delphi, the National Highway follows the outline of the Gulf of Evoikos (which separates the Greek mainland from the island of Evia) and the Gulf of Pagassitikos, past the port of Volos, and across the plain to Larissa. The capital of Thessaly, **Larissa** has several fine hotels, which make it a convenient base for exploring, but the main attraction in these parts is almost 70 kilometers to the west—Meteora.

Long before they reach **Meteora**, visitors can see what the place's fascination is all about—great columns of rock soar almost 2,000 feet into the air, and topping them off are precariously perched monasteries. In all, there are 24 of these eyrie-like monasteries at Meteora; only two of them are still functioning as monasteries, but several of them are open to·visitors. Inside (once you make it up the hill), you can tour the refectories and cells arranged in rows with balconies and galleries, the chapels with their ikons and frescoes dating from the 14th century.

To the west of Meteora, the magnets for tourists are **Ioannina,** capital of the region known as Epirus, noted for the baronial mansions that dot its narrow streets; **Nikopolis,** which was built by Octavius Caesar to honor his own victory over the combined fleets of Antony and Cleopatra at the Battle of Actium in 31 B.C.; and **Missolonghi,** which has gone down in the annals of Greek history because of its stubborn resistance to the Turks during the War of Independence—and because Lord Byron died there.

The major landmark between central Greece and the northern provinces is **Mount Olympus** itself, the very eyrie of the gods and the highest point (9,793 feet) in Greece. Here you'll see some of the most spectacular, and beautiful, scenery in Greece.

If, on the way north to Meteora or Olympus, you detour to the east, around Pagasitikos Gulf, you come to the port of **Volos** and the ancient land of the Argonauts. Today's Volos is a substantial town and resort, its spacious waterfront lined with cafes and restaurants, and it's hard to conjure up images of Jason and his crew there. The hills beyond Volos are another matter. The wild peninsula that separates the gulf from the Aegean Sea is dominated by the peaks of the Pelion range, their flanks covered by forests of beech and chestnut at the upper levels, with groves of olive, peach, and apple trees on the lower levels. On the eastern shore the mountains dip directly into the sea, dented here and there with tiny bays lined by narrow spits of beach.

There are a few modest one-taverna resorts along this coastline, but the main appeal of the Pelion range is its hill towns— **Portaria, Makrynitsa, Vizitsa, Kissos, Tsagarada**—clinging precariously to the slopes, their mule-wide cobbled streets winding between attractive balconied homes with russet roof tiles and traditional painted woodcarvings. The two most popular of these hill towns with sightseers are probably **Makrynitsa** and **Vizitsa,** both of which have historic buildings being preserved by the National Tourist Organization. Skiers head for **Hania** in winter. But lovers of solitude head for tiny towns like **Tsagarada,** teetering on its hillside, its town square dominated by an 800-year-old plane tree with church bells hanging from its massive limbs: there's a taverna up the hill behind the church, cobbled goat paths lead up and down and across the hillside (you can spend hours hiking here, but be sure you get back before dark), and the views from almost any outlook are breathtaking. There are Class B Xenia Hotels at Tsagarada (fashioned from the local stone and timber) and Portaria. The roadways are well engineered, but winding, narrow, and at times hair-raising; if you're heading for the Aegean side of the mountains, the easiest drive is not the most direct route on the map, but the seemingly longer one along the shores of the Pagasitikos Gulf and then across the mountains where they're narrower and lower. It's a trip of some five hours, and you can drive straight there, since there's little to see along the way—unless you're a devout archaeology buff.

## Northern Greece

This is where Alexander the Great was born (in the town of **Pella,** which is now noted for its recently excavated pebble mosaics, dating from the days of Alexander), and where Marc Antony and Octavius defeated Brutus and Cassius in the battle fought at **Philippi** (the ruins of the ancient agora and acropolis are still there). If you've been sampling the wines of **Naoussa** in the tavernas of the Plaka, you may also want to visit this ancient town, which is famous for peaches, apples, and weaving, as well as red wine.

**Thessaloniki,** the capital of ancient Macedonia, is a bustling modern city, with a sweeping promenade curving around the harbor; the old part of the city is built in tiers against the flank of Mount Hortisti, and here and there among the boulevards you will catch sight of the medieval ramparts, Byzantine churches, or the triumphal arch of the emperor Galerius.

But perhaps the most dramatic sight up in the north is the **Chalkidiki Peninsula,** a mountainous finger of land tipped by the unique **Mount Athos.** The "Holy Mountain," or Aghios Oros, has long been an isolated monastic community which has its own republican government and police force of monks. To visit Mount Athos you must have a special permit (the National Tourist Organization will tell you where to apply), and you must be over 21. Ladies of any age may not enter the monasteries—even female animals are forbidden!

The Chalkidiki Peninsula is one of the newest "in" spots in

Greece, and there are several stunning resorts where the ladies can console themselves while the men are off to Athos.

## Beaches, Mountains, Villages

Those are only a few of the highlights of the Greek hinterlands. Everywhere you travel, of course, you'll be close to quiet beaches and coves, or spas and resorts, mountains, villages with tavernas and folk festivals, and ruins of temples and fortresses. Again, the National Tourist Organization of Greece can ply you with leaflets, photographs, and details of every corner of the land. In addition, they'll give you up-to-the-minute details of new hotels, tourist villages, beaches, and marinas which are popping up like Doric columns all over the landscape. You can now find first-rate or close to first-rate accommodations in every region of Greece. All at bargain prices. Many of them will remind you of Florida or the Caribbean rather than the Parthenon, but no matter—you'll have your eyes shut, sunning yourself on the beach.

## Getting Around by Bus and Train

There's now an efficient network of bus routes fanning out from Athens through the country to 66 cities and towns. The buses are big, comfortable, mostly pullman-type, and the fares are remarkably low. Athens to Naoussa in the north is less than $15 round trip, Athens to Corinth is about $2.50 one way. The services operate several times a day—for example, 13 departures daily to Missolonghi, eight a day to Pyrgos (for Olympia), six a day to four different towns in Thessaly.

Greek State Railways operates diesel trains to the Peloponnese and the north, and supplements them with pullman coaches into the smaller towns. There are five trains daily to Pyrgos (437 drachmas, $11.50; one way, first class) and to Thessaloniki (627 drachmas, $16.50, first class; 418 drachmas, $11, second class, one way). These are the least expensive ways of getting around in Greece.

## Sightseeing Tours by Coach

Most of the tour companies in Athens also offer a choice of conducted tours of the hinterlands lasting for anywhere from three to nine days. Check with your hotel concierge for details of tours by CHAT, American Express, and Key Tours, and by

Viking's for budget-priced tours. Meantime, here are some samples of the *range* of tours and typical prices available.

**4-Day Classical Tour:** Corinth, Mycenae (lunch), Epidaurus, Nauplia (overnight), Tripolis, Vytina, Olympia (lunch, dinner, overnight), Patras, ferry ride from Aegion to Itea, Delphi (lunch, dinner, overnight), Ossios Lucas. $191 in first-class hotels, $169 in tourist-class hotels.

**5-Day Archaeological Tour:** Corinth, Mycenae (lunch), Epidaurus, Nauplia (dinner, overnight), Tripolis, Sparta (lunch), Mystra, Sparta or Tripolis (dinner, overnight), Vytina, Olympia (lunch, dinner, overnight), Patras, ferry ride Aegion to Itea, Delphi (lunch, dinner, overnight), Ossios Lucas. $233 in first-class hotels, $197 in tourist-class hotels.

**5-Day Classical Tour plus Meteora:** Same itinerary as Classical Tour (above) with an additional day spent in Meteora, Kalambaka, Trikala, and Thermopilae. $283 in first-class hotels, $261 in tourist-class hotels, full-board throughout.

**6-Day Northern Greece Tour:** Thebes, Arakhova, Delphi (lunch, dinner, overnight), Amphissa, Lamia, Trikala, Kalambaka (dinner, overnight), Meteora, Larissa, Valley of Tempi, Platamon, Thessaloniki (dinner, overnight), Amphipolis, Philippi, Kavala (dinner, overnight), Thassos (lunch), Kavala, Thessaloniki (dinner, overnight), Pella, Larissa (lunch), Thermopilae, Kammena, Vourla. $295, full board, first-class hotels.

**9-Day Grand Tour of Greece:** Corinth, Mycenae (lunch), Epidaurus, Nauplia (dinner, overnight), Tripolis, Sparta (lunch), Mystra, Sparta or Tripolis (dinner, overnight), Olympia (lunch, dinner, overnight), Patras, ferry ride from Aegion to Itea, Delphi (lunch, dinner, overnight), Amphissa, Lamia, Trikala, Kalambaka (dinner, overnight), Meteora, Kalambaka (lunch), Larissa, Valley of Tempi, Platamon, Thessaloniki (dinner, overnight), Amphissa, Philippi, Kavala (dinner, overnight), Thassos (lunch), Kavala, Thessaloniki (dinner, overnight), Pella, Larissa (lunch), Thermopilae. $440, full board, first-class hotels.

## Touring Greece by Car

In the end, if you have the time, the cash, and the inclination, the best way to tour Greece is by car. The Greek government has been forging ahead with its road-building program, and although there are only limited stretches of expressway, there are now good, comfortable roads linking all the major tourist areas. There's an expressway of sorts, National Highway #1, all the way from Athens, along the eastern shores of Attica, through Lamia, Larissa, and Kateria to Thessaloniki—a distance of just over 300 miles. And another from Athens, round the Gulf of Saronica to Corinth, and along the northern shore of the Peloponnese to Patras (where you can catch a ferry boat to Italy). There's also a new extension of the expressway which goes from Corinth south to the city of Epidaurus. These highways are considered expressways in Greece, and you have to pay tolls (trifling amounts) on some stretches, but don't zoom onto them expecting an interstate highway or you'll be disappointed—in addition to which you'll have your timetable thrown for a loop. The stretch of National Highway #1 from Athens to Thebes (the turnoff for Delphi) is a four-lane highway, without dividers and with an unmarked shoulder on the right, so that most drivers seem to position themselves halfway between the right lane and the passing lane. Also, the standard of driving in Greece is probably the most immature this side of the Middle East. This doesn't mean that you shouldn't drive in Greece—it's simply a warning to drive with extra care, and not to plan on averaging more than 40 miles an hour.

But you don't need an expressway to enjoy some pleasurable driving. The coastal road from Athens to Sounion, for example, is a well-engineered corniche-type highway with many bends but no tricky corners, and there are some fine, scenic roads in the mountains of Arcadia and around Olympia.

Distances in Greece are manageable, and you can cover a lot of territory even with leisurely driving. Here are three suggestions for car tours from Athens:

1. **3-day to 5-day tour** could include Corinth, Epidaurus, Nauplia, Mycenae, Arcadia, Sparta, Kalamata, Pyrgos, Olympia, Patras (from which you can head across to Italy or return to Athens). How long you spend on that tour will depend on how much time you spend snooping around the ruins, or nipping off to the beach for a dip.

2. **5-day to 7-day tour** could take you up through Delphi and Amfissa to Missolonghi, Agrinion, and Arta to Ioannina in Epirus, then back via Trikala and Karditsa to Lamia, where you pick up the expressway to Athens. That itinerary gives you a nice mixture of antiquity, resorts, and scenery.

3. This itinerary, again for **5 to 7 days,** would take you along the old scenic road through Boeotia to Delphi and Lamia, then to Karditsa and Trikala, over a stretch of less than first-rate highway to Grevena and Kozana, with a sidetrip to Naoussa on

the way to Thessaloniki, and returning via Alexandria, Katerina, and Larissa, to Lamia and Athens—on expressway all the way back. Again, a mixture of antiquity, scenery, and resorts.

There are several reliable companies renting cars (see below), and you'll have a wide choice of cars—from Volkswagens to Mercedes with automatic transmissions. There are very few cars with air conditioning, however. Check out several rates before you decide which company you're going to choose from. Note particularly such features as unlimited mileage rates, seasons, tax (usually 10%, although Hellascars charges only 7%), minimum age (usually 25, but 21 with Hellascars), insurance, and special weekend or low-season rates.

You'll recognize a few old faithfuls among the list of rental companies, like Avis and Hertz, both of which have the most convenient locations (including desks at the airport arrival hall), but the largest company in Greece may not be familiar to you—Hellascars. It's actually linked up with National/Tilden in the U.S.A., who'll take your reservation; you can also book your car through a travel agent, or direct by cable (in which case, send it collect and Hellascars will pay). They have 400 cars, all less than two years old, including VW 1303s, Fiat 127s and 124s, Peugeots, Ford Escorts, VW Minibuses, and Mercedes automatics. They offer 24-hour service, they'll deliver the car to your hotel (even if you're staying in Vouliagmeni), and you can park your car *free* in their garages at night.

*Note:* Not all the rental cars come equipped with seat belts, so specify *in advance* if you want them.

## Some Sample Rental Rates in Athens

|  | Per day (24 hrs) | Per km |
|---|---|---|
| Fiat 127, VW 1303 | $ 9.50 | 12¢ |
| Fiat 124, P 104, VW Polo | $11.20 | 13¢ |
| P 204/304, VW Golf Ford Escort L | $15.50 | 15¢ |
| P 404 Family Estate VW Minibus | $22.50 | 21¢ |
| Mercedes Automatic | $30.00 | 28¢ |

There are also unlimited mileage rates, from $145 a week for a VW in the off-season, $172 in summer.

Remember to add 18% for tax and duty stamp to the above rates. All prices subject to change without notice.

## Car Rental Companies in Athens

**Avis,** 48 Amalias Avenue (tel. 3224-951), and at the Athens Hilton

**Hellascars,** 7 Stadiou Street (tel. 3233-487)

**Hertz,** 12 Syngrou Avenue (tel. 9220-102)

**Batek,** 43 Syngrou Avenue (tel. 9221-440)

**Tourent,** 6 Syngrou Avenue (tel. 9238-821)

**Athens Cars,** 10 Filellinon Street (tel. 3233-783)

## Distance by Road from Athens to Various Points in Greece

The figures below are in kilometers, the measurement used on Greek maps and road signs. A kilometer equals ⅝ of a mile, but the simplest way to translate kilometers into miles is to multiply by 6 and divide by 10. It's not a precise figure, but close enough for most purposes.

| From Athens to: | Kilometers |
| --- | --- |
| Corinth | 84 |
| Ioannina | 444 |
| Kalamata | 283 |
| Karditsa | 302 |
| Katerina | 440 |
| Lamia | 215 |
| Larissa | 356 |
| Messolonghi | 248 |
| Nauplia | 145 |
| Naoussa | 533 |
| Patras | 217 |
| Thessaloniki | 539 |

*Chapter XIV*

# THE ISLANDS

### And How to Reach Them from Athens

GO DOWN TO PIRAEUS any day of the week and you can take your pick of a score of cruise ships or ferryboats waiting to take you to some offshore Elysium. Or go to the airport and hop on a jet to any of a dozen islands. In some cases, you can fly over and back in the same day. So your vacation in Athens can easily include a day or two on the Greek islands as well. The question is: Which one? That's an impossible question to answer. Start with the numbers.

There are 1,425 Greek islands. Of these, 166 are inhabited, including the privately owned islets such as Niarchos' Spetsopoulos and Onassis' Skorpios, but only about three dozen are visited regularly by tourists from abroad.

Within that three dozen you have a choice of highly sophisticated, swinging resorts or unspoiled one-taverna-one-guesthouse-and-a-handful-of-fishermen islands.

The islands all have a few things in common. Sun. Torrential sun. About 300 days of sunshine a year, and many of the islands are warm enough for sunbathing or swimming in January. They all have their typically Greek villages, with whitewashed houses huddling around narrow alleyways leading to a tiny harbor confettied with the red, blue, and yellow awnings of cafes and tavernas. Many are dotted with remnants of antiquity—temple columns, Byzantine churches, Crusader fortresses; others have little besides secluded coves and beaches, and valleys filled with olives, lemon trees, and vineyards.

Whatever type of island you choose, they're all great places to be . . . day or night.

**GETTING YOUR BEARINGS:** It's no easy matter charting your way through all these islands, even on paper. Begin by breaking them down into groups.

There are eight groups—from west to east (more or less). They are the Ionians, the Saronics, the Sporades, the Cyclades, the North Aegeans, the Eastern Aegeans, the Dodecanese and Rhodes, and Crete (which is one island, but large enough to be ranked with the groups).

The Saronic Islands are in the Gulf of Saronica, just off Piraeus, and you've already read all about them in the chapter on one-day tours from Athens—Aegina, Poros, Hydra, and Spetsai.

Now here's a brief preview of the others. Very brief, because this is a book about Athens, and the islands really deserve a volume all to themselves, but you'll read about half a dozen island highlights in the next chapter.

## The Ionian Islands

Greece's seven islands in the Ionian Sea (at the southern end of the Adriatic Sea) are Corfu (or Kerkyra), Paxi, Lefkas, Cephalonia, Ithaca, Zante, and Kythera (or Cerigo). **Ithaca** was the birthplace and kingdom of Odysseus, and **Lefkas** is the closest island to Skorpios, the new kingdom of Onassis.

But the island most visitors flock to is the largest in the group, **Corfu.** It's one of the most beautiful (unlike the Aegean islands, Corfu has lots of greenery), and one of the most interesting (it has been held variously by the French, the Venetians, the British, and the Greeks, and it's only a few miles from Albania). Turn to the next chapter for more detials on Corfu.

## The Sporades and Euboea

The islands known as the Sporades—Skiathos, Skopelos, Alonissos, and Skyros—lie to the northeast of **Euboea,** which looks like a peninsula off the eastern shore of central Greece but is, in fact, the second-largest Greek island after Crete. It's joined to the mainland by a swing bridge over the Straits of Euripos, which are famous for an unusual tidal current that zips through in alternate directions roughly every six hours, at speeds that vary from four to six knots, depending on the moon. If you don't see it, you'll hear it.

**Skyros** is the island where Odysseus discovered Achilles, who had been hidden there, disguised as a girl by his mother to protect him from the ravages of the Trojan War; you can also see the tomb of Rupert Brooke, another of those English poets who died unheroically of fever or blood poisoning in Greece. There's nothing you really must see on these islands—you simply go there to lounge on the beach by day and live it up in the tavernas by night. All of them are acquiring new hotels and resorts at a rate to match that tidal current. Euboea now has six Class A hotels. For more information on Skiathos, turn to the following chapter.

## The Cyclades (or Kyklades) Islands

Next to the Saronics these are the islands closest to Athens, and therefore the most popular and the most developed. Some of their names are probably familiar—Mykonos, Delos, Kea, Serifos, Kimolos, Milos, Paros, Naxos, Kythmos, Siphnos, Ios, Sikinos, Andros, Tinos, Syros, Antiparos, Anafi, Santorini, Amorgos, Pholegendros. They get their collective name from an ancient Greek word meaning "wheeling ones," because they seem to whirl, like one of the islands' famous white windmills, around Delos.

**Delos** is accessible only by caique, or fishing boat, from Mykonos (unless it's included on a cruise itinerary); it was the birthplace of Apollo, the god of the sun, among other things, and was, therefore, a sacred island. Its most famous features are a line of marble lions, and three temples dedicated to Apollo and his twin sister Artemis. The island is now uninhabited—and because of a pronouncement from Delphi, no one has been born there or died there since the sixth century B.C.

**Kea** is the Cyclade closest to the mainland (a mere 13 miles from Cape Sounion), but because tourists have to catch the ferryboat from Lavrion, near Sounion, rather than convenient Piraeus, it's almost totally unspoiled, the way Mykonos was until it was discovered. Unspoiled maybe, but it can offer you fine accommodations in two class B and two class C hotels; otherwise you can enjoy the beaches, the snorkeling, the walks, and the tavernas without being crowded out by tourists, Greek or otherwise.

**Tinos** was the legendary abode of Poseidon, the god of the sea, but in more recent years it has acquired a reputation as the island of the Virgin Mary, and Greeks come from all over the country on her feast day, August 15 (an interesting day to visit the island, but no time to turn up without a hotel reservation).

Syros was an old shipbuilding center, and is now the home for wealthy shipowners who can't quite afford a Skorpios or Spetsopoulos. **Andros, Naxos,** and **Paros** are all dreamy and idyllic, the way Greek islands are supposed to look, and still undiscovered. **Santorini** is, in many ways, the most fascinating of the Cyclades, and you'll read more about it, and Mykonos, in the highlights chapter that follows.

Santorini still has three hotels, which is about par for most of the Cyclade islands—except Mykonos and Tinos which are well endowed with accommodations up to Class A hotels.

## The Northern Aegean Islands

Sometimes called the Thracian Islands because they're way up north off the coast of Thrace: Samothrace, Thassos, and Lemnos. **Samothrace** is a mountainous island (5,000 feet and more) which was the home of the *Winged Victory;* most of the island's hotels are now booked by archaeologists who're busy digging up all sorts of fascinating relics from B.C. eras.

**Thassos** is just off the coast of Macedonia; this is where the Phoenicians got their gold, and where modern Greeks now spend their vacations (it's one of the up-and-coming resort areas). **Lemnos** is the island where Hephaestus, the god of goldsmiths, landed when his old man, Zeus, tossed him off Olympus, and where Jason and the Argonauts came searching for the Golden Fleece and found an island populated only by women who had killed all their men. The Argonauts stayed a year. You'll probably want to stick around, too. Especially if you're staying in the island's sole deluxe-class hotel. Thassos is well supplied with budget-priced hotels; Samothrace has only a small number of beds for visitors.

## The Eastern Aegeans

There are four of them, all tucked in close to the coast of Turkey—Samos, Ikaria, Chios, and Lesvos (sometimes spelled Lesbos, and sometimes called Mytilene after its biggest village). Sappho the greatest poetess of antiquity, and Aesop, the greatest yarnspinner of antiquity, were both born on **Lesvos;** there are various ruins, galleries, and museums there, but it's really a place to go to lie on the beach and read Sappho and Aesop.

Chios (sometimes spelled Hios) is one of the larger Greek islands, with a population of 60,000, most of them descendants of generations of seafarers. Both **Samos** and **Ikaria** have been bypassed by history—ancient and modern. All four islands have a range of budget-priced hotels.

## The Dodecanese Islands and Rhodes

Rhodes is the largest, and the others include Patmos, Leros, Astypalaea, Karpathos, Kassos, Nisyros, Castellorizo, Kalymnos, Kos, and Symi. **Kos,** the second-largest, is the island of Hippocrates, the father of medicine, and you can still see the ruins of his school and the temple to Asclepius. This is another relatively lush island, plump with figs, pomegranates, bananas, mulberries, cherries, oranges, and lemons—and, of course, grapes. **Patmos** is sometimes called the Island of the Donkey because every family owns one (there are even some two-donkey families); most of the donkeys are used to carrying tourists up the hill to the 11th-century monastery of St. John, a unique fortress-like place with priceless manuscripts, and the Cave of the Apocalypse, where St. John wrote the divinely inspired Revelations.

**Patmos, Kalymnos,** and **Kos** are the only other islands with a wide range of accommodations. The others have hotels or rooms in private homes—but only in limited quantities. That's why they're unspoiled. Rhodes is featured in the "Islands Highlights" chapter that follows.

## Crete

Crete is the fourth-largest island in the Mediterranean (technically, it's surrounded by its own sea, the Cretan), and it's full of ruins and historic sites from the days of the Minoan civilization right up to World War II. The main town is **Heraklion,** which has interesting museums and churches, but the goal of most visitors is the great palace at **Knossos** to see the royal apartments, drainage system, terraces, and traces of the dreaded Labyrinth where the Minotaur gobbled up its human prey. Knossos is one of the great sights of the Mediterranean, so you'll read more about Crete in the next chapter.

## How to Get to the Islands

Olympic Airways and Greek shipping companies operate "bus" services by plane or ferry to many of the islands, and between them they cover most of the islands tourists are likely to visit. However, some of the islands mentioned in the previous pages cannot be reached directly, either by sea or air from Athens, and if you have an urge to visit any of those spots, check out possible transportation with the National Tourist Organization.

**BY SEA:** In an area of the world where so much history was written by seafarers for so many centuries you'll probably want to sail from the mainland to the islands. That's no problem, as you'll see from the following table. There are plenty of boats, lots of departures, accommodations to suit every budget; an island like Mykonos, for example, is only six or seven hours away by sea, and you can get to the farthest islands, such as Rhodes, within 24 hours.

The ferryboats and ships that carry passengers from Piraeus to the islands vary considerably (some of them have been around for a long time), and it's not possible in these few pages to give you a listing of the best craft—you'll have to get that information from your travel agent, or the National Tourist Organization, or from someone standing in line at the American Express office on Syntagma. Generally speaking, you'll be able to choose between private cabins, shared cabins, bunks, lounges, or deck class (which may be rugged but in some ways is the most fun). Most ferryboats have some kind of snackbar on board, but to be on the safe side take along some kind of simple picnic.

Theoretically, the boats operate on a fixed schedule but since so many indirect factors may affect their performance (weather and cargo, to name two) you should never rely on precise timing. Getting around the islands is strictly for people with time to spare.

There's a more reliable (and more comfortable) way of seeing the islands by boat, and that's by taking one of the dozens of cruise ships on three-day, four-day, or longer voyages, which you'll read about later. But the great advantages of ferryboats and interisland boats are frequency of schedules and *economy,* as you can see from the chart below.

## Ferryboat Services from Piraeus

| To | # of sailings per week | duration of trip (hours) | One-way fares (drachmas)* 2nd | Tourist |
|---|---|---|---|---|
| Crete |  |  |  |  |
| (Heraklion) | 14 | 12 | 691 | 508 |
| Hios | 5 | 10 | 567 | 406 |
| Ios | 3 | 8-10 | 507 | 400 |
| Kos | 4 | 15 | 738 | 553 |
| Mykonos | 3 | 5-7 | 404 | 313 |
| Rhodes | 7 | 19½ | 807 | 614 |
| Santorini |  |  |  |  |
| (Thera) | 4 | 9½ | 507 | 400 |
| Siros | 12 | 23½ | 339 | 232 |

* The Tourist Class fare is for the young and adventurous; most travelers will prefer the comfort of the more expensive class of accommodations—"expensive" in this case being a mere, say, $11 for the trip to magical Mykonos; first-class fares vary from vessel to vessel and are not available at press time—but they are usually 25% to 30% more expensive than 2nd class fares.

Again, always check details of shipping company, name of vessel and destination before you leave the ticket office, otherwise you may have to pay again to get to where you really want to go.

**BY AIR:** Olympic Airways operates the internal Greek flights with modern jets and twin-engined aircraft: Boeing 707s, Boeing 720s, Nihon YS-11As, Skyvan SC-7s, and Britten-Norman Islanders. All services are economy class only; since flights are crowded in summer and mistakes can be made even with confirmed reservations it's always wise to get to the airport early—the *West* Terminal, remember. If you're impatient to get to your dream island, you can charter a Piper Aztec five-seater or an Alouette helicopter. The table below will give you some idea of the scope and frequency of these Olympic services. For more details, check with your travel agent, or the main Olympic office on Syntagma—6 Othonos Street (tel. 9292-444).

## Flights to the Islands
## (summer schedules)*

| From Athens to: | # of flights weekly | Duration of flight | One-way fare* (drachmas) |
|---|---|---|---|
| Chios (Hios) | 27 | 50 mins. | 755 ($21) |
| Corfu (Kerkyra) | 30 | 1 hr. 20 mins. | 1130 ($31) |
| Crete (Heraklion) | 63 | 1 hr. 10 mins. | 890 ($25) |
| Kos | 19 | 1 hr. 10 mins. | 960 ($27) |
| Lemnos | 14 | 1 hr. 5 mins. | 780 ($22) |
| Lesbos (Mytiline) | 34 | 1 hr. 5 mins. | 870 ($24) |
| Mykonos | 22 | 55 mins. | 630 ($18) |
| Rhodes | 49 | 55 mins. | 1220 ($34) |
| Samos | 19 | 1 hr. 5 mins. | 875 ($24) |
| Skiathos | 21 | 40 mins. | 630 ($18) |

* Subject to change; check with your travel agent.

# Chapter XV

# ISLAND HIGHLIGHTS

AS WE MENTIONED earlier, choosing which island to visit is a ticklish problem. They all have something to offer—antiquity, glamor, beaches, or, in some cases, just plain isolation. If you're having trouble making a decision, here are some notes on half a dozen islands based on recent visits.

## Corfu

This is the green Greek island. Because of its location in the Ionian Sea, a few miles from the coast of Albania, Corfu has much more foliage than most of the other islands. (It also rains more often here, but that still adds up to only a few showers in winter.)

The main town of Corfu, also called Corfu (or **Kerkyra** to the Greeks), has arcaded streets modeled on the Rue Rivoli, palazzos in the style of Venice, and cricket fields in the style of Eton—all holdovers from the centuries of conquerors from different parts of Europe.

It's an old town, relatively unchanged through the ages, and, to this day, its cobbled back alleys, or cantounias, are accessible only to pedestrians. It's a great place for walking and exploring (houses built in the style of Naples or Paris or London, Byzantine churches and fortresses), but once you get beyond the cantounias there's a lot to see on the island.

Corfu has its own patron saint, St. Spyridon, who lies in a richly decorated sarcophagus with his mummified, slippered feet sticking out; four times a year (Palm Sunday, Easter, August 11, and the first Sunday in November) his body is carried through the streets, and anyone who has a favor to ask whispers it to his slippered feet. St. Spyridon is credited with several miracles.

At **Gastori**, a few miles from the town of Corfu, you can see the remains of the Kaiser's Bridge, which crosses the main road and allowed Kaiser Wilhelm to walk from his royal yacht directly to Achilleion Palace; this sumptuous palace, which was built by Empress Elizabeth of Austria in 1890, is now a gambling casino. Mon Repos, a more modest villa built by a British governor in the 19th century, was the birthplace of Prince Philip, duke of Edinburgh.

But in the end, it's the natural beauty of the island that will probably make the most lasting impression on you. A spectacular spiral road will bring you to **Aghios Gordis,** one of the island's most beautiful beaches, surrounded by rugged almost spooky nature; readers of Henry Miller will know about **Palaekastritsa** even before they reach its beautiful beach—small tavernas where you can select a meal from tanks of live lobsters, the 13th-century fortress of Angelokastio, and the panoramic view from "Bella Vista," a natural balcony overlooking the town and the sea. The island has lots of seafood restaurants, of course, besides the tavernas of Palaekastritsa. One of the most famous is **Giannis,** which hangs over the edge of a cliff, in the aristocratic quarter of the island, Perama, about five miles from the town.

Before you go exploring the island, check out your plans with the tourist office in the new Government Building next door to the post office on Samara Street. They'll give you information on how to get around the island by scheduled bus, or by tourist boats to the various coves along the west coast. You can also rent a car (Autorent Corfu has Fiat 124s for $23 a day plus 12¢ for each additional kilometer) and try to find your own way—no easy matter because the signposting is unreliable or nonexistent, and out in the countryside you won't find too many people who speak English.

**HOTELS ON CORFU:** When it comes to a place to stay your only problem will be choosing among several attractive locations and hotels. You can stay in the town itself, or at some of the new hotels and resorts out on the island. In town, the top choices are the deluxe **Corfu Palace** where the management is Swiss and most of the 110 rooms look out to the sea; swimmers have a choice of the hotel pool or the beach at the Miramare Beach Hotel (12 miles away but linked by free shuttle bus). Summer half-board rates are $60 single, $88 double; or just $44 single, $65 double in the off-season. One of the loveliest hotels in town is the 50-room Class A **Cavalieri,** converted from a 17th-century nobleman's mansion (or what remained of it after it was hit by a bomb in World War II); all the public rooms and most of the guest rooms are decorated with reproduction period furniture, and the dining room serves some of the finest meals on the island. Half-board rates are $44 double in season. The **Corfu Hilton Hotel** is located on a plateau a few kilometers south of the town; each of its 274 rooms has balcony, well-equipped bathroom, telephone, individual controls for heating and air conditioning; resort facilities include two swimming pools (one indoors), bowling alleys, two tennis courts (with lights for night play) health club, and an 18-hole golf course a short shuttle-bus ride away. Summer rates are around $72 double, half-board.

Other leading hotels on the island are the deluxe **Miramare Beach** at Moraitike) with 149 beachside bungalows; the 122-room deluxe **Eva Palace** at Dafnila; the 72-room deluxe **Castello** at Dassia, a converted manor house with splendid antique furnishings; and the 308-room deluxe **Astir Palace Corfu.** Other Class A hotels include a pair of Chandris hotels—the **Chandris Corfu** and **Chandris Dassia,** where summer room rates are under $50 double, with breakfast and dinner. In addition, there are scores of Class B, C, and D hotels throughout the island, with new ones opening every year. Room rates are from $15 double in summer, but in most cases you'll be expected to settle for a half-board rate.

**HOW TO GET TO CORFU:** The quickest way, of course, is by Olympic Airways—four flights from Athens every day in summer, the first one leaving early in the morning to give you a full day on the beach. The slowest way is by car or bus across the mountains to Igoumenitsa, where you board a ferry for a short trip to the island. There is also ferryboat service once a week from Patras.

## Skiathos

Think of a tiny island covered with wild strawberries and pine trees and rimmed with—wait for it—66 beaches. Beautiful beaches, most of them, particularly Koukounaries, a half-mile combination of dazzling sand and clear water, named for the stone pines which separate the sea from a freshwater lagoon. And so that you can enjoy this beach to the fullest, fortune has perched two luxury hotels there—one at each end of the beach. The **Skiathos Palace** has 200 rooms and 15 suites, heated swimming pool, discotheque, beauty parlor, and sauna. Guest rooms are decorated in white with cinnamon and turquoise highlights, and come equipped with two-channel radio, telephone, refrigerator prestocked with everything from ice and beer to cognac and creme de menthe miniatures. It's open all year. Rates are from 2,200 to 3,000 drachmas for a double, half-pension in season. The 32-room **Xenia** is open only during the summer, when doubles are from $35 half-pension. There are another half-dozen hotels in town, offering double rooms for less than $15 for a double in-season, half-pension.

Nightlife on Skiathos consists of a couple of clubs, a couple of tavernas with bouzouki, and lots of waterfront cafes where you can watch the fishing boats in the harbor and the brightly colored nets hanging in the trees to dry.

## Mykonos

Everyone has heard of Mykonos—and when you get there, you won't be disappointed—it's everything you've hoped for . . . maybe even more: whitewashed waterfront, disappearing in whitewashed cobblestoned alleys, lined with whitewashed houses and balconies with blue or yellow trim; tiny cobblestoned squares with whitewashed churches. There are no cars in this part of town, just hundreds of spindly tables and chairs, sun umbrellas, little old ladies in long black dresses, and tourists in next to nothing; take a bus and a boat to Paradise Beach (about 50¢) or Super Paradise Beach (75¢) and you'll find yourself among tourists in nothing at all. Or wander around the island and admire its famed windmills (whitewashed, of course), or some of its 300-odd churches and chapels. Where to stay?

When you set foot on the island you'll probably be surrounded by dozens of those little old ladies in black offering rooms in their cottages, most of which are simply furnished but spotlessly clean and inexpensive; if you want to play it safe, go first to the tourist police office, right on the harbor, and ask them to recommend some rooms. Otherwise, you have a choice of pensions: **Philippi,** otherwise known as **Angelique Kontiza Pension** (tel. 0289-22295; 20 rooms, some with private bath) in the center of town is recommended—at 11 Kalogera Street; the Class C **Mykonos Beach,** where a double room with breakfast costs 494 drachmas ($14); any of the three Class B hotels **Theoxenia, Afroditi, Alkistis**—the latter two bungalow-style accommodations—or the Class A **Leto.** In any of the Afroditi's 110 modern bungalows, room and half-board for a single is $24 in high season, $35 for a double. Full board costs 951 drachmas and 1,556 drachmas, respectively. Rates at the Theoxenia are a dollar higher.

Try to avoid half-pension rates if you can, because there are so many delightful little restaurants on the island—such as Maria's and Zanni's, both on the waterfront, the touristy Taverna Mykonos (also on the waterfront), and the Taverna Antonini (on the square). Afters is a pleasant pub for after-dinner drinks.

Some of the best shopping in Greece is to be found on Mykonos—a branch of the famed jeweler Lalaounis (see chapter on "Shopping in Athens"), Galatis (more jewelery), George Konteous (still more jewelery), Nikis for ladies' fashions, and Panos for superb handwoven bedspreads ($60 double), shoulder bags ($9.50), placemats ($1.50)—all with exquisite combinations of earth-and-sea-inspired colors.

**HOW TO GET TO MYKONOS:** Two or three flights daily in summer (45 minutes flying time), or 24 crossings a week by boat from Piraeus (six to seven hours).

## Santorini

Alias Thira. Alias, perhaps, Atlantis. No island in the Mediterranean offers a more dramatic landfall than this one: you sail into what remains of the crater of the volcano created when, as you read back in the chapter on museums, "Enkeladus in the bowels of the Earth was roused with undescribable fury," past a flat island of brown-black lava to the towering cliffs of Santorini itself, topped by the gleaming, whitewashed churches and homes of the village. When you go ashore here you still haven't arrived—you still have to get up that almost-vertical 600-foot cliff. There's a zigzag path to the top, and most people negotiate it on the back of a donkey in about 20 minutes. Some foolhardy people, like us, *walk* up (despite what the muleteers tell you, "one hour, one hour" it's only *half* an hour to the top, even with picture stops), but walking is not really recommended, especially if your ship has put lots of people ashore, in which case the 100-odd donkeys are working overtime and the path becomes the setting for a donkey stampede; the only reward for dodging the hooves and the droppings is that the muleteers assume that anyone who has reached the top has paid his 100 drachmas for the round-trip ride, so you can treat yourself to a free ride down. Once you get to the top, the thing to do is ignore the souvenir shops, find a cliffside taverna, and over a glass of Santorini white marvel over the history of this extraordinary, legendary island.

Scientists speculate that Santorini/Thira was destroyed by a gigantic earthquake, volcanic explosion, *and* tidal wave, which left only the tips of the volcanic cone behind. That became Santorini and its satellite islands. The tidal wave, according to some estimates, may have been as high as 600 feet, which would make it the largest natural convulsion in the recorded history of mankind; some scientists and archaeologists speculate that this same convulsion wiped out the civilization of Knossos on Crete, caused the parting of the Red Sea (the same one recorded in the Bible), and sent that giant wave all the way to the Sahara where it gathered up some desert sands before sweeping all the way back to deposit the sands on Crete. (If this seems farfetched, compare it with history's most recent counterpart, the eruption of Java's Krakatoa in 1883, when so much red-hot pumice was forced into the air that skies turned red in *North America* . . . so red that fire departments in Poughkeepsie, New York, and New Haven, Connecticut, were called out twice because people thought those towns were on fire, and a Dutch ocean-going freighter was carried off by the tidal wave and dumped intact in the jungle *two miles away.* ) Anyway, it's romantic to speculate that somewhere far beneath this gleaming, white clifftop village there may rest the lost continent of Atlantis.

As it happens, **Atlantis** is the name of the better of the town's two hotels. It's in Class B, and costs 1,494 drachmas ($37) for a double, half-pension, with a big terrace overlooking the town and the sea.

If you come to Santorini on one of the cruise ships, you will not (by the time you've made your way up the hill on donkey-back) be able to see much more than the whitewashed village at the edge of the crater—which for most people may be experience enough for one day, since it *is* such an extraordinary place. Visitors who stay for a few days may want to explore some of the quiet coves and beaches on the opposite side of the island, linger in the tavernas drinking the local wines (Vissanto and Nihteri), or explore the site of Ancient Thira—the agora, theater, temples, and shrines. On July 20, the feast day of the Prophet Elijah, the islanders celebrate at the monastery of the same name, and the evening is given over to the local dances—the syrtos and the repati. Join them. You'll soon learn the syrtos and repati.

**HOW TO GET TO SANTORINI:** There are·daily flights (55 minutes) by Olympic from Athens, but the only way to arrive in Santorini is by boat—either ferryboat (once a day from Piraeus) or cruise ship. If you come by ferryboat, make sure you get off at the right port Thira (not Ia).

## Crete

Zorba's island is the largest of the Greek islands, with half-a-million people. Its 3,000 square miles are mostly mountains, which rise to 7,500 feet at their highest peak. Crete lies equidistant from Europe, Asia, and Africa (which is only 200 miles to the south), another of those islands with a mishmash history—except that this one goes back farther than the others. As Cretans will constantly remind you, the *first* civilization in Europe was on Crete—the legendary Minoan kingdom with its bull-oriented culture that flourished here 3,000 years before the birth of Christ. All that remains of this culture are·the ruins of the **Palace of Knossos,** one of the outstanding archaeological sites of Europe—what was once·a five-story structure (4,000 years ago!), with private bathrooms and flushing toilets (4,000 years ago!). The most striking remnant of the civilization is the modest throne of the king, which still stands against the wall of the throne room after all these centuries, and which Cretans claim is the oldest throne in existence. The palace is only 20 minutes by bus from the town of Heraklion (where you'll probably arrive, whether you come by air or sea), but before you dash over to check out the ruins and the labyrinths, pay a visit to the downtown **Archaeological Museum** first, because after you've inspected its exhibits (frescoes, artifacts, and models visualizing the original palace) you'll appreciate the ruins even more. The Palace of Knossos is open weekdays from 8 a.m. to sunset, and on Sundays and holidays from 10 to·1 and 2:30 to 7; admission is 25 drachmas. The museum is open from 9 to 1 and 2 to 4 daily (except Monday afternoon); on Sundays and holidays, from 10 to 1; admission is 25 drachmas, which includes entry fees to other archaeological sites (including the Palace of Knossos). Sightseeing tours to the museum and palace, with English-speaking guides, cost about $5, including admissions, but the regular bus to the palace is only 2.50 drachmas.

There are several other Minoan sites on Crete, most notably the secondary palace of Phaestos; otherwise the things to see are the natural beauties of the island, wild headlands and rugged mountains, valleys filled with olive trees and cypresses, a plain filled with windmills, and the whitewashed villages. Crete is the island of El Greco, who was born Domenico Theotokopoulos in the village of Fodele, before heading off for Italy, Spain, and immortality. Its second most famous son is Nikos Kazantizakis, who wrote many distinguished novels before one of them, *Zorba the Greek* was made into a movie earning him international fame.

If you're coming to Crete mainly to see Knossos and wallow in the Minoan Civilization, you'll probably want to stay in downtown Heraklion, where you'll find dozens of hotels, most of them built within the past ten years. But if you've come for a vacation, to mix the sand and the sea with the quest for culture, stay at **Aghios Nikolaos,** 40 miles east of Heraklion, a pretty resort town poised between the sea and a lake. There are several new hotels here, too, in every price range, but top honors go to the deluxe bungalow-hotel **Minos Beach,** one of the finest resorts anywhere in the Mediterranean. Its nearest rival is the deluxe **Mirabello Village,** where the 128 bungalow rooms rent for 1,750 drachmas double for two ($49), including breakfast and dinner—slightly less than the Minos Beach. At Elounda, the **Astir Palace Elounda Beach Hotel** sprinkles its bayside site with 112 deluxe rooms. Elsewhere on the island there are scores of hotels in the A, B, and C categories, but you'd still be wise to make a reservation far in advance in summer.

**HOW TO GET TO CRETE:** Olympic Airways has seven or eight Boeing 737 flights every day during the summer months (50 minutes flight time, $45 round trip), and seafarers have a choice of two boats daily from Piraeus.

## Rhodes

If you go to Rhodes by sea, so much the better, because that way you can more readily capture the flavor of this, one of the great crossroads of history. You sail into another dramatic harbor, past the 15th-century fortress/lighthouse of St. Nicholas, past three small stone windmills guarding the old harbor, almost right up to the turreted walls of the old city, which at this point is virtually concealed behind its battlements, except for its minarets and the magnificient **Palace of the Grand Masters.** The Grand Masters, that is, of the Knights of St. John, who built these fortifications so thoroughly that they were able to rule the island, behind those walls, for two centuries.

Rhodes is half a dozen Mediterraneans rolled into one—Saracen, Crusader, Turkish, Venetian, Ancient Greek, Modern European. It's the largest of the Dodecanese, and its recorded history goes back all the way to the 11th century B.C. It has one of the pleasantest climates in Europe, with warm days ten months of the year, which makes it a favorite winter resort for Europeans living in northern climes. Fortunately, it's a simple matter to enjoy both the historic and the resort side of the island. The old city of Rhodes is a delightful experience (alleys and courtyards, bazaars, tavernas, fountains, squares, wrought-iron balconies, ornate doorways, mosques, churches, mansions), with a couple of interesting museums, but it won't take you long to complete your tour. The only other sight on the island (but some sight) is **Lindos**—a circular harbor and a whitewashed village, topped by a Crusader fortress and an even more ancient acropolis which is today not much more than a few toppled columns and some well-trodden steps. You get to the acropolis either by donkey along a special path, or on foot (the best way) up through cobbled streets not much wider than your shoulders, and lined with a phalanx of handicraft and sourvenir shops. It's quite a hike, but the view from the top is breathtaking—the town and the harbor on one side, an even tinier harbor on the other, with a pair of fishing boats and a toy-sized chapel marking the spot where Saint Paul came ashore to preach to the Rhodians.

Accommodations in Lindos, as of this date, are confined to rooms in private houses (or complete houses for longer stays), but elsewhere on the island you have a choice of almost a hundred hotels in every class, and more are being put up every year. The grandest of all is the renowned **Grand Hotel Astir Palace**, a vast, deluxe complex, with 380 rooms, a casino, a tennis court, and a new indoor swimming pool. A single room with half-board here runs from 1,200 drachmas ($33) to 1,350 drachmas ($37) in high season; doubles are 2,000 to 2,300 drachmas ($55 to $64). These prices include service and taxes.

**HOW TO GET TO RHODES:** Six flights every day from Athens in summer (65 minutes each way, $54 round trip); five companies operate regular sea service to the island all year round (trips take 20 hours nonstop, up to 28 hours with intermediate stops).

# Chapter XVI

# CRUISES THROUGH THE GREEK ISLANDS

IN THE PREVIOUS two chapters you learned about the various Greek islands and how to get to them by scheduled ferryboat and plane, but there's still another way of seeing these gleaming sunny islands . . . on an island cruise. You board a luxury cruise ship in Piraeus and set off for a few days of relaxed island-hopping—without having to pack and unpack more than once, without having to dash out to airports to catch flights. These island cruises are a happy combination of touring and vacationing—you have a chance to see the sights, but you also get to lounge around the pool or sunbathe on the deck between ports of call.

Usually the longer stretches between islands are covered during the night, when you can't really do much sightseeing anyway, and the time you do have to spend on shore varies, depending on all sorts of factors—time of departure from Piraeus, availability of berths on tenders, arrangement of itinerary. Some stops you'll find too short—obviously on a three-day cruise, for example, you can't include everything. However, a stop on Crete will always allow you time at least to visit the Minoan ruins at Knossos, and in Rhodes you'll be able to visit the old walled city and its museums, and you'll probably have time also to take the four-hour coach tour to Lindos.

Here are some sample cruise itineraries:

## 3-Day Cruise

| | | | |
|---|---|---|---|
| Friday | Piraeus | | dep. 1 p.m. |
| | Mykonos | arr. 7 p.m. | dep. midnight |
| Saturday | Rhodes | arr. noon | dep. 7 p.m. |
| Sunday | Crete | arr. 8 a.m. | dep. noon |

|  | Santorini | arr. | 5 p.m. | dep. 9 p.m. |
| Monday | Piraeus | arr. | 7 a.m. | |

## 4-Day Cruise

| Monday | Piraeus | | | dep. 1 p.m. |
| | Mykonos | arr. | 7 p.m. | dep. midnight |
| Tuesday | Ephesus | arr. | 7 a.m. | dep. noon |
| | Patmos | arr. | 5 p.m. | dep. midnight |
| Wednesday | Rhodes | arr. | 8 a.m. | dep. 8 p.m. |
| Thursday | Crete | arr. | 8 a.m. | dep. noon |
| | Santorini | arr. | 5 p.m. | dep. 9 p.m. |
| Friday | Piraeus | arr. | 7 a.m. | |

## 7-Day Cruise

| Wednesday | Piraeus | | | dep. 6 p.m. |
| Thursday | Crete | arr. | 8 a.m. | dep. noon |
| | Santorini | arr. | 5 p.m. | dep. 8 p.m. |
| Friday | Rhodes | arr. | 7 a.m. | dep. 9 p.m. |
| Saturday | Ephesus | arr. | 7 a.m. | dep. noon |
| Sunday | Istanbul | arr. | 2 p.m. | (overnight) |
| Monday | Istanbul | | | dep. noon |
| Tuesday | Delos | arr. | 10 a.m. | dep. 1:30 p.m. |
| | Mykonos | arr. | 3 p.m. | dep. 11 p.m. |
| Wednesday | Piraeus | arr. | 7 a.m. | |

Other seven-day itineraries include Santorini, Crete, Rhodes, Cos, Patmos, Samos, Kusadasi, Mount Athos, Chalkidiki, Delos, Mykonos; or Istanbul, Izmir, Ephesus, Delos, Mykonos, Rhodes, Crete, and Santorini.

## The Cruise Ships

There are half a dozen shipping companies operating cruises through the Greek Islands—hence the wide range of departures and itineraries. There are several newcomers to the flotilla of cruise ships for longer trips, such as the TSS *Atlas* of Epirotiki Lines and the *Aquarius* and *Castalia* of Hellenic Mediterranean Lines: some of the ships you may recognize from their winter assignments in the Caribbean—such as Sun Lines' fine *Stella Solaris, Stella Maris,* and *Stella Oceanis.* The largest single fleet, however, belongs to the Epirotiki Line, which was founded in 1919 and claims to have started the fashion for cruising the

Greek Islands two decades ago. It probably offers you the widest choice of cruises, ships, accommodations, and, most important, departures.

Most of these cruise ships are equipped with all the facilities you would find in a resort hotel—swimming pool, air conditioning, dining rooms that can usually sit the entire quota of passengers at one sitting, beauty salon, nightclub, bars and lounges, discotheques, and in some cases cinemas. On most of the ships, some or all of the cabins are equipped with wall-to-wall carpeting, private toilets and showers, telephones, and two-channel radios. Stewards, cruise directors, tour guides, and most other members of the crew who come in contact with passengers speak fluent or adequate English. Recent additions to the cruising fleet are almost ocean liners: the Epirotiki Lines' *Atlas* is a 16,000-ton vessel with 289 cabins, nine decks, a 300-seat cinema and *three* swimming pools—all for a seven-day Mediterranean cruise! At least one of the ships *was* at one time a transatlantic liner: it's the *Navarino* (formerly the *Gripsholm* ) of the Karageorgi Line, a 23,000-ton "Greek Island," as they call it, that sails on 14-day cruises through the Greek Islands, to Venice, Yugoslavia, and Istanbul.

**WHAT IT WILL COST:** Rates vary enormously, of course, depending on the duration of the cruise, the size and facilities of the ship, the type of cabin accommodations. Your travel agent will be able to show you deck plans when you get around to choosing a specific cruise and a specific ship, at the same time giving you up-to-date details of the fares. Meantime, here are some guidelines.

Fares for a three-day cruise will vary from $180 per person with three or four passengers in a cabin, to $350 per person with two in a stateroom with private bath. The *average* fare for such a cruise will be about $210 to $220, sharing a double cabin.

On a typical four-day cruise, fares vary from $225 with three or four passengers to a cabin, to $484 per person with two in a stateroom with private bath. The *average* fare for one of these four-day cruises is likely to be between $300 and $400 per person, sharing a double cabin—or roughly $75 to $100 per person *per day*, for meals, accommodations, *and* transportation.

When deciding how much you ought to pay, keep these points in mind: You spend most of your time on deck or ashore, so the size and luxury of your cabin is of minor importance; most of these ships are modern and air-conditioned so you don't have to be on an upper deck, and you don't need an outside cabin (in most cases, you can't open the portholes anyway because of the air conditioning); even the least expensive accommodations have private showers and toilets. So don't think that you can't afford to take one of these cruises unless you can afford the most expensive cabins. In fact, in some cases cabins one deck down are a better value than cabins on the boat deck because that part of the ship is wider and the cabins have more space—but they may cost $30 or $40 less.

Remember also that these fares include all your meals for three or four days—a total of nine meals, for example, on a three-day cruise. The food is usually international fare, with a touch of Greek at most meals; at least one poolside buffet; and usually one Greek evening when the entire meal is Greek and the crew entertains you with folk music and dancing.

Shore excursions are extra (you don't have to take them if you don't want to), and tips for a three-day cruise usually add up to another $10—but, of course, that figure is up to you.

Think about it. A cruise is a great way to see several islands on a short vacation. It's a great way to get some sun. The sea is usually calm. (*Usually.*) You see the sights. You meet new friends. You eat heartily. Chances are, you'll probably find the three-day cruise too short and decide to stretch the trip to four days, at least.

**SEVEN-DAY YACHT CRUISE:** There's another way to cruise the Greek Islands, more in the spirit of the Argonauts but with much less effort. It's on one of **Viking Tours'** seven-day "Fascinating Yacht Cruises," aboard an 85-foot motor-yacht, the *Viking of Kos*. This *Viking* is equipped with twin Rolls-Royce diesel engines; the cabins have showers and toilets, the main saloon doubles as bar and dining room, and there's ample deck space for sunning and lazing. One of these seven-day *Viking* cruises takes in the islands of Mykonos, Delos, Santorini, Ios, Paros, Tinos, and Naxos, with four nights in hotels, three nights on the yacht. The fare, $250, includes bed and breakfast (no meals; most passengers prefer the option of dining ashore), hotel accommodations, services of an English-speaking tour leader (but not shore excursions), all port fees and transfers, round-trip steamer ticket to Mykonos. The second *Viking* cruise (during July, August, and September) visits Corfu, Parga, Paxi, Lefkas, Skorpios, Kefa-

Ionia, and Ithaka—with accommodations ashore each night in island *pensions.* Fare: $291. Your travel agent can give you full details, or write to Viking's Travel Bureau, 3 Filellinon Street, (Syntagma, in the Arcade) Athens.

## Last Word

As we said earlier, every care has been taken to check and cross-check prices, dates, opening hours, and other facts in this guide. . Inevitably, some of them may change before you sit down to plan your trip; there's little the author or publisher can do about such variations, which are the responsibility of governments, economies, oil sheiks, and other quirky factors. Nevertheless, the prices should not be off by more than 5% or 10%, except in unprecedented circumstances; use the figures in these pages as a basic guide, and if precise dollar-and-cent calculations are a critical matter, check out the detailed prices with your travel agent before you leave home.

# CAPSULE VOCABULARY

### And Calendar of Events

LEARN A FEW BASIC words and phrases in Greek before you go (you could memorize the following list, for example, on the flight over). You'll be amazed how much difference this will make to your reception in shops, restaurants, and hotels. Greeks *really* appreciate it when foreigners make an effort to speak a few words of their language. When you go into a shop, for example, say *"KaliMEra"*—good day (you can use it any time up to, say, 4 o'clock). Good evening is *"KaliSPEra."* When you are introduced to someone, say *"HEropoLEE,"* and at the end of that first meeting you say *"HArika"* which means 'pleased to have met you.' Greeks are much more formal about such basic courtesies, as you can see.

Because the Greek alphabet is different from our own, we are including in this guide a phonetical vocabulary of useful expressions to assist you in your everyday dealings.

To aid your **pronunciation,** we have written the *accented syllable in capital letters,* the rest of the word in lowercase. As a general rule, in modern Greek the *accent of the word is on the middle or last syllable,* unlike English, where you usually find the accent on the first syllable of a word. This simple difference in pronunciation often determines whether or not you will be understood. Don't worry too much, though. So many people in Athens learn English in school that you may find you need this handy vocabulary only for courtesy or fun.

## EVERYDAY EXPRESSIONS

| | |
|---|---|
| **Good morning** | kaliMEra |
| **Good evening** | kaliSPEra |

| | |
|---|---|
| Hello or goodbye (informal) | YAsaas! |
| Hello or goodbye (formal) | HErete |
| What is your name? | POSSssas LEne? |
| I have enjoyed myself very much | HArika poLEE |
| Yes | neh |
| No | Ohi |
| Excuse me | sigNOmee |
| Does anyone speak English? | MiLEYE kanEES angliKA? |
| Thank you (very much) | efharistO (PArapolee) |
| Please | parakaLO |
| You're welcome | parakaLO |
| Good health! (cheers!) | steeneeYAsou (singular) |
| | steeneeYAsass (plural) |
| | steeneeYAmas (us) |
| I don't understand | THENkatalaVEHno |
| Please repeat it | PEHstehtoh PAlee, parakaLO |
| What time is it? | TEE ORah EEneh? |
| How much is it? | POso EHee? |
| | POso KAnee? |
| It's all right | enDAXi |
| It's not all right | THEN EEnai enDAXi |
| I'm sorry | liPAmai |
| Men's room | ANfhron |
| Ladies' room | yiNAIkon |
| What? | TEE? |
| Why? | yaTEE? |
| When? | POteh? |
| How? | POHSS? |
| How far? | POHso mahkreeAH? |
| How long? | POsso KeRO? |
| Good | kaLO |
| Can you tell me? | boREEte namooPEEtah? |
| I am lost | EHkhasa tahTHROmo |
| I am sorry | leePOOme |

## TRAVEL EXPRESSIONS

| | |
|---|---|
| I want to go to the airport. | THEHlo na PAo sto ahehroTHROmeeo |
| Please call a taxi for me. | sass parakaLO foNAXTeh EHna afhtohKEEnee toh |
| Show me on the map. | THEEKstehmoo sto KHARtee |

| | |
|---|---|
| Am I going in the right direction for . . .? | peeyeno kaLA YA .? |
| Please tell me where to get off. | parakaLO PEHstehmoo poo na VGHO |

## SHOPPING

| | |
|---|---|
| I'm just looking. | ahpLOSS keeTAHzo |
| May I try this one? | boRO na toh thokeeMAHso? |
| It does not fit me. | then moo YEEnehteh |
| Will this fade (shrink)? | tha ksehVApsee (maZETsee)? |
| Will you please wrap this? | moo toh teeLEEyehteh paraka LO? |
| Where do I pay? | POO tha pleeROso? |
| My (mailing) address is . . . | ee (takheethromeeKEE) theeEFtheenseemoo EEneh |

## TELEPHONE

| | |
|---|---|
| Where can I telephone? | POO boRO nateelefoNEEso? |
| Will you telephone for me? | teelefoNEEteh ya MEHna? |
| Give me the long distance operator. | THOstehmo tohn teelefonee TEE maKRASS ahpo STAsehohs. |
| Hello | ehmBROHSS |
| May I speak to . . . | boRO nameeLEEsto . . . |
| Please speak more slowly. | parakaLO meeLAteh PYO arGHA |

## CALENDAR OF EVENTS

The following is only a sampling of the hundreds of special events—folkloric, religious, festive, cultural—that take place throughout the year all over Greece. For a complete list, contact the National Tourist Organization of Greece.

**JANUARY:** Feast of St. Basil—a general celebration with traditional New Year's cake and national costumes (1st).

Epiphany—the "Blessing of the Waters" ceremony throughout Greece. The most spectacular spot to visit is Piraeus (6th).

**FEBRUARY:** In mid-February it's carnival time throughout Greece.

**MARCH:** Greek National Holiday, honoring, the War of Independence with military parades throughout the country (25th).

**APRIL:** Sound and Light performances in Athens, Corfu, and Rhodes (through October).

Anniversaries dedicated to Saint Spyridon, patron saint of Corfu (midmonth).

Easter Sunday in the Greek Orthodox church, a public holiday and the most important religious holiday in the Greek calendar (22nd).

**MAY:** Labor Day and Flower Festival, a public holiday (1st).

The anniversary of the union of the Ionian Islands with Greece, celebrated mostly on Corfu (21st).

"Hadjipetria" Festival in Trikkali, in the province of Thessaly (end of month).

**JUNE:** Wine Festivals at Daphni (11 kilometers from Athens), Rhodes, and other locations—wine-tasting, tavernas, dancing.

**JULY:** Wine Festival at Alexandroupolis (midmonth).

Athens Festival—drama, concerts, opera, ballet at Herod Atticus Theater (through September).

Epidaurus Festival—performances of ancient Greek drama in open-air theater (through August).

Northern Greece National Theater performances of ancient Greek drama in the open-air theaters at Philippi and on the island of Thassos.

"Dionysia" Wine Festival on island of Naxos (midmonth).

**AUGUST:** Ancient Greek dramas performed in the open-air theater at Diou, near Mount Olympus (midmonth).

Art exhibition on Skiros island (first week of month).

Holiday honoring the Virgin Mary, celebrated on the island of Tinos (15th).

**SEPTEMBER:** Thessaloniki International Trade Fair.
Film Festival and Festival of Light Music, Thessaloniki.

**OCTOBER:** Demetrius Festival—music, opera, ballet—in Thessaloniki.
National Anniversary (28th).

**NOVEMBER:** St. Andrew's Day, celebrating the patron saint of Patras (30th).